POCKET

SINGAPORE

TOP EXPERIENCES · LOCAL LIFE

T0018254

RIA DE JONG

Contents

Performer at Chingay festival (p24)
SAM'S STUDIO/SHUTTERSTOCK ©

Explore Singapore 33

Worth a Trip

Survival Guide 177

COVID-19

We have re-checked every business in this book before publication to ensure that it is still open after the COVID-19 outbreak. However, the economic and social impacts of COVID-19 will continue to be felt long after the outbreak has been contained, and many businesses, services and events referenced in this guide may experience ongoing restrictions. Some may be temporarily closed, have changed their opening hours and services, or require bookings; some unfortunately could have closed permanently. We suggest you check with venues before visiting for the latest information.

Top Experiences

Find Treasures at the Asian Civilisations Museum
Magnificent collection of pan-Asian treasures. **p36**

Clear Your Mind at Gardens by the Bay
Singapore's high-tech futuristic garden. **p38**

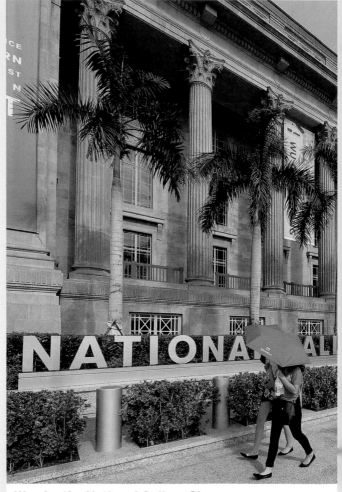

Wander the National Gallery Singapore

World's leading collection of Southeast Asian art. **p40**

Walk With the Animals at Singapore Zoo

A world-class tropical wonderland. **p96**

Spot Leopards at the Night Safari

An exciting nocturnal adventure. **p98**

Relax in Singapore Botanic Gardens
Spectacular gardens. **p102**

Time Travel at the Chinatown Heritage Centre
Step into the past. **p138**

Get Your Thrills at Universal Studios

The city's biggest, busiest amusement park. **p128**

Take in Stunning Vistas at Southern Ridges

Singapore's most picturesque jungle trek. **p116**

Dining Out

Singaporeans are obsessed with makan (food), whether it's talking incessantly about their last meal to feverishly posting about it online. From eye-wateringly priced cutting-edge fine dining to dirt-cheap mouth-watering hawker fare, Singapore's cultural diversity has created one of the world's most varied culinary landscapes.

Hawker Grub

Hawker centres are usually standalone, open-air (or at least open-sided) structures with a raucous vibe and rows upon rows of food stalls peddling any number of local cuisines.

Often found in malls, food courts are basically air-conditioned hawker centres with marginally higher prices, while coffeeshops, also called *kopitiams,* are open-shopfront cafes, usually with a handful of stalls.

Wherever you are just dive in and get ordering (p149). Local wisdom suggests stalls with the longest queues are well worth the wait.

The Next Generation

As the older generation of hawkers barrel towards retirement, a new breed of innovative hawkers are taking up the challenge of dishing out great meals on the cheap. You'll find everything from Japanese ramen and Mexican street food, both with Singaporean twists, to old-school British fare and flavour-hit traditional sock-brewed *kopi* (coffee).

Fancy Fare

Singapore's restaurant scene is booming. From the ever-growing list of local and international celebrity-chef nosheries to a new breed of midrange eateries, delivering sharp, produce-driven menus in more relaxed settings, the options are endless. Clusters of big-hitters have transformed the areas around China-town's Amoy St and Keong Saik Rd into dining 'it' spots.

EQROY/SHUTTERSTOCK ©

Best New-Gen Hawkers

Timbre+ A hawker hub with food trucks, craft suds and live tunes. (p122)

A Noodle Story Ramen with a Singaporean twist in Chinatown. (p147)

Coffee Break Singapore *kopi* meets hipster flavours at this Chinatown drink stall. (p141)

Best Hawker Eats

Maxwell Food Centre Chinatown's most tourist-friendly hawker centre. (p148)

Chinatown Complex The hard-core hawker experience. (p148)

Lau Pa Sat Worth a visit for its magnificent wrought-iron architecture alone. (pictured; p150)

Takashimaya Food Village A fabulous basement food hall on Orchard Rd. (p90)

Ya Kun Kaya Toast Historic hang-out serving Singapore's best runny eggs and *kaya* (coconut jam) toast. (p150)

Best Fusion & Western

Neon Pigeon Japanese iza-kaya share plates in Keong Saik. (p149)

Super Loco Customs House Mexican street food with a killer Marina Bay Sands view. (p52)

Butcher Boy Wow-oh-wow Asian-inspired creations for meat lovers. (p148)

Best Celeb-Chef Hot Spots

National Kitchen by Violet Oon Much-loved Peranakan favourites from the Julia Childs of Singapore. (p51)

Odette Modern French from Gallic superstar Julien Royer. (p51)

Iggy's Orchard Rd's most desirable culinary address helmed by Aitor Jeronimo Orive. (p87)

Burnt Ends Extraordinary barbecued meats from Australian expat Dave Pynt. (p147)

Waku Ghin Refined Japanese by acclaimed chef Tetsuya Wakuda. (p52)

Bar Open

From speakeasy cocktail bars to boutique beer stalls to artisan coffee roasters, Singapore is discovering the finer points of drinking. The clubbing scene is no less competent, with newcomers including a futuristic club in the clouds, a basement hot spot fit for the streets of Tokyo, and a techno refuge in Boat Quay.

Cut-Price Drinks

Singapore is an expensive city to drink in. A beer at most city bars will set you back between S$10 and S$18, with cocktails commonly ringing in between S$20 and S$30. That said, many bars offer decent happy-hour deals, typically stretching from around 5pm to 8pm, sometimes starting earlier and finishing later. Those who don't mind plastic tables can always swill S$7 bottles of Tiger at the local hawker centre.

Kopi Culture

Single-origin beans and siphon brews may be all the rage among local hipsters, but Singapore's old-school *kopitiams* (coffeeshops) deliver the real local deal. Before heading in, it's a good idea to learn the lingo. *Kopi* means coffee with condensed milk, *kopi-o* is black coffee with sugar, while *kopi-c* gets you coffee with evaporated milk and sugar. If you need some cooling down, opt for a *kopi-peng* (iced coffee). Replace the word *kopi* with *teh* and

you have the same variation for tea. One local tea concoction worth sipping is *teh tarik* – literally 'pulled tea' – a sweet spiced Indian tea.

Best Wine Bars

Ginett Buzzing bar pouring possibly the cheapest glass of French plonk in town. (p77)

Que Pasa Classy little wine bar with an Iberian vibe in heritage Emerald Hill Rd. (p92)

Best Cocktails

Tippling Club Boundary-pushing libations from the bar that raised the bar. (pictured; p153)

BOAZ ROTTEM/ALAMY ©

28 HongKong Street Passionate mixologists turning grog into greatness. (p54)

Native Surprising ingredients and clever twists in trendy Amoy St. (p153)

Manhattan Long-forgotten cocktails are given a new lease on life in this Orchard Rd heavyweight. (p91)

Best Clubs

Zouk A multivenue classic west of Robertson Quay. (p55)

Headquarters by the Council Thumping techno and house beats in this Boat Quay shophouse. (p56)

Taboo Hot bods and themed nights at Singapore's classic gay club. (p154)

Best Beers

Level 33 The world's highest craft brewery with a bird's-eye view of Marina Bay below. (p56)

Smith Street Taps A rotating cast of craft suds in a Chinatown hawker centre. (p154)

Druggists Twenty-three taps pouring craft brews in trendy Jalan Besar. (p74)

Best Coffee

Chye Seng Huat Hardware Superlative espresso, filter coffee, on-site roasting and classes. (p74)

Nylon Coffee Roasters A small, mighty espresso bar and roaster in Everton Park. (p152)

Coffee Break Singapore *kopi* meets hipster flavours in this Amoy St hawker stall. (p141)

The Singapore Sling

There's no denying the celebrity status of Singapore's most famous drink. Created by Raffles Hotel (p47) barman Ngiam Tong Boon, the Singapore sling first hit the bar in 1915. The recipe, once a tightly held secret, has long been out and now many Singapore bars peddle a modern twist on the original

Treasure Hunt

While its shopping scene might not match the edge of Hong Kong's or Bangkok's, Singapore is no retail slouch. Look beyond the malls and you'll find everything from sharply curated local boutiques to vintage map peddlers and clued-in contemporary galleries.

Retail Road Map

While mall-heavy Orchard Rd is Singapore's retail queen, it's only one of several retail hubs. For electronics, hit tech mall Sim Lim Square. Good places for antiques include Tanglin Shopping Centre, Dempsey Hill and Chinatown. For fabrics and textiles, scour Little India and Kampong Glam; the latter is also known for perfume traders and indie-cool Haji Lane. For independent fashion, design and books, explore Tiong Bahru.

Bagging a Bargain

While Singapore is no longer a cut-price electronics nirvana, it can offer savings. Know the price of things beforehand, then browse and compare. Ask vendors what they can do to sweeten the deal; at the very least, they should be able to throw in a camera case or memory cards. Sim Lim Square mall is known for its range and negotiable prices, though it's also known for taking the uninitiated for a ride, not to mention for occasionally selling 'new' equipment that isn't quite new: a quick internet search will bring up blacklisted businesses. The best deals are on computers and cameras, with prices often 20% lower than major stores.

Best for Design

Kapok Innovative threads and lifestyle objects at the National Design Centre. (p59)

Supermama Contemporary designer pieces with a Singaporean theme. (p79)

Bynd Artisan Handmade journals, leather travel accessories and jewellery. (p111)

SAM'S STUDIO/SHUTTERSTOCK ©

Best for Tech

Sim Lim Square Six levels of laptops, cameras and more at Singapore's biggest tech mall. (p81)

Mustafa Centre No shortage of electronic gizmos, available 24 hours a day. (p80)

Best Souvenirs

Raffles Hotel Gift Shop Everything from vintage poster prints to tea and tomes. (p59)

Antiques of the Orient Beautiful old maps, prints and photos of Singapore and the region. (p93)

National Gallery Singapore The museum store stocks tasteful, design-savvy gifts, including specially commissioned pieces. (p40)

Best Luxury Malls

ION Orchard Mall A-list boutiques in Singapore's most impressive consumer temple. (p93)

Shoppes at Marina Bay Sands Bayside luxury – and the world's first floating Louis Vuitton store. (pictured; p59)

Paragon Polished brands and a dedicated children's floor in the heart of Orchard Rd. (p93)

Best Midrange Malls

ION Orchard Mall ION's lower levels are dedicated to midrange fashion and accessories. (p93)

VivoCity Accessible labels galore at Singapore's biggest mall, just across from Sentosa. (p125)

Best for Art & Antiques

Tanglin Shopping Centre Quality Asian antiques and art in a mall off Orchard Rd. (p93)

Shang Antique Evocative temple artefacts and vintage Asian knick-knacks in Dempsey Hill. (p112)

For Kids

Safe, respectable, reliable Singapore would make an admirable babysitter. From interactive museums to an island packed with theme-park thrills, young ones are rarely an afterthought. Hotels supply cots, most cafes provide high-chairs and modern malls have family rooms. If you're after family time, the Little Red Dot has you covered.

Sentosa: Pleasure Island

While kid-friendly attractions are spread out across Singapore, you'll find the greatest concentration on the island of Sentosa. Here you'll find the LA-style Universal Studios theme park, plus a long list of supporting attractions, from the ambitious SEA Aquarium to zip-lining. You'll need at least a full day to experience everything Sentosa has to offer, not to mention a well-stocked wallet, as most activities, rides and shows cost extra.

Discounts

Kids receive up to 50% discount at most tourist venues. Those aged six years and under enjoy free entry to many of Singapore's top museums, including the National Gallery Singapore, National Museum of Singapore and the Asian Civilisations Museum. Kids under 0.9m tall can ride the MRT for free. Full-time students with photo ID cards also enjoy discounts at many attractions.

Best Thrills

Universal Studios Hollywood-inspired rides, roller coasters and shows for the young and young-at-heart. (p128)

iFly Plummet a virtual 2746m without a plane in sight at this indoor sky-diving centre. (p132)

Pinnacle@Duxton Affordable, family-friendly skypark with breathtaking city views and space to run around. (p146)

Best Museums

National Museum of Singapore An evocative exploration of Singaporean history and culture, with audiovisual displays, artefacts and child-friendly signs. (p46)

PUMPZA/SHUTTERSTOCK ©

ArtScience Museum
World-class art and science exhibitions with interactive kids' programs. (p40)

Lee Kong Chian Natural History Museum Engaging exhibits, complete with giant dinosaurs and fantastical displays of exotic beasts from both land and sea. (p120)

MINT Museum of Toys An impressive, Technicolor collection of over 50,000 rare, collectable toys. (p48)

Outdoor Adventures

Gardens by the Bay Space-age bio-domes, crazy Super-trees, bird's-eye Skyway and a 1-hectare Children's Garden, complete with wet play zones. (p38)

Southern Ridges Complete with dedicated children's playground, a treetop walk and the occasional monkey sighting. (p116)

Pulau Ubin Hop on a bike and cycle through forest and past colourful shacks on this tranquil, relatively flat, stuck-in-time island. (p174)

Singapore Ducktours Embarrassingly fun tours on a brightly coloured amphibious former military vehicle. (p49)

Best Animal Watching

Singapore Zoo Breakfast with orang-utans at one of the world's role-model zoological gardens. (p96)

Night Safari Spend the evening with leopards, lions and Himalayan blue sheep at this atmospheric wildlife oasis. (p98)

SEA Aquarium A spectacular, comprehensive aquarium. (pictured; p131)

Strolling Around

Singapore is a dream for families using strollers. Footpaths are well maintained, accessing public transport is a breeze (wheel straight onto trains and buses) and large attractions often have strollers for hire.

History & Culture

Singapore's history and culture is show-cased in its numerous and extremely well-curated museums and sights. You'll find the biggest and the best in the Colonial District, where collections dive into the area's history, culture and art. Beyond them are unexpected treasures, from reconstructed Chinatown slums to haunting wartime memorials.

WWII Sites

Singapore's WWII experience was a watershed period in its history. It's covered in depth in many museums, including the National Museum of Singapore and Former Ford Factory. It's also commemorated at several wartime sites, including a British fort on Sentosa, the battleground of Bukit Chandu (Opium Hill) and a former bunker in Fort Canning Park. Not surprisingly, the trauma of occupation and Singapore's tetchy postwar relations with its larger neighbours have fuelled its obsession with security today.

Best Peranakan Pickings

Peranakan Museum Delve into the Peranakan world of marriage, storytelling, fashion, feasting and mourning in atmospheric, multimedia galleries. (p46)

Baba House Step into the private world of a wealthy Peranakan family, c 1928, at one of Singapore's most beautiful historic homes. (p144)

Katong Antique House A cluttered collection of historical objects and stories from one of Singapore's leading Peranakan historians. (p165)

Best for War History

Fort Siloso Slip into subterranean tunnels at this ill-fated defence fort on Sentosa Island. (p131)

Reflections at Bukit Chandu A gripping retelling of the Japanese invasion atop former battlefield Opium Hill. (p117)

Battlebox This haunting underground complex documents the swift fall of Singapore. (p46)

Best for Art & Handicrafts

National Gallery Singapore Singapore's biggest cultural asset showcases 19th- and 20th-century regional art. (p40)

EQROY/SHUTTERSTOCK ©

Asian Civilisations Museum A pan-Asian treasure trove of decorative arts, religious artefacts, art and textiles. (p36)

Gillman Barracks A rambling artillery of private galleries exhibiting modern and contemporary art. (p120)

Best for Old Singapore

National Museum of Singapore Explore centuries of Singaporean history, from exiled Sumatran princes to independence. (p46)

Chinatown Heritage Centre Relive the gritty, chaotic and overcrowded Chinatown of yesteryear. (p138)

Images of Singapore Live A child-friendly interactive panorama spanning six centuries of local history. (p131)

Indian Heritage Centre A state-of-the-art museum showcasing the origins and heritage of Singapore's Indian community. (p66)

Best Temples, Mosques & Churches

Thian Hock Keng Temple Stands proud with its stone lions and elaborately carved beams. (p144)

Sultan Mosque The golden-domed hub that holds Kampong Glam together. (p66)

Sri Veeramakaliamman Temple Little India's most colourful, and stunning Hindu temple. (pictured; p67)

St Andrew's Cathedral Whitewashed wedding-cake elegance of Singapore's most famous church. (p43)

Former Ford Factory

The former Ford Motors assembly plant is best remembered as the place where Britain surrendered Singapore to Japan on 15 February 1942. It's now home to an exhibition that charts Singapore's descent into war, the three dark years of Japanese occupation and Singapore's path to independence.

Show Time

Singapore's nightlife calendar is generally booked solid. There's live music, theatre and adrenalin-pumping activities year-round, but at certain times of the year the city explodes into a flurry of car racing, cultural festivals and hot-ticket music events. When that all gets too much, Singapore's spas are waiting in the wings.

Film

Singaporeans love to watch movies and, at around S$12.50 per ticket, it's great value. Multiplex cinemas abound with many located in larger malls. The annual Singapore International Film Festival screens independent and art-house films. Singapore's cinemas are chilly, so wear something warm.

Live Music

An enthusiastic local music scene thrives (to a point). Esplanade – Theatres on the Bay hosts regular free performances and is home to the Singapore Symphony Orchestra. Top-tier international talent is showcased at both the Singapore International Jazz Festival and indie favourite St Jerome's Laneway Festival.

Booking Events

Check what's on and buy tickets at www. sistic.com.sg. Expect to pay from S$20 to S$70 for a ticket to a local theatre production, S$100 to S$300 for international music acts, and S$65 to S$200 for big-budget musicals. Gigs by local music acts are often free, though some places have a small cover charge.

Best for Live Music

BluJaz Café Consistently good jazz and blues in Kampong Glam. (p78)

Crazy Elephant Rock and blues in party-central Clarke Quay. (p58)

Esplanade – Theatres on the Bay Polished performances spanning classical to rock. (pictured; p49)

Timbre+ Live music at this New Age hawker centre. (p122)

TERENCE WONG/SHUTTERSTOCK © ARCHITECTS: MICHAEL WILFORD AND RUSSELL JOHNSON

Best for Theatre

Singapore Repertory Theatre A world-class repertoire that includes seasonal Shakespeare at Fort Canning Park. (p58)

Wild Rice Reinterpreted classics, new works and striking sets. (p79)

TheatreWorks New commissions and international collaborations. (p58)

Necessary Stage Locally flavoured, thought-provoking theatre. (p171)

Best for Chinese Performance

Chinese Theatre Circle Chinese opera, talks, performances and meals in Chinatown. (p155)

Singapore Chinese Orchestra Classical Chinese concerts performed with traditional instruments. (p155)

Best Spectator Sports

Singapore Formula One Grand Prix The F1 night race screams around Marina Bay in late September. (p24)

Rugby Sevens Singapore joined the list of host countries for the World Rugby Cup series in 2016.

Best for Classic & Indie Films

Rex Cinemas Bollywood hits on the edge of Little India. (p78)

Worth a Trip

Though not quite as manic as the Hong Kong races, a trip to **Singapore Turf Club** (☑ 6879 1008; www.turfclub.com.sg; 1 Turf Club Ave; from S$6; Ⓜ Kranji) is a hugely popular day out. Race times vary but usually run on Friday evenings and Sunday afternoons. A dress code is enforced (see website details) and entry is over 18s only, so bring photo ID.

Tours

ALEKSANDRA TOKARZ/SHUTTERSTOCK ©

Although Singapore is one of the world's easiest cities for self-navigation, guided tours can open up the city and its history in unexpected ways. Tours and cruises span everything from fun, family-friendly overviews to specialised themed adventures.

Best Themed Tours

Betel Box: The Real Singapore Tours Led by Tony Tan and the team at the Betel Box hostel. (p167)

Jane's SG Tours Insightful tours offering a unique look into Singapore's history, architecture, religions, botany and culture. (p88)

Battlebox Head underground to discover the tunnels and rooms of this historic WWII bunker. (pictured; p46)

Best Hop-On, Hop-Off Tours

Singapore 7 Sightseeing (www.singapore7.com) Passing major tourist areas on several routes, this double-decker, open-top tourist bus allows you to hop on and off as many times as you like.

SIA Hop-On (www.siahop on.com) Traversing the main tourist arteries every 15 to 60 minutes daily, Singapore Airlines' tourist bus runs four different lines.

Best Neighbourhood Tours

Original Singapore Walks (www.singaporewalks.com) Knowledgable on-foot excursions through Chinatown, Little India, Kampong Glam, the Colonial District, Boat Quay, Haw Par Villa and war-related sites. Most tours last from 2½ to three hours and do not require a booking;

check the website for meeting times and places.

Chinatown Trishaw Night Tour (www.viator.com) An atmospheric four-hour tour of Chinatown including dinner, on-foot exploration, a trishaw ride and a bumboat river cruise along the Singapore River.

Best River Tours

Singapore River Cruise Relaxing, 40-minute bumboat cruises that ply the stretch between the Quays and Marina Bay with spectacular views of the city. (p49)

Singapore Ducktours Embarrassingly fun tours on a brightly coloured amphibious former military vehicle. (pictured; p49)

Under the Radar

With a well-worn tourist trail, and often just a few days to complete it in, many visitors only manage to tick off Singapore's must-see highlights. However, if you dare to deviate off the path Singapore is more than happy to divulge many of its best-kept secrets.

CHRIS HOWEY/SHUTTERSTOCK ©

Jalan Besar

This foodie micro-burb is chockfull of stunning shophouses, vibrant street art, funky cafes and famous local eats.

Admire **Petain Road's** row of 18 pre-war shophouses (pictured, p67), decked in vibrant Peranakan tiles, nature-inspired bas-reliefs and ornate window decorations. Then seek out one of the city's most lauded coffee spots and roaster **Chye Seng Huat Hardware** (p74).

Steps away, you'll find 23 taps pouring an interesting selection of rotating craft brews at **Druggists** (p74).

Unmissable local foodie haunts include laksa at **Sungei Road Laksa** (p63), the glorious mess that is a meal at **Beach Road Scissor Cut Curry Rice** (p75), and dim sum at **Swee Choon Tim Sum.**(p71),

---

Best Under-the-Radar Attractions

Lorong Buangkok The city's last remaining mainland kampong (village) in the island's north. A visit to this tiny settlement is an evocative way to see what life was like for many Singaporeans before independence.
Gillman Barracks A former British military camp turned contemporary arts enclave.
Lee Kong Chian Natural History Museum A jaw-dropping display of the region's biologically diverse ecosystem complete with specimens and high-tech exhibits.

Festivals

Singapore is the ultimate melting pot. With four official languages, it's a place where mosques sidle up to temples, European chefs experiment with Chinese spices, and local English is peppered with Hokkien, Tamil and Malay. This rich, vibrant multicultural heritage is celebrated year-round through a plethora of diverse festivals.

SAM'S STUDIO/SHUTTERSTOCK ©

Best Music Festivals

St Jerome's Laneway Festival (January; http://singapore.lanewayfestival.com) Uberhip one-day indie music fest.

Singapore International Jazz Festival (April; www.sing-jazz.com) Three-day showcase of jazz talent.

ZoukOut (December; www.zoukout.com) Singapore's biggest outdoor dance party, held over two nights on Sentosa with A-list international DJs.

Best Chinese Festivals

Chinese New Year (February) Dragon dances, fireworks, food and spectacular street decorations.

Mid-Autumn Festival (August/September) Lanterns light up Chinatown as revellers nibble on mooncakes. Held on the full moon of the 8th lunar month.

Best Hindu Festivals

Thaipusam (February) Kavadis (heavy metal frames) pierce parading devotees.

Diwali (October/November) Little India glows for the 'Festival of Lights'.

Thimithi (October/November) Hindus walk over white-hot coals at Sri Mariamman Temple.

Best for Foodies

Singapore Food Festival (July; www.yoursingapore.com) Two weeks of tastings, special dinners and food-themed tours.

World Gourmet Summit (March/April; www.worldgourmetsummit.com) Four weeks of top chefs, workshops and lavish dinners.

Best Unique Singapore Festivals

Chingay (February; www.chingay.org.sg) Singapore's biggest street party, held on the 22nd day after Chinese New Year.

Singapore National Day (9 August) Extravagant processions and fireworks. Buy tickets in advance.

Singapore Formula One Grand Prix (September; www.singaporegp.sg) Spectacular after-dark F1 racing.

Views & Vistas

Admit it: posting hot travel shots online to torture friends is fun – and Singapore makes the perfect partner in crime. From dramatic skyline panoramas to close-up shots of brightly coloured shutters, food and lurid tropical flora, the city is ridiculously photogenic. So take aim, shoot and expect no shortage of gratifying Likes.

BULE SKY STUDIO/SHUTTERSTOCK ©

Best Skyline Vistas

Smoke & Mirrors Point-blank views of the Padang and Marina Bay skyline from this stylish rooftop bar at the National Gallery of Singapore. (p54)

ION Sky Observation deck on level 56 of the ION Orchard Mall. (p93)

CÉ LA VI SkyBar Cocktails and gobsmacking city vistas from this bar perched atop Marina Bay Sands. (p55)

1-Altitude Rooftop Gallery & Bar 360-degree island views await at the world's highest alfresco bar, 282m above CBD traffic. (p56)

Best for Architecture Buffs

Gardens by the Bay High-tech trees, epic bio-domes, a soaring indoor waterfall and striking sculptures. (p38)

National Gallery Singapore A breathtaking synergy of colonial architecture and innovative contemporary design. (p40)

Chinatown Ornate heritage shophouses and smoky temples with stories to tell. (p137)

Marina Bay Sands A three-tower sci-fi fantasy. (p46)

Emerald Hill Rd An evocative mix of lantern-lit shophouses and elegant, early 20th-century residences. (p86)

Best Is-This-Really Singapore?

Little India Colouring-book facades, shrines and garland stalls, mini mountains of spice and dazzling saris. (p61)

Kampong Glam An *Arabian Nights* fantasy of late-night cafes, intricate Persian rugs and a whimsical, golden-domed mosque. (p61)

Pulau Ubin Tin-roof shacks, free-roaming farm animals and rambling jungle wilderness channel a Singapore long since lost. (p174)

Geylang Road An after-dark world of neon-lit karaoke bars, *kopitiams* (coffeeshops) and seedy side streets with temples and sex workers. (p160)

Four Perfect Days

Day 1

SAIKO3P/SHUTTERSTOCK ©

Take a morning stroll on the **Quays** (p53) for a stunning panorama of brazen skyscrapers and refined colonial buildings, before exploring the remarkable **Asian Civilisations Museum** (p36). Sample some Peranakan perfection at **National Kitchen by Violet Oon** (p51), before seeing the world-class collection of Southeast Asian art at the **National Gallery Singapore** (p40).

In the afternoon discover the temples of **Chinatown** (p137). **Sri Mariamman Temple** (p146) and **Buddha Tooth Relic Temple** (pictured; p144) offer glimpses into neighbourhood life. Then have a pre-dinner tipple on Club St and an early dinner of iconic chilli crab at **Jumbo Seafood** (p51).

Complete your evening with a visit to the nocturnal **Night Safari** (p98).

Day 2

TK KURIKAWA/SHUTTERSTOCK © ARCHITECTS: BENOY

Little India (p61) will erase every preconceived notion of Singapore as a sterile, OCD metropolis. Take in the colours and chanting of **Sri Veeramakaliamman Temple** (p67) before visiting the **Indian Heritage Centre** (p66), to learn the area's fascinating backstory. For lunch turn up the heat at curry house **Lagnaa Barefoot Dining** (p71).

Beat the afternoon heat by heading to the air-conditioned **ION Orchard Mall** (pictured; p83) before enjoying a happy-hour tipple on heritage beauty **Emerald Hill Road** (p86).

When your tummy starts to rumble head to **Satay by the Bay** (p53) and then go exploring the futuristic **Gardens by the Bay** (p38) – don't miss the Supertrees light show (7.45pm and 8.45pm).

Day 3

I VIEWFINDER/SHUTTERSTOCK ©

Wake up early to join the orangutans for **Jungle Breakfast with Wildlife** (p97) at the world-class **Singapore Zoo** (p96). Note feeding times, as the animals are more active then and you have the opportunity to get up-close and personal.

After all that wildlife, it's time for some pure, unadulterated fun on **Sentosa Island** (pictured; p127). Tackle rides at movie theme park **Universal Studios** (p128) or book an indoor skydive at **iFly** (p132).

Finally slow down the pace with evening drinks and dinner on a palm-fringed Sentosa beach. Options include family-friendly **Coastes** (p135) or the more secluded **Tanjong Beach Club** (p134).

Day 4

JOYFULL/SHUTTERSTOCK ©

For a taste of 1950s Singapore, indulge in a local breakfast of *kaya* (coconut jam) toast, runny eggs and strong *kopi* (coffee) at **Chin Mee Chin Confectionery** (p169). Then wander the shop-house-lined streets of **Joo Chiat (Katong)** (p163). Don't miss the pastel beauties on **Koon Seng Road** (p165), before slurping a bowl of cult-status laksa from **328 Katong Laksa** (p168).

Work off lunch by renting a bicycle and cycling the peaceful **East Coast Park** (p167), watching the numerous ships cruising the Strait of Singapore.

In the evening, swap tranquillity for neon-lit **Geylang** (p160), a red-light district juxtaposed with temples, mosques and some of the best food in Singapore. End your night at rooftop bar **Smoke & Mirrors** (p54), where you'll enjoy commanding city views.

Need to Know

For detailed information, see Survival Guide (p177)

Currency
Singapore dollar (S$)

Language
English, Mandarin,
Bahasa Malaysia, Tamil

Visas
Citizens of most
countries are granted
90-day entry on arrival.

Money
ATMs and money-
changers are widely
available. Credit cards
are widely accepted.

Mobile Phones
Numbers start with 9
or 8. Buy tourist SIM
cards (around S$15)
from post offices,
convenience stores
and telco stores – by
law you must show
your passport.

Time
Singapore is (GMT/
UTC plus eight hours

Tipping
Generally not
customary, and
prohibited at
Changi Airport.

Daily Budget

Budget: Less than S$200

Dorm bed: S$25–45

Meals at hawker centres and food courts: around S$6

One-hour foot reflexology at People's Park Complex: S$25

Ticket to a major museum: S$6–20

Midrange: S$200–400

Double room in midrange hotel: S$150–300

Singapore Ducktour: S$43

Two-course dinner with wine: S$80

Cocktail at a decent bar: S$20–28

Top End: More than S$400

Four- or five-star double room: S$350–800

Massage at Remède Spa: S$105

Degustation in top restaurant: S$300-plus

Theatre ticket: S$150

Advance Planning

Two months before Book big-ticket events
such as the Formula One race. Reserve a table
at a hot top-end restaurant.

One month before Book a bed if you're planning to stay in a dorm over the weekend.

One week before Look for last-minute deals
on Singapore accommodation and check
for any events or festivals. Book a posh hotel
brunch or high tea.

Arriving in Singapore

✈ Changi Airport

MRT trains run into town from the airport from 5.30am to 11.18pm; public buses run from 6am to midnight. Both the train and bus trips cost from S$1.69. The airport shuttle bus (adult/child S$9/6) runs 24 hours a day. A taxi into the city will cost anywhere from S$20 to S$40, and up to 50% more between midnight and 6am, plus airport surcharges. A four-seater limousine taxi is S$55, plus a S$15 surcharge per additional stop.

⚓ Harbour Front Cruise Ferry Terminal

MRT trains into town cost from S$1.07. A taxi will cost from S$8 to S$13, plus any surcharges.

🚌 Woodlands Train Checkpoint

Taxis into town cost from S$25 to S$30, plus any surcharges.

Getting Around

Ⓜ MRT

The local subway – the most convenient way to get around between 5.30am and midnight.

🚌 Bus

Go everywhere the trains do and more. Great for views. Run from 5am to 1am the following day, plus some later night buses from the city.

🚕 Taxi

These are fairly cheap if you're used to Sydney or London prices, though there are hefty surcharges during peak hours and from midnight to 6am. Flag one on the street or at a taxi stand. Good luck getting one on rainy days.

🚗 Grab

Singapore's answer to Uber, which it took over in 2018.

Singapore Neighbourhoods

Singapore Zoo &
Night Safari
(12km)

West & Southwest Singapore (p115)
An urban getaway of jungle canopy walks, hilltop cocktails, historic war sites – an off-the-radar cultural gem.

Holland Village, Dempsey Hill & the Botanic Gardens (p101)
Latte-sipping expats, boutique antiques in converted colonial barracks and the luxurious sprawl of Singapore Botanic Gardens.

Singapore Botanic Gardens ◉

Southern Ridges ◉

◉
Universal Studios

Sentosa Island (p127)
Welcome to Fantasy Island, a 'think big' playground of theme parks, activities and shows, sunset beach bars and marina-side dining.

Orchard Road (p83)

Malls, malls, malls – from the futuristic to the downright retro, this air-conditioned thoroughfare is to retail what Las Vegas' Strip is to gambling.

Little India & Kampong Glam (p61)

The Singapore you didn't think existed: gritty, Technicolor laneways bursting with life, sheesha cafes and independent boutiques.

Joo Chiat (Katong) (p163)

Spiritual home of Singapore's Peranakan community, peppered with multicoloured shophouses, shrines and some of the island's best local food spots.

● National Gallery Singapore
● Asian Civilisations Museum

● Chinatown Heritage Centre

● Gardens by the Bay

Colonial District, the Quays & Marina Bay (p35)

Dashing colonial buildings mixed with modern marvels, world-class museums and riverfront dining.

Chinatown & the CBD (p137)

A mix of incense-heady temples and sizzling hawker centres, sky-scrapers and shophouses and jammed with trendy restaurants and bars.

Explore
Singapore

Explore ⊚
Colonial District, the Quays & Marina Bay

The former British administrative enclave is Singapore's showcase, home to a swath of grand colonial buildings, modern architectural marvels, and superlative museums and parks. The Singapore River connects the three quays, which bring a buzzing nocturnal life to the area.

The Short List

○ **Asian Civilisations Museum (p36)** Admiring Southeast Asia's finest collection of pan-Asian treasures.

○ **Gardens by the Bay (p38)** Leaping into a sci-fi future at Singapore's spectacular botanic gardens.

○ **National Gallery Singapore (p40)** Wandering the grand home of the world's largest public display of modern Southeast Asian art.

○ **Marina Bay Sands (p46)** Pondering Singaporean ambition from the top of one of the world's greatest engineering feats.

○ **Peranakan Museum (p46)** Exploring the colour-saturated culture of the Peranakans.

Getting There & Around

Ⓜ The MRT is centred on City Hall, an interchange station that's also connected via underground malls towards the Esplanade, from where you can cut across to Marina Bay. Raffles Place (East–West Line) is the next stop for the Quays. The Bayfront MRT (Downtown Line) serves Marina Bay Sands, Gardens by the Bay and Fort Canning.

Neighbourhood Map on p44

Downtown Singapore TAPANUTH/SHUTTERSTOCK ©

Top Experience 📷

Find Treasures at the Asian Civilisations Museum

The remarkable Asian Civilisations Museum houses the region's most comprehensive collection of pan-Asian treasures. Over three levels, its beautifully curated galleries explore Singapore's heritage as a port city and the connections, history, cultures and religions of Southeast Asia, China, the Indian subcontinent and Islamic west Asia.

◉ MAP P44, D4

📞 6332 7798; 1 Empress Pl

www.acm.org.sg

adult/student/child under 6yr S$20/15/free, 7-9pm Fri half price

🕙 10am-7pm Sat-Thu, to 9pm Fri

Ⓜ Raffles Place, City Hall

Tang Shipwreck

Having sunk more than 1000 years ago, the Tang Shipwreck offers an insight into the history of trade throughout Asia in the 9th century. Laden with exquisite objects and over 60,000 Tang dynasty ceramics, its discovery was literally finding hidden treasure. The mesmerising sea of Changsha bowls surround a replica wooden plank boat, held together by coconut husk rope. Don't bother trying to see your reflection in the ornate bronze mirrors – their silvery alloy has been blackened from centuries underwater. One was even an antique before setting sail and is now over 2000 years old!

Trade Gallery

As people migrated around the region, so did their ideas, tastes and goods. The collection of porcelain is especially strong, covering the history of the different regions in which it was produced. Don't miss the intense blue-and-white Chinese and Middle Eastern ceramics. One for slightly different tastes is the brightly coloured boar's-head tureen and under dish – complete with open nostrils for the steam to escape, it must have made quite the spectacle on its owner's dinner table. It wasn't all about porcelain in the Tang dynasty era, though – the intricate silver tea set was made in China and is one of the few remaining still with its original box.

Ancient Religions Gallery

Ancient Indian religions also spread throughout Asia from the 3rd century BC, specifically Hinduism and Buddhism, and this gallery showcases the changes in religious images that occurred as the new was meshed with the old. Don't miss the terracotta head of a Bodhisattva, whose mane of hair, beard and headdress is incredibly detailed. This gallery is still a work in progress as the museum intends to delve further into the transformations of these religions and others in Asia.

★ Top Tips

o The 3rd-level galleries are only accessible from the stairs and the lift at the rear of the building.

o Mornings are the quietest time to visit to avoid crowds.

o If you enter via the River Entrance, make sure you exit out the main lobby doors to see the building's impressive facade.

✗ Take a Break

An outlet of the Privé (p92) chain can be found in the museum lobby, perfect for a spot of coffee with a nice view of the Singapore River.

Top Experience 📷
Clear Your Mind at Gardens by the Bay

Welcome to the botanic gardens of the future, a fantasy land of space-age bio-domes, high-tech Supertrees and whimsical sculptures. Costing S$1 billion and sprawling across 101 hectares of reclaimed land, Gardens by the Bay is more than a mind-clearing patch of green. This ambitious masterpiece of urban planning is as thrilling to architecture buffs as it is to nature lovers.

◎ MAP P44, H6

☏ 6420 6848

www.gardensbythebay.
com.sg

18 Marina Gardens Dr

gardens free, conservatories adult/child under 13 yr S$28/15

The Conservatories

Housing 226,000 plants from 800 species, the Gardens' asymmetrical conservatories rise like giant paper nautilus shells beside Marina Bay. The Flower Dome replicates a dry, Mediterranean climate and includes ancient olive trees. It's also home to sophisticated restaurant Pollen, which sources ingredients from the Gardens. Cloud Forest Dome is a steamy affair, re-creating the tropical montane climate found at elevations between 1500m and 3000m. Its centrepiece is a 35m-high mountain complete with waterfall.

Supertrees & Sculptures

Sci-fi meets botany at the Supertrees, 18 steel-clad concrete structures adorned with over 162,900 plants. Actually massive exhausts for the Gardens' bio-mass steam turbines, they're used to generate electricity to cool the conservatories. For a sweeping view, walk across the 22m-high **OCBC Skyway** (adult/child under 13 yr S$8/5) connecting six Supertrees at Supertree Grove, where tickets can be bought (cash only, last ticket sale 8pm). Each night at 7.45pm and 8.45pm, the Supertrees become the glowing protagonists of Garden Rhapsody, a light-and-sound spectacular. The most visually arresting of the Gardens' numerous artworks is Mark Quinn's colossal *Planet*. Created in 2008, the sculpture is a giant seven-month-old infant (modelled on Quinn's own son), fast asleep and seemingly floating above the ground.

Far East Organization Children's Garden

Little ones are wonderfully catered for at this interactive garden, specifically designed for kids up to 13 years old. Let them go wild on the obstacle-dotted Adventure Trail and suspension-bridge-linked Treehouses. Finally cool down at the Water Play Zone, complete with motion-sensing water effects and piped-in music.

★ **Top Tips**

o The nearest MRT station to the Gardens is Bayfront.

o Gardens by the Bay operates a handy, on-site **shuttle bus** (⏲9am-9pm, 1st Mon of month from 12.30pm). Buy tickets on board (small denominations of cash only).

o The conservatories are open 5am-2am and the OCBC Skyway is open 9am-9pm.

✗ **Take a Break**

Fine dine in the Flower Dome at **Pollen** (📞6604 9988; www.pollen.com.sg; a la carte 2/3 courses S$88/98, set lunch 3/5 courses S$55/85, 6-course dinner tasting menu S$155; ⏲noon-2.30pm & 6-9.30pm Wed-Mon, Pollen Terrace cafe 9am-9pm Wed-Mon). The restaurant also hosts an excellent afternoon tea.

For a cheaper feed, opt for alfresco hawker centre Satay by the Bay (p53).

Top Experience 📷
Wander the National Gallery Singapore

Ten years in the making, the S$530 million National Gallery is a fitting home for what is one of the world's most important surveys of colonial and post-colonial Southeast Asian art. Housed in the historic City Hall and Old Supreme Court buildings, its 8000-plus collection of 19th-century and modern Southeast Asian art fills two major gallery spaces.

◉ MAP P44, D3

📲 6271 7000

www.nationalgallery.sg

St Andrew's Rd

adult/child S$20/15

🕙 10am-7pm Sat-Thu, to 9pm Fri

🅿; Ⓜ City Hall

The Buildings

Unified by a striking aluminium and glass canopy, Singapore's former City Hall (p43) and Old Supreme Court buildings are now joined to create the country's largest visual arts venue spanning a whopping 64,000 sq metres. Enter via the St Andrew's Rd door to get a real appreciation of how these colonial giants have been seamlessly connected. The two buildings have played pivotal roles in Singapore's journey; City Hall was where the Japanese surrendered to Singapore in 1945 and where Singapore's first prime minister, Lee Kuan Yew, was sworn in. Tours are held daily; don't miss the court holding cells, where many of Singapore's accused waited to hear their fates.

DBS Singapore Gallery

Titled 'Siapa Nama Kamu?' (Malay for 'What Is Your Name?'), this gallery showcases a comprehensive overview of Singaporean art from the 19th century to today. Don't miss Chua Mia Tee's *Portrait of Lee Boon Ngan* in Gallery Two; take note of how her collar sparkles. Also in this gallery, look out for the black-and-white woodblock prints; *Seascape* was a collaboration of six artists; Finally, have your mind bent by Matthew Ngui's *Walks Through a Chair,* remade especially for the gallery.

UOB Southeast Asia Gallery

Examining the art and artistic contexts of the greater Southeast Asian region, this gallery is housed in the Old Supreme Court. Keep an eye on the architecture as well as the walls while you wander around. The darkened Gallery One was once a courtroom but is now filled with art and pieces from the second half of the 19th century when most of Southeast Asia was under colonial rule. Be confronted in Gallery Three by Raden Saleh's wall-filling *Forest Fire;* however, it's the *Wounded Lion,* also by Saleh, that may give you a fright.

★ Top Tip

o The museum runs free one-hour tours through the galleries and also of the building's highlights; highly recommended. Only 20 slots are available on a first-come, first-served basis. Registration opens 20 minutes before each tour at the Tour Desk, B1 Concourse. Check the website for start times.

✕ Take a Break

If you need a quick pit stop head to **Gallery & Co.** (☎6385 6683; www.galleryand.co; 01-17 National Gallery Singapore; ⏲10am-7pm Sat-Thu, to 9pm Fri) for an array of Southeast Asian–inspired dishes and desserts, plus great coffee. Once you've finished chowing down browse the eclectic range of designer books, accessories and souvenirs.

For something a little fancier head to Peranakan favourite National Kitchen by Violet Oon (p51).

Walking Tour 🥾

Colonial Singapore

In a city firmly fixed on the future, the Colonial District offers a glimpse of a romanticised era and its architectural legacies. This is the Singapore of far-flung missionaries and churches, high-society cricket clubs, Palladian-inspired buildings and the legendary Raffles Hotel. This walk takes in some of the city's most beautiful heritage buildings, swaths of soothing greenery, spectacular skyline views and even a spot of contemporary Asian art.

Walk Facts

Start Singapore Art Museum (Ⓜ Bras Basah)

Finish Old Hill Street Police Station (Ⓜ Fort Canning, Clarke Quay)

Length 2.6km; three to four hours

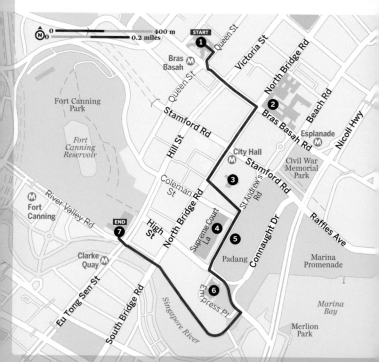

❶ Singapore Art Museum

The **Singapore Art Museum** (SAM; 📱6589 9580; www.singapore artmuseum.sg; 71 Bras Basah Rd) occupies a former Catholic boys school. Original features include the shuttered windows, ceramic floor tiles and inner quadrangle. The central dome and arcade portico were early 20th-century additions.

❷ Raffles Hotel

Head southeast along Bras Basah Rd, passing the Renaissance-inspired Cathedral of the Good Shepherd and the English Gothic Chijmes, a convent-turned-restaurant complex. Diagonally opposite Chijmes is the legendary Raffles Hotel (p47).

❸ St Andrew's Cathedral

You'll find wedding-cake-like **St Andrew's Cathedral** (📱6337 6104; www.cathedral.org.sg; 11 St Andrew's Rd; ⏰9am-5pm) further south on North Bridge Rd. Completed in 1838, it was torn down after being struck by lightning (twice!), and rebuilt by Indian convicts in 1862. It's one of Singapore's few surviving examples of English Gothic architecture.

❹ City Hall

Built in 1928, **City Hall** (1 St Andrew's Rd) is where Lord Louis Mountbatten announced the Japa-nese surrender in 1945 and Lee Kuan Yew declared Singapore's independence in 1965. City Hall and the Old Supreme Court, built in 1939, now house the National Gallery Singapore (p40).

❺ Padang

Opposite City Hall is the open field of the Padang, home to the Singapore Cricket Club and Singapore Recreation Club. It was here that the invading Japanese herded the European community together before marching them off to Changi Prison.

❻ Victoria Theatre

Below where St Andrew's Rd curves to the left stand a group of colonial-era buildings, including the Victoria Theatre & Concert Hall (p57). Completed in 1862, it was originally the Town Hall. It was also one of Singapore's first Victorian Revivalist buildings.

❼ Old Hill Street Police Station

Hang a right to hit the Singapore River. The multicoloured building on the corner of Hill St is the **Old Hill Street Police Station** (formerly MICA Bldg; 140 Hill St; admission free; ⏰10am-7pm). Dubbed a 'skyscraper' when built in 1934, it's now home to a string of private contemporary art galleries.

A

B Orchard Rd

C

D Bencoolen M

Bencoolen St

Waterloo St

Penang Rd

1 Oxley Rd

Oxley Rise

Fort Canning Rd

Canning Walk

National Museum of Singapore

Queen St

Fort Canning Tunnel

3 Battlebox

National Museum of Singapore **1**

Bras Basah M

Victoria St

River Valley Rd

Jln Rumbia

Fort Canning Park

Peranakan Museum

Stamford Rd

2 Tank Rd

Fort Canning Reservoir

Cox Tce

Peranakan Museum **2**

Canning Rise

Armenian St

Stamford Rd

City Hall M

St Andrew's Cathedral

Mohamed Sultan Rd

Merbau Rd

Unity St

17

Robertson Quay

Clemenceau Ave

Fort Canning

River Valley Rd

Hill St

Coleman St

North Bridge Rd

3 30

31

Robertson Quay

Singapore River

Ord Bridge

21

Clarke Quay

24 **32** **8** Singapore River Cruise

High St

National Gallery Singapore

11

14

St Andrew's Rd

Coleman Bridge

Magazine Rd

12

Read Bridge

Merchant Rd

Clarke Quay M

Upper Circular Rd

Elgin Bridge

29

Asian Civilisations Museum

4 Havelock Rd

Cumming St

Eu Tong Sen St

Carpenter St

South Bridge Rd

Circular Rd

27

Boat Quay

Singapore River

Hongkong St

20

North Canal Rd

Hong Lim Park

George St

Cavenagh Bridge

Havelock Square

Upper Pickering St

Chulia St

5 Upper Cross St

Park Cres

Upper Hokien St

Pickering St

Church St

Phillip St

Market St

28

Chinatown M

Upper Cross St

Hokien St

Nankin St

China St

Pekin St

Raffles Place M

6 Eu Tong Sen St

New Bridge Rd

South Bridge Rd

Cross St

Telok Ayer M

Market St

Raffles Quay

A Neil Rd

B

Amoy St

Telok Ayer St

C Cecil St

D

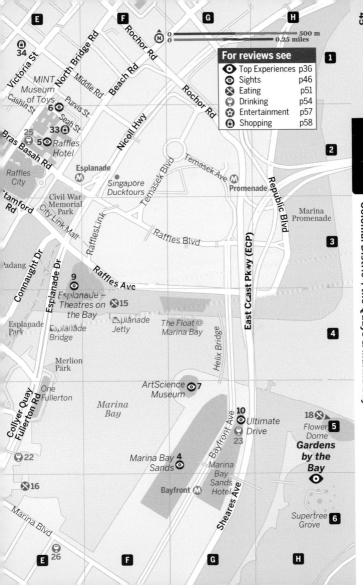

500 m
0.25 miles

For reviews see

◉	Top Experiences	p36
◉	Sights	p46
✖	Eating	p51
●	Drinking	p54
✪	Entertainment	p57
🔒	Shopping	p58

Victoria St

🔒 34

MINT
Museum
of Toys

North Bridge Rd

Middle Rd

Rochor Rd

Beach Rd

Cashin St

Purvis St

Rochor Rd

6 ◉

Seah St

33 🔒

Bras Basah Rd

25 🔒

5 ◉ Raffles
Hotel

Raffles
City

Nicoll Hwy

Esplanade
Ⓜ

Temasek Blvd

Temasek Ave

Promenade Ⓜ

Republic Blvd

Marina
Promenade

Stamford Rd

Civil War
Memorial
Park

City Link Mall

Singapore
Ducktours

Temasek Blvd

Raffles Blvd

3

Connaught Dr

Padang

Esplanade Dr

RafflesLink

Raffles Ave

East Coast Pkwy (ECP)

9 ◉

Esplanade –
Theatres on
the Bay

✖ 15

Esplanade
Jetty

The Float @
Marina Bay

Helix Bridge

4

Esplanade
Park

Esplanade
Bridge

Merlion
Park

ArtScience
Museum

◉ 7

Collyer Quay

Fullerton Rd

One
Fullerton

Marina
Bay

Bayfront
Ave

10
◉ Ultimate
Drive

23

18 ✖
Flower
Dome 5

Gardens
by the
Bay

● 22

Marina Bay
Sands

4
◉

Marina
Bay
Sands
Hotel

Sheares Ave

◉

✖ 16

Bayfront Ⓜ

Supertree
Grove

6

Marina Blvd

● 26

Sights

National Museum of Singapore

MUSEUM

1 ◉ MAP P44, C1

Imaginative and immersive, Singapore's rebooted National Museum is good enough to warrant two visits. At once cutting edge and classical, the space ditches staid exhibits for lively multimedia galleries that bring Singapore's jam-packed biography to vivid life. It's a colourful journey, spanning ancient Malay royalty, wartime occupation, nation-building, food and fashion. Look out for interactive artwork *GoHead/GoStan: Panorama Singapura,* which offers an audiovisual trip through the city-state's many periods. Free guided tours are offered daily; check the website for times. (☏6332 3659; www.nationalmuseum.sg; 93 Stamford Rd; adult/child S$15/10; ◔10am-7pm, last admission 6.30pm; P; MDhoby Ghaut, Bencoolen)

Peranakan Museum

MUSEUM

2 ◉ MAP P44, C2

This is the best spot to explore the rich heritage of the Peranakans (Straits Chinese descendants). Thematic galleries cover various aspects of Peranakan culture, from the traditional 12-day wedding ceremony to crafts, spirituality and feasting. Look out for intricately detailed ceremonial costumes and beadwork, beautifully carved wedding beds and rare dining porcelain. An especially curious example of Peranakan fusion culture is a pair of Victorian bell jars in which statues of Christ and the Madonna are adorned with Chinese-style flowers and vines. At the time of research, the museum was closed for renovations. (☏6332 7591; www.peranakan museum.org.sg; 39 Armenian St; adult/child under 7yr S$10/6, 7-9pm Fri half price; ◔10am-7pm, to 9pm Fri; MCity Hall, Bras Basah)

Battlebox

MUSEUM

3 ◉ MAP P44, C2

Take a tour through the Battlebox Museum, the former command post of the British during WWII, and get lost in the eerie and deathly quiet 26-room underground complex. War veterans and Britain's Imperial War Museum helped re-create the authentic bunker environs; life-size models re-enact the fateful surrender to the Japanese on 15 February 1942. Japanese Morse codes are still etched on the walls. Due to the tour length and underground location, the museum is recommended for children over eight years old. (☏6338 6133; www.battlebox.com.sg; 2 Cox Tce; adult/child S$18/9; ◔tours 1.30pm, 2.45pm & 4pm Mon, 9.45am, 11am, 1.30pm, 2.45pm & 4pm Tue-Sun; MDhoby Ghaut)

Marina Bay Sands

AREA

4 ◉ MAP P44, G5

Designed by Israeli-born architect Moshe Safdie, Marina Bay Sands is a sprawling hotel, casino, mall, theatre, exhibition and museum complex. Star of the show is the **Marina Bay Sands** hotel (📞6688 8888; r from S$550; 🅿️ ❄️ @ 🛜 🏊); its three 55-storey towers connected by a cantilevered **SkyPark** (📞6688 8826; www.marinabaysands.com/sands-skypark; Level 57, Marina Bay Sands Hotel Tower 3; adult/child under 13yr S$23/17; ⏰9.30am-10pm Mon-Thu, to 11pm Fri-Sun). Head up for a drink and stellar views at CÉ LA VI (p55), before catching a show at the MasterCard Theatres or doing serious damage to your credit card at the Shoppes (p59). (www.marinabaysands.com; 10 Bayfront Ave, Marina Bay; 🅿️; Ⓜ️Bayfront)

Raffles Hotel NOTABLE BUILDING

5 ◉ MAP P44, E2

Although its resplendent lobby is only accessible to hotel guests, Singapore's most iconic slumber palace is worth a quick visit for its magnificent ivory frontage, famous Sikh doorman and lush, hushed tropical grounds. It is also peppered with notable retailers and restaurants.

The hotel started life in 1887 as a modest 10-room bungalow fronting the beach (long gone thanks to land reclamation).

Behind the hotel were the Sarkies brothers, immigrants from Armenia and proprietors of two other grand colonial hotels – the Strand in Yangon (Rangoon) and the Eastern & Oriental in Penang.

The hotel's heyday began in 1899 with the opening of the main building, the same one that guests stay in today. Before long, 'Raffles' became a byword for oriental

Marina Bay Sands hotel

MBZUR TRAVEL/SHUTTERSTOCK ©

Colonial District, the Quays & Marina Bay Sights

Raffles Revival

Singapore's most iconic hotel has remained synonymous with Oriental luxury for over a century. Having shut her doors in late 2017, the grand old dame underwent a nearly two-year restoration and renovation (the cost of which is still under wraps, but is considerably more than her 1991 S$160 million facelift!), which will ensure she continues to dazzle visitors with her colonial grandeur, decadence and lashings of luxury.

luxury – 'A legendary symbol for all the fables of the Exotic East', went the publicity blurb – and was featured in novels by Joseph Conrad and Somerset Maugham.

The famous Singapore sling was first concocted here by bartender Ngiam Tong Boon in 1915, and (far less gloriously) a Singaporean tiger, having escaped from a travelling circus nearby, was shot beneath the Billiard Room in 1902. By the 1970s the hotel had become a shabby relic, but dodged the wrecking ball in 1987 when it received National Monument designation and reopened in 1991. (6337 1886; www.rafflessingapore. com; 1 Beach Rd; City Hall, Esplanade)

MINT Museum of Toys   MUSEUM

6 ◎ MAP P44, E2

Nostalgia rules at this slinky ode to playtime, its four skinny floors home to over 50,000 vintage toys. You'll see everything from rare Flash Gordon comics and supersonic toy guns to original Mickey Mouse dolls and oh-so-wrong golliwogs from 1930s Japan. Stock up on whimsical toys at the lobby shop or head to the adjacent **Mr Punch Rooftop Bar** (6339 6266; www.mrpunch. com; 3-11.30pm Mon-Thu, noon-1am Fri, to 11.30pm Sat, to 6.30pm Sun) to celebrate adulthood with a stiff drink. (6339 0660; www. emint.com; 26 Seah St; adult/child S$15/7.50; 9.30am-6.30pm, last Sat of month to 9.30pm; City Hall, Esplanade)

ArtScience Museum   MUSEUM

7 ◎ MAP P44, G5

Designed by prolific Moshe Safdie and looking like a giant white lotus, the lily-pond-framed ArtScience Museum hosts major international travelling exhibitions in fields as varied as art, design, media, science and technology. Expect anything from explorations of deep-sea creatures to retrospectives of world-famous industrial designers. (6688 8826; www.marinabaysands.com; Marina Bay Sands, 10 Bayfront Ave, Marina Bay; adult/child under 13yr from S$16/12;

⏱10am-7pm, last admission 6pm; Ⓜ Bayfront)

Singapore River Cruise

BOATING

8 ◎ MAP P44, C3

This outfit runs 40-minute bumboat tours of the Singapore River and Marina Bay. The boats depart roughly every 15 minutes from various locations, including Clarke Quay, Boat Quay and Marina Bay.

A cheaper option is to catch one of the company's river taxis – commuter boats running a similar route on weekdays; see the website for stops and times. (☏6336 6111; www.rivercruise.com.sg; bumboat river cruise adult/child S$25/15; Ⓜ Clarke Quay)

Esplanade – Theatres on the Bay

ARTS CENTRE

9 ◎ MAP P44, E3

Singapore's S$600 million Esplanade – Theatres on the Bay offers a nonstop program of international and local performances, and free outdoor shows. Book tickets through **SISTIC** (☏6348 5555; www.sistic.com.sg; Level 4 Concierge, ION Orchard, 2 Orchard Turn; Ⓜ Orchard). The controversial aluminium shades – which have been compared to flies' eyes, melting honeycomb and two upturned durians – reference Asian reed-weaving geometries and maximise natural light. Since its opening in 2002, the building has slowly but surely become accepted as part of the local landscape. (☏6828 8377; www.esplanade.com; 1 Esplanade Dr; ⏱box office noon-8.30pm; 🅿; Ⓜ Esplanade, City Hall)

Ultimate Drive

ADVENTURE SPORTS

10 ◎ MAP P44, G5

Dress to kill, then make a show of sliding into the plush interior of a high-end supercar – choose from a range of brightly coloured Ferraris and Lamborghinis – before tearing out for a spin. A taste of luxury can be yours, if only for 15 to 60 minutes. Rides also depart from Suntec City at the convention centre entrance (01-K27) between 10am and 8pm. (☏6688 7997; www.ultimatedrive.com; Tower 3, 01-14 Marina Bay Sands Hotel, 10 Bayfront Avenue as driver/passenger from S$375/300; ⏱9am-10pm; Ⓜ Bayfront)

Singapore Ducktours

Jump into a remodelled WWII amphibious Vietnamese craft for a surprisingly informative and engaging one-hour land-and-water tour. The route focuses on Marina Bay and the Colonial District. (Map p44, F2; ☏6338 6877; www.ducktours.com.sg; Tower 5, 01-330 Suntec City, 3 Temasek Blvd; adult/child under 13yr S$43/33; ⏱10am-6pm; Ⓜ Esplanade)

Architecture

Despite the wrecking-ball rampage of the 1960s and 1970s, Singapore still lays claim to a handful of heritage gems. An ever-expanding list of ambitious contemporary projects has the world watching.

Colonial Legacy

As the administrative HQ of British Malaya, Singapore gained a wave of buildings on a scale unprecedented in the colony. European aesthetics dominated, from the neoclassicism of City Hall, the Fullerton Building and the National Museum of Singapore to the Palladian-inspired Empress Building, now home to the Asian Civilisations Museum. While many other buildings adopted these styles, they were often tweaked to better suit the tropical climate, from the *porte cochère* (carriage porch) of St Andrew's Cathedral to the porticoes of the former St Joseph's Institution, now the location of the Singapore Art Museum.

Shophouses

Singapore's narrow-fronted shophouses are among its most distinctive and charming architectural trademarks. Traditionally a ground-floor business topped by one or two residential floors, these contiguous blocks roughly span six styles from the 1840s to the 1960s. The true scene stealers are those built in the so-called Late Shophouse Style, with richly detailed facades often including colourful wall tiles, stucco flourishes, pilasters and elaborately shuttered windows. Fine examples grace Koon Seng Rd in Joo Chiat (Katong).

Singapore Now

Chinese American IM Pei is behind the iconic brutalist skyscraper OCBC Centre, the silvery Raffles City, and the razor-sharp Gateway twin towers. Britain's Sir Norman Foster designed the UFO-like Expo MRT station and Supreme Court, as well as the South Beach mixed-use development (opposite Raffles Hotel), its two curving towers sliced with densely planted sky gardens. Designed by local studio Woha, the Parkroyal on Pickering hotel features dramatic hanging gardens, while Israeli-born Moshe Safdie's Marina Bay Sands turns heads with its record-breaking, 340m-long cantilevered SkyPark.

Eating

National Kitchen by Violet Oon

PERANAKAN $$

11 🍴 MAP P44, D3

Chef Violet Oon is a national treasure, much loved for her faithful Peranakan dishes – so much so that she was chosen to open her latest venture inside Singapore's showcase National Gallery (p40). Feast on made-from-scratch beauties like sweet, spicy *kueh pie ti* (pastry cups stuffed with prawns and yam beans), dry laksa and beef *rendang*. Bookings two weeks in advance essential. (📞9834 9935; www.violetoon.com; 02-01 National Gallery Singapore, 1 St Andrew's Rd; dishes S$15-42; ⏱noon-2.30pm & 6-9.30pm, high tea 3-4.30pm; Ⓜ City Hall)

Jumbo Seafood

CHINESE $$$

12 🍴 MAP P44, B4

If you're lusting after chilli crab – and you should be – this is a good place to indulge. The gravy is sweet and nutty, with just the right amount of chilli. Just make sure you order some *mantou* (fried buns) to soak it up. While all of Jumbo's outlets have the dish down to an art, this one has the best riverside location. (📞6532 3435; www.jumboseafood.com.sg; 01-01/02 Riverside Point, 30 Merchant Rd; dishes from S$15, chilli crab per kg around S$88; ⏱noon-2.15pm & 6-11.15pm; Ⓜ Clarke Quay)

Whitegrass

AUSTRALIAN $$$

13 🍴 MAP P44, D2

It's all about the details in this fine-dining establishment helmed by chef-owner Sam Aisbett. From the Australian produce to the Roland Lannier steak knives and mural by local illustrator MessyMsxi (it's not wallpaper!), everything is effort-lessly chic. The ever-evolving menu has Japanese and Asian influences and uses only the best produce available; it's truly a dining experi-ence worth booking in for.

Be sure to check the cancel-lation fees on the website before committing to a reservation. (📞6837 0402; www.whitegrass.com.sg; 01-26/27 Chijmes, 30 Victoria St, 2-/3-/5-/8-course lunch S$54/70/142/235, 3-/5-/8-course dinner S$116/170/265; ⏱noon-2pm Wed-Sat, 6-9.30pm Tue-Sat; 🗷; Ⓜ City Hall, Bras Basah)

Odette

FRENCH $$$

14 🍴 MAP P44, D4

Cementing its place in the upper echelons of Singapore's saturat-ed fine-dining scene, this modern French restaurant keeps people talking with its two Michelin stars. With former **Jaan** (📞6837 3322; www.jaan.com.sg) chef Julien Royer at the helm, menus are guided by the seasons and expertly crafted. The space is visually stunning, with a soft colour palette and floating aerial installation by local artist Dawn Ng. (📞6385 0498; www.odetterestaurant.com; 01-04 National

Gallery Singapore, 1 St Andrew's Rd; lunch/dinner from S$128/268; ⊘noon-1.30pm Tue-Sat, 7-9pm Mon-Sat; ⚲; Ⓜ City Hall)

Gluttons Bay
HAWKER $

15 ⊗ MAP P44, F4

Selected by the *Makansutra Food Guide,* this row of alfresco hawker stalls is a great place to start your Singapore food odyssey. Get indecisive over classics like oyster omelette, satay, barbecue stingray and carrot cake (opt for the black version). Its central, bayside location makes it a huge hit, so head in early or late to avoid the frustrating hunt for a table. (www.makansutra.com; 01-15 Esplanade Mall, 8 Raffles Ave; dishes from S$4.50; ⊘5pm-2am Mon-Thu, to 3am Fri & Sat, 4pm-1am Sun; Ⓜ Esplanade, City Hall)

Waku Ghin
JAPANESE $$$

The refinement and exquisiteness of the 10-course degustation menu by acclaimed chef Tetsuya Wakuda is nothing short of breathtaking, and the two Michelin stars only adds to the appeal of this elusive restaurant at Marina Bay Sands (see 4 ⊙ Map p44, G5). Using only the freshest ingredients, the modern Japanese-European repertoire changes daily, though the signature marinated Botan shrimp topped with sea urchin and Oscietra caviar remains a permanent show-stopper. (⚲6688 8507; www.tetsuyas.com; L2-01 Shoppes at Marina Bay Sands, 2 Bayfront

Ave, access via lift A or B; degustation S$450, bar dishes S$20-60; ⊘5.30pm & 8pm seatings, bar 5.30-11.45pm; Ⓜ Bayfront)

Super Loco Customs House
MEXICAN $$

16 ⊗ MAP P44, E6

With a perfect harbourside location and twinkling string lights, this Mexican restaurant injects a laid-back vibe into Singapore's super-corporate CBD. Tacos are the house speciality and the *de baja* with crispy fish and chilli mango salsa is a winner; wash it down with a margarita (choose from eight flavours) while admiring the in-your-face Marina Bay Sands view. (⚲6532 2090; www.super-loco. com; 01-04 Customs House, 70 Collyer Quay; dishes S$8-38, set lunch from S$35; ⊘noon-3pm & 5-10.30pm Mon-Thu, noon-11pm Fri, 5-11pm Sat; ⚲; Ⓜ Raffles Place, Downtown)

Common Man Coffee Roasters
CAFE $$

17 ⊗ MAP P44, A3

While this airy, industrial-cool cafe roasts and serves top-class coffee, it also serves seriously scrumptious grub. Produce is super fresh and the combinations simple yet inspired, from all-day brekkie winners like filo-wrapped soft-boiled eggs paired with creamy hummus, feta, olives, cucumber and tomato, to a lunchtime quinoa salad with grilled sweet potato, spinach, mint, coriander, goat cheese and honey-raisin yoghurt. (⚲6836 4695;

Quays of the City

The stretch of riverfront that separates the Colonial District from the CBD is known as the Quays.

Boat Quay (Map p44, D4; Ⓜ Raffles Place, Clarke Quay) Boat Quay was once Singapore's centre of commerce, and remained an important economic area into the 1960s. The area became a major entertainment district in the 1990s, filled with touristy bars, shops and menu-clutching touts. Discerning punters ditch these for the growing number of clued-in cafes and drinking dens dotting the streets behind the main strip.

Clarke Quay (Map p44, B3; Ⓜ Clarke Quay, Fort Canning) How much time you spend in Clarke Quay really depends upon your personal taste in aesthetics. If pastel hues, Dr Seuss–style design and lad-and-ladette hang-outs are your schtick, you'll be in your element. Fans of understated cool, however, should steer well clear.

Robertson Quay (Map p44, A3; Ⓜ Clarke Quay, Fort Canning) At the furthest reach of the river, Robertson Quay was once used for the storage of goods. Now some of the old *godown* (warehouses) have found new purposes as bars and members-only party places. The vibe here is more 'grown up' than Clarke Quay, attracting a 30-plus crowd generally more interested in wining, dining and conversation than getting hammered to Top 40 hits.

www.commonmancoffeeroasters. com; 22 Martin Rd; mains S$14-29; ⏱7.30am-5pm Mon-Fri, to 5.30pm Sat & Sun; 🛜🍽; Ⓜ Fort Canning)

Satay by the Bay HAWKER $

18 Ⓧ MAP P44, H5

Gardens by the Bay's own hawker centre has an enviable location, alongside Marina Bay and far from the roar of city traffic. Especially evocative at night, it's known for its satay, best devoured under open skies on the spacious wooden deck. The bulk of the food stalls are open 11am to 10.30pm. (☎6538 9956; www. sataybythebay.com.sg; Gardens by the Bay, 18 Marina Gardens Dr, dishes from S$4; ⏱ stall hours vary, drinks stall 24hr; Ⓜ Bayfront)

Song Fa Bak Kut Teh CHINESE $

19 Ⓧ MAP P44, C4

If you need a hug, this cult-status eatery delivers with its *bak kut teh*. Literally 'meat bone tea', it's a soothing concoction of fleshy pork ribs simmered in a peppery broth of herbs, spices and whole garlic cloves. The ribs are sublimely sweet and melt-in-the-mouth, and staff will happily refill your bowl with broth. (☎ 6533 6128; www.songfa.com.sg; 11 New Bridge Rd; dishes S$3.20-11.50; ⏱9am-9.15pm Tue-Sun; Ⓜ Clarke Quay)

Drinking

Smoke & Mirrors BAR

Oozing style, this rooftop bar (see 11 ✕ Map p44, D3) offers one of the best views of Singapore. Perched on the top of the National Gallery, the vista looks out over the Padang (p43) to Marina Bay Sands (p46) and is flanked by skyscrapers on either side. Arrive before sunset so you can sit, drink in hand, and watch the city transition from day to night. Book ahead. (☎ 9234 8122; www.

smokeandmirrors.com.sg; 06-01 National Gallery Singapore, 1 St Andrew's Rd; ⏱3pm-1am Mon-Thu, to 2am Fri, noon-2am Sat, to 1am Sun; Ⓜ City Hall)

28 HongKong Street COCKTAIL BAR

20 🍸 MAP P44, C4

Softly lit 28HKS plays hide and seek inside an unmarked 1960s shophouse. Slip inside and into a slinky scene of cosy booths and passionate mixologists turning grog into greatness. Marked with their alcohol strength, cocktails are seamless and sublime, among them the fruity '93 'til Infinity' with pisco, pineapple, lime and cypress. House-barrelled clas-

Clarke Quay (p53)

sics, hard-to-find beers and lip-smacking grub seal the deal.

Email findus@28hks.com for reservations. (www.28hks.com; 28 Hongkong St; ⏱5.30pm-1am Mon-Thu, to 3am Fri & Sat; Ⓜ Clarke Quay)

Zouk
CLUB

21 Ⓣ MAP P44, B3

Drawing some of the world's biggest DJs and Singapore's see-and-be-seen crowd, this is the place to go to if you want to let loose. Choose between the main two-level club with pumping dance floor and insane lighting, or the hip-hop-centric, graffiti-splashed Phuture. (⏱6738 2988; www.zouk-club.com; 3C River Valley Rd; women/men from S$30/35 redeemable for drinks; ⏱Zouk 10pm-4am Fri, Sat & Wed, Phuture 10pm-3am Wed & Fri, to 2am Thu, to 4am Sat; Ⓜ Clarke Quay, Fort Canning)

Landing Point
LOUNGE

22 Ⓣ MAP P44, E5

For a decadent high tea, it's hard to beat the one at this chichi water-side lounge. Book ahead (one week for weekdays, one month for weekends), style up, and head in on an empty stomach. Steaming pots of TWG tea are paired with delectable morsels like truffled-egg sandwiches, melt-in-your-mouth quiche, brioche buns topped with duck and blueberries, and caramel-filled dark-chocolate tarts. (⏱6333 8388; www.fullerton hotels.com; Fullerton Bay Hotel, 80

Collyer Quay; high tea per adult/child under 12yr S$48/24; ⏱9am-midnight Sun-Thu, to 1am Fri & Sat, high tea 3-5.30pm Mon-Fri, noon-2pm & 3-5pm Sat & Sun; 📶 Ⓜ Raffles Place)

CÉ LA VI SkyBar
BAR

23 Ⓣ MAP P44, G5

Perched on Marina Bay Sands' cantilevered SkyPark, this bar offers a jaw-dropping panorama of the Singapore skyline and beyond. A dress code kicks in from 6pm (no shorts, singlets or flip-flops) and live DJ sets pump from late afternoon. Tip: skip the S$23 entry fee to the SkyPark Observation Deck (p47) – come here, order a cocktail and enjoy the same view. (⏱6508 2188; www.sg.celavi.com; Level 57, Marina Bay Sands Hotel Tower 3, 10 Bayfront Ave; admission S$20, redeemable on food or drinks; ⏱noon-late; Ⓜ Bayfront)

Fleek
CLUB

24 Ⓣ MAP P44, B3

When you're 'on fleek' you're at the pinnacle and this shrine to hip-hop is just that. Tiny compared to neighbouring Clarke Quay megaclubs, Fleek packs a megapunch with a potent formula of pumping beats, cheap drinks and an off-the-hook dance floor. It's the place you go to lose yourself in the music; the Thursday night S$10 house pours will help you on your way. (⏱8808 0854; www.facebook.com/fleeksg; 01-10, 3C River Valley Rd; ⏱6pm-4am Wed-Sat; Ⓜ Clarke Quay, Fort Canning)

Colonial District, the Quays & Marina Bay Drinking

Long Bar

BAR

25 📍 MAP P44, E2

Famous the world over, the Raffles Hotel Long Bar is the very place that bartender Ngiam Tong Boon invented the now legendary Singapore sling in 1915. Having undergone a sensitive restoration, the colonial plantation-inspired bar reopened in September 2018. Thankfully the beloved sling remains the same, as does the tradition of discarding peanut shells directly on the floor. (📞6337 1886; www.rafflessingapore.com; Raffles Hotel, 1 Beach Rd; ⏰11am-11pm; Ⓜ City Hall, Esplanade)

Level 33

MICROBREWERY

26 📍 MAP P44, E6

In a country obsessed with unique selling points, this brewery takes the cake – no, keg. Claiming to be the world's highest 'urban craft brewery', Level 33 brews its own lager, pale ale, stout, porter and wheat beer – order the tasting paddle to try them all. It's all yours to slurp alfresco with a marvellous view over Marina Bay. (📞6834 3133; www.level33.com.sg; Level 33, Marina Bay Financial Tower 1, 8 Marina Blvd; ⏰11.30am-midnight Mon-Thu, to 2am Fri & Sat, noon-midnight Sun; 🛜; Ⓜ Downtown)

Headquarters by the Council

CLUB

27 📍 MAP P44, C4

Don't let the unassuming facade of this shophouse fool you. Follow the just audible thumping beat and look for the Morse code on the pillar till you find yourself joining one of Singapore's hot-test dance floors. Pumping out mainly techno and house, with a dash of disco, this is the place to head to if you want to dance, dance, dance. (📞8125 8880; www.facebook.com/headquarters.sg; Level 2, 66 Boat Quay; ⏰6pm-3am Wed-Fri, 10pm-4am Sat; Ⓜ Clarke Quay)

1-Altitude Rooftop Gallery & Bar

BAR

28 📍 MAP P44, D5

Wedged across a triangle-shaped deck 282m above street level, this is the world's highest alfresco bar, its 360-degree panorama taking in soaring towers, colonial landmarks and a ship-clogged sea. Women enjoy free entry and all-night S$10 martinis on Wednesday, while Get Busy Thursday pumps out hip-hop and R&B hits. Dress up: no shorts or open shoes, gents. (📞6438 0410; www.1-altitude.com; Level 63, 1 Raffles Pl; admission incl 1 drink S$30, from 9pm S$35; ⏰6pm-2am Sun-Tue, to 3am Thu, to 4am Wed, Fri & Sat; Ⓜ Raffles Place)

Singlish, lah!

While there isn't a Singlish grammar as such, there are definite characteristics. Verb tenses tend to be nonexistent. Past, present and future are indicated instead by time indicators, so in Singlish it's 'I go tomorrow' or 'I go yesterday'. Long stress is placed on the last syllable of phrases, so that the standard English 'government' becomes 'guvva-men'.

Words ending in consonants are often syncopated and vowels are often distorted. A Chinese-speaking taxi driver might not immediately understand that you want to go to Perak Rd, since they know it as 'Pera Roh'.

A typical exchange might – confusingly – go something like this: 'Eh, this Sunday you going *cheong* (party), *anot*? No, *ah*? Why like that? Don't be so boring, *lah*!' Prepositions and pronouns are dropped, word order is flipped, phrases are clipped short and stress and cadence are unconventional, to say the least.

The particle *lah* is often tagged on to the end of sentences for emphasis, as in 'No good, *lah*'. Requests or questions may be marked with a tag ending, since direct questioning can be rude. As a result, questions that are formed to be more polite often come across to Westerners as rude. 'Would you like a beer?' becomes 'You wan beer or not?'

For more, check out the Coxford Singlish Dictionary on the satirical website Talking Cock (www.talkingcock.com).

Entertainment

Singapore Symphony Orchestra
CLASSICAL MUSIC

The neo-classical **Victoria Theatre & Concert Hall** (☏6908 8810; www.vtvch.com; ☉10am-9pm) is home to Singapore's well-respected flagship orchestra, which makes its performing home at the 1800-seat state-of-the-art Esplanade – Theatres on the Bay (p49). It plays at least weekly; check the website or SISTIC (p49) for details and book ahead. There is a box office on-site. Student and senior (over 55) discounts available; kids under six years not permitted. (SSO; ☏6602 4245; www.sso.org.sg; 01-02 Victoria Concert Hall, 9 Empress Pl; ☉box office 9am-6.30pm Mon-Fri, 1hr before performances at Victoria Concert Hall; Ⓜ Raffles Place, City Hall)

TheatreWorks THEATRE

30 ⭐ MAP P44, A3

One of the more experimental theatre companies in Singapore, TheatreWorks is led by enigmatic artistic director Ong Keng Sen. A mix of fresh local work and international collaborations, performances are housed in the company's headquarters, a former rice warehouse just off Robertson Quay. See the website for updates. (📞6737 7213; www.theatreworks.org.sg; 72-13 Mohamed Sultan Rd; Ⓜ Fort Canning)

Singapore Repertory Theatre THEATRE

31 ⭐ MAP P44, A3

Based at the KC Arts Centre but also performing at other venues, the SRT produces international repertory standards as well as modern Singaporean plays. Check the website for upcoming productions. (SRT; 📞6733 8166; www.srt.com.sg; KC Arts Centre, 20 Merbau Rd; Ⓜ Fort Canning)

Crazy Elephant LIVE MUSIC

32 ⭐ MAP P44, C3

Anywhere that bills itself as 'crazy' should set the alarm bells ringing, but you won't hear them once you're inside. This touristy, graffiti-lined rock bar is beery, blokey and loud. Music ranges from rock to deep funky blues. Happy hour runs 5pm to 9pm and the musicians hit the stage from 9pm Monday to Saturday and from 8pm Sunday. (📞6337 7859; www.crazyelephant.sg; 01-03/04 3E River Valley Rd; ⏱5pm-2am Tue-Thu & Sun, to 1am Mon, to 3am Fri & Sat; Ⓜ Clarke Quay, Fort Canning)

Shopping

Raffles Boutique GIFTS & SOUVENIRS

33 🔒 MAP P44, E2

It might sound like a tourist trap, but the Raffles Hotel gift shop is a good spot for quality souvenirs, whatever your budget. Pick up anything from vintage hotel posters to handcrafted silk cushions, and branded Raffles stationery, tea sets and toiletries. (📞6412 1143; www.rafflesarcade.com.sg/raffles-boutique; 328 North Bridge Rd, (Seah St Driverway); ⏱9am-8pm; Ⓜ City Hall, Esplanade)

Shoppes at Marina Bay Sands

Shoppes at Marina Bay Sands

GIFTS & SOUVENIRS → MALL

From Miu Miu pumps and Prada frocks to Boggi Milano blazers, this sprawling temple of aspiration (see 4 ◉ Map p44, G5) gives credit cards a thorough workout. Despite being one of Singapore's largest luxury malls, it's relatively thin on crowds – great if you're not a fan of the Orchard Rd pandemonium. The world's first floating Louis Vuitton store is also here, right on Marina Bay. (☏6688 8868; www.marinabaysands.com; 10 Bayfront Ave; ⏱10.30am-11pm Sun-Thu, to 11.30pm Fri & Sat; 🛜; Ⓜ Bayfront)

Kapok

GIFTS & SOUVENIRS

04 🔒 MAP P44, E1

Inside the National Design Centre, Kapok showcases beautifully designed products from Singapore and beyond. Restyle your world with local jewellery from Amado

Free Concerts

If you're hankering for wallet-friendly diversions, Esplanade – Theatres on the Bay (p49) offers free live performances throughout the week, and the Sing-apore Symphony Orchestra (p57) performs free at the Singapore Botanic Gardens (p102) monthly. Check online for details.

Gudek and Lorem Ipsum Store and a flattering dress by GINLEE Studio. Imports include anything from seamless Italian wallets to British striped tees and Spanish backpacks. When you're shopped out, recharge at the on-site cafe. (☏9060 9107; www.ka-pok.com; 01-05 National Design Centre, 111 Middle Rd; ⏱11am-8pm; Ⓜ Bugis, Bras Basah)

Explore

Little India & Kampong Glam

Little India is Singapore trapped in its gritty past – it's frenetic, messy and fun. Spice traders spill their wares across its five-foot ways and Indian labourers swarm into the area each weekend. Kampong Glam, the former home of the local sultan, is an eclectic mix of Islamic stores and eateries, hipster bars and boutiques.

The Short List

○ **Lagnaa Barefoot Dining (p71)** Braving your choice of mouth-burning spice levels at this famous curry house.

○ **Tekka Centre (p73)** Shopping for saris followed by authentic street eats at the downstairs hawker market.

○ **Sri Veeramakaliamman Temple (p67)** Experiencing this atmospheric Hindu temple.

○ **Sifr Aromatics (p79)** Customising the perfect fragrance at this perfume lab.

Getting There & Around

Ⓜ Little India MRT station is right by the Tekka Centre. You can walk here from Rochor, Jalan Besar, Bugis and Farrer Park MRT stations.

Ⓜ Bugis is best for Kampong Glam, and the busy, up-and-coming Jalan Besar area (clustered just south of Lavender St) is easily reached from Bendemeer, Lavender or Farrer Park MRT stations.

Neighbourhood Map on p64

Sultan Mosque (p66) RONNIE CHUA/SHUTTERSTOCK ©

Walking Tour 🥾

A Stroll in Little India

Loud, colourful and refreshingly raffish, Little India stands in contrast to the more sanitised parts of the city. Dive into a gritty, pungent wonderland of dusty grocery shops, gold and sari traders, haggling Indian families and heady Hindu temples. Jumble them all together with a gut-busting booty of fiery eateries and you have Singapore's most hypnotic, electrifying urban experience.

Walk Facts

Start Corner of Buffalo and Race Course Rds (Ⓜ Little India)

Finish Sungei Road Laksa (Ⓜ Jalan Besar)

Length 1.5km; two hours with stops

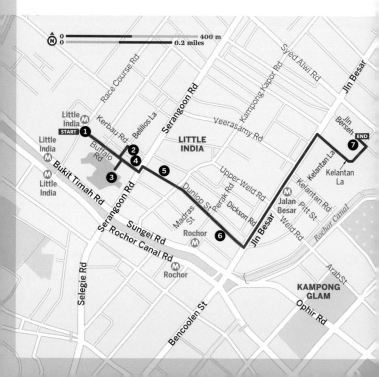

❶ Buffalo Road

Plunge into subcontinental Singapore on Buffalo Rd, a bustling strip packed with brightly coloured facades, Indian produce shops and garland stalls. Flowers used to make the garlands are highly symbolic: both the lotus and the white jasmine spell purity, while the yellow marigold denotes peace.

❷ Tan House

As you walk up Buffalo Rd towards Serangoon Rd, look for an alley on your left leading to Kerbau Rd. Take a quick detour down it and be dazzled by Tan House, quite possibly Singapore's most colourful building. When you're Instagrammed out, head back to Buffalo Rd.

❸ Tekka Centre Wet Market

If it's morning, scour the wet market inside Tekka Centre (p73), where locals battle it out for the city's freshest produce. It's an intense place, stocking everything from fresh yoghurt to dried curry spices. If you're after a sari, the top floor has a swarm of vendors.

❹ Nalli

For quality cotton and silk saris, many locals head to **Nalli** (☑6299 3949; www.nallisingapore.com.sg; 10 Buffalo Rd; ☺10am-9.30pm Mon-Sat, to 7.30pm Sun) directly opposite the Tekka Centre. It's a small, industrious shop where you can pick up cotton saris for as little as S$40. If money isn't an issue, consider opting for a beautiful silk version, which usually go for between S$100 and S$1000.

❺ Thandapani Co

Slip into Dunlop St and look for **Thandapani Co** (☑6292 3163; 124 Dunlop St; ☺9.30am-9.30pm). Adorned with hessian bags packed with chillies, fennel seeds and other Indian staples, this grocery shop is considered one of the city's best spice vendors and stocks ingredients you won't find elsewhere.

❻ Abdul Gafoor Mosque

Equally enticing is **Abdul Gafoor Mosque** (☑6295 4209; www.face book.com/masjidabdulgafoor; 41 Dunlop St; admission free; ☺10am-noon & 2-4pm Sat-Thu, 2.30-4pm Fri), with its peculiar mix of Islamic and Victorian architecture. Completed in 1910, it features an elaborate sundial crowning its main entrance; each of the 25 rays is decorated with Arabic calligraphy denoting the names of 25 prophets.

❼ Sungei Road Laksa

End your local adventure with a cheap, steamy fix at **Sungei Road Laksa** (www.sungeiroadlaksa.com.sg; 01-100, Block 27, Jln Berseh; laksa S$3; ☺9am-6pm, closed 1st & 3rd Wed of the month). The fragrant, savoury, coconut-base soup enjoys a cult following, and only charcoal is used to keep the precious gravy warm. To avoid the lunchtime crowds, head in before 11.30am or after 2pm.

Little India & Kampong Glam

For reviews see
⊙ Sights	p66
⊗ Eating	p71
⊗ Drinking	p76
⊗ Entertainment	p78
⊕ Shopping	p79

Chye Seng
Huat Hardware

Two
Bakers

Jln
Besar
Stadium

Druggists

Sturdee Rd
Petain
Road
Terraces

Petain Rd

Sri Srinivasa
Perumal Temple

Serangoon Rd

Serangoon
Plaza

41

LITTLE
INDIA

Sri
Veeramakalliamman
Temple

3

10 Amrita Ayurveda
& Yoga

21

Farrer
Park Fields

Little
India

37

25

Kerbau Rd

Buffalo Rd

Farrer
Park

Owen Rd

Burmah Rd

Birch Rd

Roberts La

Kinta Rd

Race Course La

Klang Rd

Chander Rd

Race Course Rd

Northumberland Rd

Hampshire Rd

Upper
Dickson
Rd

Norris Rd

Veerasamy Rd

Cuff Rd

Kampong Kapor Rd

Desker Rd

Rowell Rd

Baboo La

Hindoo Rd

Syed Alwi Rd

Verdun Rd

Sam Leong Rd

Kitchener Rd

Desker Rd

Rowell Rd

Jln Besar

16

24

Plumer Rd

Maude Rd

Kitchener Rd

Townshend Rd

Syed Alwi Rd

King George's Ave

Jln Besar

Foch Rd

Tyrwhitt Rd

Horne Rd

Tyrwhitt Rd

Jln Besar

0.2 miles

400 m

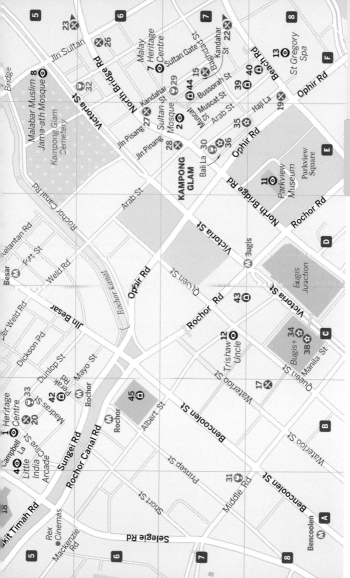

Little India & Kampong Glam

Sights

Indian Heritage Centre
MUSEUM

1  MAP P64, B5

Delve into the origins and heritage of Singapore's Indian community at this S$12 million state-of-the-art museum. Divided into five themes, its hundreds of historical and cultural artefacts, maps, archival footage and multimedia displays explore everything from early interactions between South Asia and Southeast Asia to Indian cultural traditions and the contributions of Indian Singaporeans to the development of the island nation. Among the more extraordinary objects is a 19th-century Chettinad doorway, intricately adorned with 5000 minute carvings. (📞6291 1601; www.indianheritage.org.sg; 5 Campbell Lane; adult/child under 6yr S$6/free; ⏰10am-7pm Tue-Thu, to 8pm Fri & Sat, to 4pm Sun; Ⓜ Little India, Jalan Besar)

Sultan Mosque
MOSQUE

2  MAP P64, E7

Seemingly pulled from the pages of the *Arabian Nights,* Singapore's largest mosque is nothing short of enchanting, designed in the Saracenic style and topped by a golden dome. It was originally built in 1825 with the aid of a grant from Raffles and the East India Company, after Raffles' treaty with the sultan of Singapore allowed the Malay leader to retain sovereignty over the area. In 1928 the original mosque was replaced by

Sri Veeramakaliamman Temple

the present magnificent building, designed by an Irish architect.

Non-Muslims are asked to refrain from entering the prayer hall at any time, and all visitors are expected to be dressed suitably (cloaks are available at the entrance). Pointing cameras at people during prayer time is never appropriate. (📞6293 4405; www.sultanmosque.sg; 3 Muscat St; admission free; ⏰10am-noon & 2-4pm Sat-Thu, 2.30-4pm Fri; Ⓜ Bugis)

Sri Veeramakaliamman Temple
HINDU TEMPLE

3 ◉ MAP P64, B4

Little India's most colourful, visually stunning temple is dedicated to the ferocious goddess Kali, depicted wearing a garland of skulls, ripping out the insides of her victims, and sharing more tranquil family moments with her sons Ganesh and Murugan. The bloodthirsty consort of Shiva has always been popular in Bengal, the birthplace of the labourers who built the structure in 1881. The temple is at its most evocative during each of the four daily *puja* (prayer) sessions. (📞6295 4538; www.sriveeramakaliamman. com; 141 Serangoon Rd; admission free; ⏰5.30am-12.30pm & 4-9.30pm; Ⓜ Little India, Jalan Besar)

Little India Arcade
MARKET

4 ◉ MAP P64, B5

This modest but colourful area of wall-to-wall shops, pungent aromas and Hindi film music is

Petain Road Terraces

Between Jln Besar and Sturdee Rd is an extraordinary row of lavishly decorated double-storey **terraces** (Map p64, E1; Petain Rd; Ⓜ Farrer Park, Bendemeer) dating back to the 1920s. They're a gasp-inducing explosion of colour, from the floral-motif ceramic wall tiles to the pillar bas-reliefs adorned with flowers, birds and trees. The hyper-ornate decoration is typical of what's known as Late Shophouse Style.

a welcome contrast to the prim modernity of many parts of the city. The arcade has an inside section as well as shops running along Campbell Lane. It's the place to come to pick up that framed print of Krishna you've always wanted, eat great food and watch street-side cooks fry chapatis. (📞6295 5998; www.littleindiaarcade.com.sg; 48 Serangoon Rd; ⏰9am-10pm; Ⓜ Little India, Jalan Besar)

Sri Vadapathira Kaliamman Temple
HINDU TEMPLE

5 ◉ MAP P64, D1

Dedicated to Kaliamman, the Destroyer of Evil, this South Indian temple began life in 1870 as a modest shrine but underwent a significant facelift in 1969 to transform it into the beauty standing today. The carvings here – particularly on the *vimana* (domed structure within the temple) – are among the best temple artwork you'll see anywhere in Singapore. ([📞]6298 5053; www.srivadapathirakali.org; 555 Serangoon Rd; admission free; ⏲6am-9pm; [M]Farrer Park, Bendemeer)

Sri Srinivasa Perumal Temple
HINDU TEMPLE

6 [◉] MAP P64, D1

Dedicated to Vishnu, this temple dates from 1855, but the striking, 20m-tall *gopuram* (tower) is a S$300,000 1966 add-on. Inside are statues of Vishnu, Lakshmi and Andal, and Vishnu's bird-mount Garuda. The temple is the starting point for a colourful, wince-inducing street parade during the Thaipusam festival: to show their devotion, many participants pierce their bodies with hooks and skewers. ([📞]6298 5771; www.sspt.org.sg; 397 Serangoon Rd; admission free; ⏲6am-noon & 6-9pm Sun-Mon, 5.30am-12.30pm & 5.30-9.30pm Sat; [M]Farrer Park, Bendemeer)

Malay Heritage Centre
MUSEUM

7 [◉] MAP P64, F6

The Kampong Glam area is the historic seat of Malay royalty, resident here before the arrival of Raffles, and the *istana* (palace) on this site was built for the last sultan of Singapore, Ali Iskandar Shah, between 1836 and 1843. It's now a museum, its galleries exploring Malay-Singaporean culture and history, from the early migration of traders to Kampong Glam to the development of Malay-Singaporean film, theatre, music and publishing.

Free guided tours run at 2pm Tuesdays, Thursdays and Saturdays. ([📞]6391 0450; www.malayheritage.org.sg; 85 Sultan Gate; adult/child under 6yr $6/free; ⏲10am-6pm Tue-Sun; [M]Bugis)

Malabar Muslim Jama-ath Mosque
MOSQUE

8 [◉] MAP P64, F5

Architecture goes easy-wipe at the golden-domed Malabar Muslim Jama-ath Mosque, a curious creation clad entirely in striking blue geometric tiles. This is the only mosque on the island dedicated to Malabar Muslims from the South Indian state of Kerala, and though the building was commenced in 1956, it wasn't officially opened until 1963 due to cash-flow problems. The better-late-than-never motif continued with the tiling, which was only completed in 1995. ([📞]6294 3862; www.malabar.org.sg; 471 Victoria St; admission free; ⏲noon-1pm & 2-4pm Sat-Thu, from 2.30pm Fri; [M]Bugis, Lavender)

Sakya Muni Buddha Gaya Temple
BUDDHIST TEMPLE

9 [◉] MAP P64, D1

Dominating this temple is a 15m-tall, 300-tonne Buddha. Keeping him company is an eclectic cast of deities, including Kuan Yin (Guan Yin; the Chinese goddess of mercy) and, interestingly, the Hindu deities

Banksy, Asian-Style

Street artist Ernest Zacharevic (www.ernestzacharevic.com) has been dubbed the Malaysian Banksy. Born in Lithuania and based in Penang, the twenty-something artist has garnered a global following for his fantastically playful, interactive street art. From Stavanger to Singapore, his murals often incorporate real-life props, whether old bicycles, wooden chairs or even the moss growing out of cracks. In one small work opposite the Malabar Muslim Jama-ath Mosque (Map p64, F5) two exhilarated kids freewheel it on a pair of 3D supermarket trolleys. To the right, a young boy somersaults out of a box, while further south, on the corner of Victoria St and Jln Pisang, a giant girl caresses a snoozing lion cub.

Brahma and Ganesh. The yellow tigers flanking the entrance symbolise protection and vitality, while the huge mother of pearl Buddha footprint to your left as you enter is reputedly a replica of the footprint on top of Adam's Peak in Sri Lanka.

The footprint's 108 auspicious marks distinguish a Buddha foot from any other 2m-long foot. The temple, which stands opposite the Taoist **Leong San See Temple** (☑6298 9371; 371 Race Course Rd; admission free; ☉7.30am-5pm), was founded by a Thai monk in 1927. (Temple of 1000 Lights; 366 Race Course Rd; admission free; ☉8am-4.30pm; Ⓜ Farrer Park, Bendemeer)

Amrita Ayurveda & Yoga
MASSAGE

10 ◎ MAP P64, B4

If Little India's hyperactive energy leaves you frazzled, revive the Indian way with an Ayurvedic (traditional Indian medicine) massage at this modest, friendly place.

Treatments include the highly popular Abhyangam (synchronised massage using medicated oils) and the deeply relaxing Shirodhara (warm oil poured over the forehead). Yoga classes are also on offer. (☑6299 0642; www.amrita.sg; 11 Upper Dickson Rd; 30min massage from S$35; ☉9am-9pm Mon-Sat, to 3pm Sun; Ⓜ Little India, Jalan Besar)

Parkview Museum
MUSEUM

11 ◎ MAP P64, E8

This cavernous 1500-sq-metre contemporary art museum was opened in 2017 by the Parkview Group, owners of the iconic art-deco building Parkview Square in which the museum is housed. Designed to enrich the local art scene and encourage the integration and appreciation of art in everyday life, it features contemporary artworks by international artists.

Dress to impress and head to Atlas (p76), the extravagant lobby bar.(6799 6971; www.parkview-museum.com; Level 3, Parkview Sq, 600 North Bridge Rd; admission free; ⏱noon-7pm; Ⓜ Bugis)

Trishaw Uncle   TOURS

12 ◉ MAP P64, C7

Hop on a trishaw for an old-fashioned ride through China-town, Kampong Glam or Little India. The Chinatown tour also takes in the Singapore River and will drop you off at the Chinatown Heritage Centre (p138), instead of back at the tour starting point. You'll find the trishaw terminal on Queen St, between the Fu Lu Shou Complex and Albert Centre Market and Food Centre. (6337 7111; www.trishawuncle.com.sg; Albert Mall Trishaw Park, Queen St;

adult/child 30min tour from S$39/29, 45min tour S$49/39; Ⓜ Bugis)

St Gregory Spa   SPA

13 ◉ MAP P64, F8

The St Gregory group is a major player in the relaxation stakes, with three facilities in Singapore. This tranquil branch is at the Parkroyal hotel, its forest-inspired design a dreamy backdrop for treatments ranging from Swedish massage, wraps and milk baths to traditional Chinese therapies and oil-based Ayurvedic massage. (✆ 6505 5755; www.stgregoryspa.com; Level 4, Parkroyal, 7500 Beach Rd; treatments S$45-300; ⏱10am-10pm Mon-Fri, 9am-9pm Sat & Sun; Ⓜ Bugis, Nicoll Hwy)

Trishaw Uncle

Eating

Lagnaa
Barefoot Dining

INDIAN $$

14 ✖ MAP P64, B4

You can choose your level of spice at friendly Lagnaa: level three denotes standard spiciness, level four significant spiciness, and anything above admirable bravery. Whatever you opt for, you're in for finger-licking-good homestyle cooking from both ends of Mother India, devoured at Western seating downstairs or on floor cushions upstairs. If you're indecisive, order chef Kaesavan's famous Threadfin fish curry. (🕿6296 1215; www.lagnaa.com; 6 Upper Dickson Rd; dishes S$8-22; ⏱11.30am-10.30pm; 🛜; Ⓜ Little India)

Cicheti

ITALIAN $$

15 ✖ MAP P64, F7

Cool-kid Cicheti is a slick, friendly, buzzing scene of young-gun pizzaioli, chic diners and seductive, contemporary Italian dishes made with hand-picked market produce. Tuck into beautifully charred wood-fired pizzas, made-from-scratch pasta and standouts like *polpette di carne* (slow-cooked meatballs). Book early in the week if heading in on a Friday or Saturday night. (🕿6292 5012; www.cicheti.com; 52 Kandahar St; pizzas S$18-25, mains S$22-56; ⏱noon-2.30pm & 6.30-10.30pm Mon-Fri, 6-10.30pm Sat; Ⓜ Bugis, Nicoll Hwy)

Swee Choon
Tim Sum

DIM SUM $

16 ✖ MAP P64, D3

What started as a single shop-house dim-sum restaurant in 1962, Swee Choon has grown to consume all the floorspace, sidewalk and back alley of four connected shophouses. It's still bursting at the seams, but don't be put off by the throngs of waiting customers as the line is well organised and moves quickly. The salted egg-yolk custard buns are like nothing you've ever tasted. (🕿6225 7788; www.sweechoon.com; 183-191 Jln Besar; dishes S$1.40-9; ⏱11am-2.30pm & 6pm-6am Mon Wed-Sat, 10am-3pm & 6pm-6am Sun; Ⓜ Jalan Besar, Rochor)

QS269 Food House

HAWKER $

17 ✖ MAP P64, B8

This is not so much a 'food house' as a loud, crowded undercover laneway lined with cult-status stalls. Work up a sweat with a bowl of award-winning coconut-curry noodle soup from **Ah Heng** (www.facebook.com/ahhengchickencurrynoodles; soup S$4.50-6.50; ⏱9.30am-10pm) or join the queue at **New Rong Liang Ge** (dishes from S$2.50; ⏱9am-8pm, closed 1st Wed of the month), with succulent roast-duck dishes that draw foodies from across the city. The laneway is down the side of the building. (Block 269B, Queen St; dishes from S$2.50; ⏱stall hours vary; Ⓜ Bugis)

The Singaporean Table

Food is one of Singapore's greatest drawcards, the nation's melting pot of cultures creating one of the world's most diverse, drool-inducing culinary landscapes.

Chinese

Thank the Hainanese for Hainanese chicken rice (steamed fowl and rice cooked in chicken stock, and served with a clear soup, slices of cucumber and ginger, chilli and soy dips), and the Hokkiens for hokkien mee (yellow Hokkien noodles with prawn) and char kway teow (stir-fried noodles with cockles, Chinese sausage and dark sauces). Teochew cuisine is famed for its rice porridge, while Cantonese classics include won-ton soup.

Indian

South Indian's hot flavours dominate. Tuck into thali, a combination of rice, curries, *rasam* (hot, sour soup) and dessert served on a banana leaf. Leave room for *roti prata* (fried flat bread served with curry sauce), *masala dosa* (thin pancake filled with spiced potato and chutney) and halal murtabak (paper-thin pancake stuffed with onion and seasoned meat, usually mutton).

Malaysian & Indonesian

Feast on Katong laksa (spicy coconut curry broth with noodles, prawns, cockles, fish cake, bean sprouts and laksa leaf), *ikan assam* (fried fish in a sour tamarind curry) and *nasi lemak* (coconut rice with fried fish and peanuts). Equally mouth-watering is *nasi padang,* which sees steamed rice paired with a choice of meat and vegetable dishes – simply pick and choose what you want and it's dolloped on a plate.

Peranakan

Peranakan (Nonya) food is a cross-cultural fusion of Chinese and Malay influences. Dishes are tangy, spicy and commonly flavoured with shallots, chillies, *belacan* (Malay fermented prawn paste), peanuts, preserved soya beans and galangal (a ginger-like root). Classics include *otak-otak,* a sausage-like blend of fish, coconut milk, chilli paste, galangal and herbs grilled in a banana leaf.

Tekka Centre

HAWKER $

18 MAP P64, A5

There's no shortage of subcontinental spice at this bustling hawker centre, wrapped around the sloshed guts and hacked bones of the wet market. Queue up for real-deal biryani, *dosa* (paper-thin lentil-flour pancake), *roti prata* (fried flatbread served with curry sauce) and *teh tarik* (sweet spiced Indian tea). Well worth seeking out is **Ah Rahman Royal Prata** (murtabak S$5-8; ⊙7am-10pm Tue-Sun), which flips some of Singapore's finest murtabak (stuffed savoury pancake). (cnr Serangoon & Buffalo Rds; dishes S$3-10; ⊙7am-11pm, stall hours vary; P ; M Little India)

Piedra Negra

MEXICAN $$

19 MAP P64, F8

Sexy Latin beats, bombastic murals and tables right on free-spirited Haji Lane: this electric Mexican joint is a brilliant spot for cheapish cocktails and a little evening people-watching. Frozen or shaken, the margaritas pack a punch, and the joint's burritos, quesadillas, tacos and other Tex-Mex staples are filling and delish. (6291 1297; www.facebook.com/piedranegrasg; cnr Beach Rd & Haji Lane; mains S$10-22; ⊙noon-midnight Sun-Thu, to 2am Fri & Sat; ; M Bugis)

Meatsmith Little India

BARBECUE $$$

20 MAP P64, B5

Often referred to as the little cousin of Burnt Ends (p147) because it's partly owned by chef David Pynt, this American barbecue joint takes inspiration from the bustling streets of Little India that surround it. Think prime meats slathered in Indian spices and rubs then smoked, grilled or charred to perfection – the double-glazed beef rib is fall-off-the-bone tender. (9625 9056; www.meatsmith.com.sg; 21 Campbell Lane; mains S$16-48; ⊙5pm-midnight Tue-Fri, 11.30am-11.30pm Sat & Sun; M Little India)

Komala Vilas

SOUTH INDIAN $

21 MAP P64, B4

This prime-position branch of the Komala Vilas chain is extremely popular because of the wallet-friendly, authentic dishes and generous portions. The wafer-thin *dosai* are legendary – order the meal and enjoy it served with three vegetable curries and condiments. Complete your feast with a warm masala tea, served in a traditional metal cup. (6293 6980; www.komalavilas.com.sg; 76-78 Serangoon Rd; dishes S$2.40-9; ⊙7am-10.30pm; ; M Little India)

Moghul Sweets

SWEETS $

If you're after a subcontinental sugar rush, tiny Moghul Sweets in the Little India Arcade (see **4** Map p64, B5) is the place to get it. Bite into luscious *gulab jamun* (syrup-soaked fried dough balls), harder-to-find *rasmalai* (paneer soaked in cardamom-infused clotted cream) and *barfi* (condensed milk and sugar slice) in flavours including pistachio, chocolate ... and carrot. (📞 6392 5797; 01-16 Little India Arcade, 48 Serangoon Rd; sweets from S$1; ⏱ 9.30am-9.30pm; Ⓜ Little India)

Charlie's Peranakan

PERANAKAN $

22 ✕ MAP P64, F7

Charlie has garnered a loyal following over the past few decades for his comforting Nonya cuisine. After an eight-year hiatus he's back doing what he loves, and Singaporeans are joyous. Tucked away in the basement of Golden Mile Food Centre, you'll find a menu overflowing with Peranakan favourites – ask Charlie or his wife what they recommend and order that. (📞 9789 6304; www.facebook.com/charliesperanakanfood;

New-School Hood

Once better known for hardware stores and boxing matches, Jalan Besar is metamorphosing into an area where heritage architecture meets new-school Singapore cool. It's a compact district, centred on Jln Besar and Tyrwhitt Rd. It's on the latter you'll find cult-status cafe-roaster **Chye Seng Huat Hardware** (CSHH Coffee Bar; Map p64, F2; 📞 6396 0609; www.cshhcoffee.com; 150 Tyrwhitt Rd; ⏱ 9am-10pm Tue-Thu & Sun, to midnight Fri & Sat; Ⓜ Bendemeer, Farrer Park, Lavender).

Around the corner, on Horne Rd, is contemporary bakery-cafe **Two Bakers** (Map p64, F2; 📞 6293 0329; www.two-bakers.com; 88 Horne Rd; pastries & cakes S$6.50-9; ⏱ 9am-6pm Mon, Wed, Thu & Sun, 10am-10pm Fri & Sat; Ⓜ Bendemeer, Lavender), where the sweet treats are created by Paris' Cordon Bleu-trained bakers. If it's late afternoon, cool down at nearby beer joint **Druggists** (Map p64, F2; 📞 6341 5967; www.facebook.com/druggistssg; 119 Tyrwhitt Rd; ⏱ 4pm-midnight Mon-Thu, to 2am Fri & Sat, 2-10pm Sun; Ⓜ Bendemeer, Farrer Park, Lavender). Its 23 taps pour a rotating selection of craft brews from microbreweries around the world.

To reach Jalan Besar, alight at Bendermeer MRT and head to Lavender St; crossing this you'll find Tyrwhitt Rd on your left as you head north.

B1-30, Golden Mile Food Centre, 505 Beach Rd; dishes S$6-20; ⏱11.30am-7.30pm; Ⓜ Lavender, Nicoll Hwy, Bugis)

Hill Street Tai Hwa Pork Noodle HAWKER $

23 ✕ MAP P64, F5

Locals have tried to keep this second-generation hawker stall – famous for Teochew-style bak chor mee (minced-pork noodles) – secret, but with its shiny Michelin star, that's now impossible. It's best to arrive early; before opening, you can grab a number instead of joining the forever-lengthening queue. Bowls come in four sizes; the S$8 option will fill you right up. (www.taihwa. sg, 01-12, Block 466, Crawford Lane, noodles S$6-10; ⏱9.30am-9pm; Ⓜ Lavender)

Beach Road Scissor Cut Curry Rice HAWKER $

24 ✕ MAP P64, E3

The eponymous rice dish is possibly the most visually displeasing plate of food you'll ever see, but after one mouthful, you're bound to dive in for more. Choose from the items displayed in the glass cabinet and then watch the scissors snip it all into bite-sized pieces. Finally, curry and braised sauces are slopped on, and it's a gloriously delicious mess. (229 Jln Besar, cnr Kitchener Rd; dishes from $3.50; ⏱11am-3.30am; Ⓜ Lavender, Farrer Park)

Gandhi Restaurant SOUTH INDIAN $

25 ✕ MAP P64, A4

It might be a canteen-style joint with erratic service and cheap decor, but who cares when the food is this good? Wash your hands by the sink at the back, and take a seat. A banana-leaf plate heaped with rice and condiments (set-meal thali) will appear; order extra items from the servers – chicken curry is a must – then tuck in. (29-31 Chander Rd; dishes S$2.50-6.50, set meals from S$4.50; ⏱11am-4pm & 6-11pm Mon-Fri, 11am-11pm Sat & Sun; Ⓜ Little India)

Nan Hwa Chong Fish-Head Steamboat Corner CHINESE $$

26 ✕ MAP P64, F6

If you only try fish-head steamboat once, do it at this noisy, open-fronted veteran. Cooked on charcoal, the large pot of fish heads is brought to you in a steaming broth spiked with tee po (dried flat sole fish). One pot is enough for three or four people, and can stretch to more with rice and side dishes. (☏6297 9319; www.facebook. com/nanhwachong; 812-816 North Bridge Rd; fish steamboats from S$20; ⏱4pm-1am; Ⓜ Bugis, Lavender)

Warong Nasi Pariaman MALAYSIAN, INDONESIAN $

27 ✕ MAP P64, E6

This no-frills corner nasi padang (rice with curries) stall is the stuff of legend. Top choices include the delicate beef *rendang,* ayam bakar (grilled chicken with coconut sauce) and spicy sambal goreng (long beans, tempeh and fried beancurd). Get here by 11am to avoid the lunch hordes and by 5pm for the dinner queue. (☑6292 2374; www.pariaman.com.sg; 736-738 North Bridge Rd; dishes from S$3; ⏱7.30am-8pm; Ⓜ Bugis)

Zam Zam   MALAYSIAN $

28 MAP P64, E7

These guys have been here since 1908, so they know what they're doing. Tenure hasn't bred complacency, though – the touts still try to herd customers in off the street, while frenetic chefs inside whip up delicious murtabak, the restaurant's speciality savoury pancakes, filled with succulent mutton, chicken, beef, venison or even sardines. Servings are epic, so order a medium between two. (☑6298 6320; www.zamzamsingapore.com; 697-699 North Bridge Rd; murtabak from S$5; ⏱7am-11pm; Ⓜ Bugis)

Drinking

Atlas   BAR

Straight out of 1920s Manhattan, this cocktail lounge in the lobby of the Parkview Museum (see 11 ⓞ Map p64, E8) is an art-deco-inspired extravaganza, adorned with ornate bronze ceilings and low-lit plush lounge seating, with a drinks menu filled with decadent champagnes, curated cocktails and some mean martinis. However, it's the 12m-high gin wall, displaying over 1000 labels, that really makes a statement – make sure you ask for a tour.

Night-time bookings are essential, but if you arrive before 6pm you should still be able to nab a table. Doors open in the morning for coffees, and European–inspired bites are served throughout the day and well into the night. The afternoon tea (3pm to 5pm, from S$52) is also worth stopping in for. Dress to impress; no shorts or slippers after 5pm. (☑6396 4466; www.atlasbar.sg; Lobby, Parkview Sq, 600 North Bridge Rd; ⏱10am-1am Mon-Thu, to 2am Fri, 3pm-2am Sat; Ⓜ Bugis)

Maison Ikkoku The Art of Mixology   COCKTAIL BAR

29 🚇 MAP P64, F7

Pimped with modern, industrial finishes and flushes of greenery, Maison Ikkoku The Art of Mixology is where real magic happens. There's no menu, so let the bartenders know what you like – a request for something sour might land you a tart, hot combo of spicy gin, grape, lemon and Japanese–chilli threads. Not cheap, but worth it. (☑6294 0078; www.ethanleslieleong.com; Level 2, 20 Kandahar St; ⏱bar 6pm-1am Sun-Thu, to 2am Fri & Sat; 🛜; Ⓜ Bugis)

Bar Stories   COCKTAIL BAR

30 🚇 MAP P64, E7

This upstairs cocktail den is as small as it is hugely popular, so call ahead if heading in later in the week. If you're lucky you'll be sitting at the bar, where gung-ho barkeeps keep it freestyle, turning whatever spirit or flavour turns you on into a smashing libation. Creative, whimsical and often brilliant. (☎ 6298 0838; www.facebook.com/barstories.sg; 57A Haji Lane; ⏰ 5pm-1am Sun-Thu, to 2am Fri & Sat; Ⓜ Bugis)

Ginett
WINE BAR

 31 ☺ MAP P64, A7

Pouring possibly the most affordable glass of wine in town (S$6), Ginett has garnered a large following of winer lovers who enjoy a decent glass of cheap French plonk. With soaring ceilings and a modern industrial bistro design, the space feels simultaneously sophisticated and casual. Take a seat

at the bar underneath row upon row of glistening hanging glasses, and sip the night away.

If you're feeling peckish, the cheese and cold cuts board will keep the hunger pangs at bay. (☎ 6809 7989; www.randblab.com; 200 Middle Rd; ⏰ 7am-11.30pm Sun-Thu, to 12.30am Fri & Sat; Ⓜ Bencoolen, Rochor)

Beast
BAR

 32 ☺ MAP P64, F6

If you're after some hard liquor and only bourbon will do, pull up a stool at a rusty drum and start working your way through the Beast's grandiose selection, including home-brewed Southern Comfort. The kitchen churns out lip-smacking American

Little India & Kampong Glam Drinking

Zam Zam

Bollywood at the Rex

Where can you catch the Bollywood blockbusters advertised all over Little India? Why, at **Rex Cinemas** (Map p64, A5; ☑6337 6607; www.carnivalcinemas.sg; 2 Mackenzie Rd; tickets S$10; Ⓜ Little India), of course. This historic theatre screens films from around the subcontinent, most subtitled in English.

Deep South–style food; the fried chicken and waffles is a standout. Live-music lovers shouldn't miss Thursday's open-mike night. (☑6295 0017; www.thebeast.sg; 17 Jln Klapa; ☺5pm-midnight Mon-Wed, to 1am Thu & Fri, 11am-midnight Sat & Sun; Ⓜ Bugis)

Prince of Wales   PUB

 33 MAP P64, B5

The closest thing to a pub in Little India, this grungy Aussie hangout is an affable, popular spot, with a small beer garden, a pool table and sports screens. Weekly staples include Wednesday quiz night (from 8pm) and live music every other night of the week. There are plenty of good drink deals to keep the good times rolling. (☑6299 0130; www.pow.com.sg; 101 Dunlop St; ☺5pm-1am Mon-Thu, 3pm-2am Fri & Sat, to 1am Sun; Ⓜ Rochor, Jalan Besar)

Entertainment

Singapore Dance Theatre   DANCE

 34 MAP P64, C8

This is the headquarters of Singapore's premier dance company, which keeps fans swooning with its repertoire of classic ballets and contemporary works, many of which are performed at Esplanade – Theatres on the Bay (p49). The true highlight is the group's Ballet under the Stars season at **Fort Canning Park** (☑1800 471 7300; www.nparks.gov.sg; bounded by Hill St, Canning Rise, Clemenceau Ave & River Valley Rd; Ⓜ Dhoby Ghaut, Clarke Quay, Fort Canning), which usually runs midyear. See the website for program details. (☑6338 0611; www.singaporedancetheatre.com; 07-02/03, Bugis+, 201 Victoria St; Ⓜ Bugis)

BluJaz Café   LIVE MUSIC

 35 MAP P64, E7

Bohemian pub BluJaz is one of the best options in town for live music, with regular jazz jams, and other acts playing anything from blues to rockabilly. Check the website for events, which includes DJ-spun funk, R&B and retro nights, as well as 'Talk Cock' open-mike comedy nights on Wednesdays and Thursdays. Cover charge for some shows. (☑6292 3800; www.blujazcafe.net; 11 Bali Lane; ☺9am-12.30am Mon-Tue, to 1am Wed-Thu, to 2.30am Fri-Sat, noon-midnight Sun; 🛜; Ⓜ Bugis)

Going Om
LIVE MUSIC

36 ⭐ MAP P64, E7

Right on Haji Lane, Going Om is a raffish, free-spirited cafe with nightly live music. It's an atmospheric spot, with candlelit tables, smooth acoustic sets (mostly well-executed covers) and no shortage of carefree punters dancing in the laneway. The boho spirit extends to the beverage list, which includes 'chakra' drinks of seven colours (one for each chakra, dude). (✆ 6396 3592; www.going-om.com.sg; 63 Haji Lane; ⏱ noon-midnight Sun-Thu, to 1am Fri & Sat; Ⓜ Bugis)

Wild Rice @ Funan
THEATRE

37 ⭐ MAP P64, A4

Singapore's sexiest theatre group is based in Kerbau Rd but performs shows elsewhere in the city (as well as abroad). A mix of home-grown and foreign works, productions range from farce to serious politics, fearlessly wading into issues not commonly on the agenda in Singapore.

Many performances take place at the LASALLE College of the Arts, located at 1 McNally St, just steps from the Rochor MRT station. (✆ 6348 5555; www.wildrice. com.sg; Level 4, Funan Mall, 107 North Bridge; Ⓜ City Hall)

Hood
LIVE MUSIC

38 ⭐ MAP P64, C8

Inside the Bugis+ mall, Hood's street-art interior sets a youth-ful scene for nightly music jams with acts such as Rush Hour and Singapore Char Siew Baos. If it's undiscovered talent you're after, head in for the weekly 'Saturday Original Session', a showcase for budding musos itching to share their singer-songwriter skills. (✆ 6221 8846; www.hoodbarandcafe. com; 05-07 Bugis+, 201 Victoria St; ⏱ 5pm-1am Sun-Thu, to 3am Fri & Sat; Ⓜ Bugis)

Shopping

Sifr Aromatics
PERFUME

39 🔒 MAP P64, F7

This Zen-like perfume laboratory belongs to third generation perfumer Johari Kazura, whose exquisite creations include the heady East (30mL S$125), a blend of oud, rose absolute, amber and neroli. The focus is on custom-made fragrances (consider calling ahead to arrange an appoint-ment), with other heavenly offerings including affordable, high-quality body balms, scented candles and vintage perfume bottles. (✆ 6392 1966; www.sifr.sg; 42 Arab St; ⏱ 11am-8pm Mon-Sat, to 5pm Sun; Ⓜ Bugis)

Supermama
GIFTS & SOUVENIRS

40 🔒 MAP P64, F8

Tucked around the corner from Arab St, this gallery-esque store is a treasure trove of contemporary giftware. Circle the huge central bench while you pore over the Singapore-inspired wares, most

Instagram Paradise

Narrow, pastel-hued **Haji Lane** (Map p106, E8; **M**Bugis) harbours a handful of quirky boutiques and plenty of colourful street art. Shops turn over fast due to exorbitant rents, however a long-term favourite is concept store Mondays Off, which stocks everything from contemporary local ceramics to art mags and geometric racks to store them on. For a sweet treat, stop off at whimsical Windowsill Pies.

created by local designers. The blue-and-white fine-porcelain dishes, made in Japan, are the headliners. (☑6291 1946; www.supermama.sg; 265 Beach Rd; ⏱11am-8pm; **M**Bugis)

Mustafa Centre DEPARTMENT STORE

41 🔒 MAP P64, C2

Little India's bustling Mustafa Centre is a magnet for budget shoppers, most of them from the subcontinent. It's a sprawling place, selling everything from electronics and garish gold jewellery to shoes, bags, luggage and beauty products. There's also a large supermarket with a great range of Indian foodstuffs. If you can't handle crowds, avoid the place on Sundays. (☑6295 5855; www.mustafa.com.sg; 145 Syed Alwi Rd; ⏱24hr; **M**Farrer Park)

Rugged Gentlemen Shoppe FASHION & ACCESSORIES

42 🔒 MAP P64, B5

A vintage-inspired ode to American working-class culture, this little menswear store offers a clued-in selection of rugged threads and accessories, including Red Wing boots, grooming products and made-in-house leather goods. Stock up on plaid shirts, sweat tops and harder-to-find denim from brands like Japan's Iron Heart and China's Red Cloud. (☑6396 4568; www.uggedgentlemenshoppe.com; 8 Perak Rd; ⏱noon-8pm Mon-Sat, by appointment Sun; **M**Rochor, Jalan Besar)

Bugis Street Market MARKET

43 🔒 MAP P64, C7

What was once Singapore's most infamous sleaze pit – packed with foreign servicemen on R&R and gambling dens – is now its most famous undercover street market, crammed with cheap clothes, shoes, accessories and manicurists. It's especially popular with teens and twenty-somethings – in a nod to its past, there's even a sex shop. (☑6338 9513; www.bugisstreet.com.sg; 3 New Bugis St; ⏱11am-10pm; **M**Bugis)

Little Shophouse ARTS & CRAFTS

44 🔒 MAP P64, F7

Traditional Peranakan beadwork is a dying art, but it's kept very much alive in this shop and workshop.

Haji Lane

The shop's colourful slippers are designed by craftsman Robert Sng and hand-beaded by himself and his sister, Irene. While they're not cheap (approximately S$1000), each pair takes a painstaking 100 hours to complete. You'll also find Peranakan-style tea sets, crockery, vases, handbags and jewellery. (☏6295 2328; 43 Bussorah St; ⏱10am-5pm; Ⓜ Bugis)

Sim Lim Square
ELECTRONICS

45 🔒 MAP P64, B6

A byword for all that is cut price and geeky, Sim Lim Square is jammed with stalls selling soundcards cameras, laptops and games consoles. If you know what you're doing, there are deals to be had, but the untutored are likely to be out of their depth. Bargain hard (but politely) and always check that the warranty is valid in your home country. (☏6338 3859; www.simlimsquare.com.sg; 1 Rochor Canal Rd; ⏱10.30am-9pm; Ⓜ Rochor, Jalan Besar)

Explore ✦

Orchard Road

What was once a dusty road lined with spice plantations and orchards is now a 2.5km torrent of magnificent malls, department stores and speciality shops. Indeed, you can shop until you drop, pick yourself up and continue spending. But wait there's more, including drool-inducing food courts and a heritage-listed side street rocking with bars and happy-hour specials.

The Short List

○ **ION Orchard Mall (p93)** *Shopping at Singapore's sleekest mall.*

○ **Tanglin Shopping Centre (p93)** *Hunting for antique treasures.*

○ **Emerald Hill Road (p86)** *Strolling this heritage-packed area.*

○ **Iggy's (p87)** *Tasting creative fusion dishes.*

○ **Killiney Kopitiam (p89)** *Enjoying breakfast at the original locals' coffeeshop.*

Getting There & Around

Ⓜ Orchard Rd is served by no less than three MRT stations: Orchard, Somerset and Dhoby Ghaut, so there's really no need to use any other form of transport.

Neighbourhood Map on p84

Orchard Road KOMAR/SHUTTERSTOCK ©

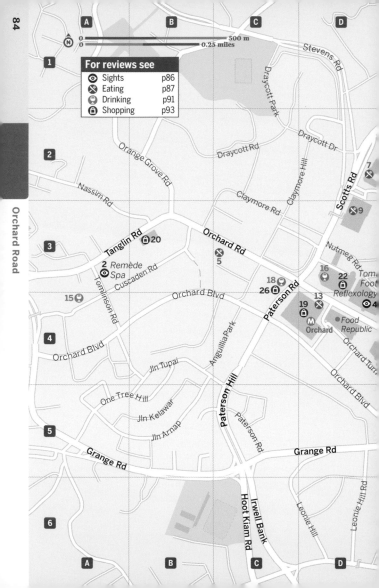

For reviews see

0 ———— 500 m
0 ———— 0.25 miles

Stevens Rd

Draycott Park

Draycott Rd

Draycott Dr

Orange Grove Rd

Nassim Rd

Claymore Hill

Claymore Rd

Scotts Rd

7

9

Tanglin Rd

20

Orchard Rd

5

Nutmeg Rd

2 Remède Spa

Cuscaden Rd

Tomlinson Rd

Orchard Blvd

18

26

Paterson Rd

16

22 Tom
Foot
Reflexology

15

19

13

4

M Orchard

Food Republic

Angullia Park

Orchard Blvd

Orchard Turf

Orchard Blvd

Jln Tupai

Paterson Hill

One Tree Hill

Jln Kelawar

Jln Arnap

Paterson Rd

Leonie Hill

Grange Rd

Grange Rd

Irwell Bank

Hoot Kiam Rd

Leonie Hill

Leonie Hill

E

F

G

H

Goodwood Hill

Scotts Rd

Bukit Timah Rd

14

1

6

Anthony Rd

Peck Hay Rd

Clemenceau Ave Nth

Monk's Hill Rd

Cavenagh Rd

2

Cairnhill Rd

Mount Elizabeth

Cairnhill Rise

Istana Park

3
Istana

3

Cairnhill Circle

Emerald Hill Rd

Cavenagh Rd

Central Expwy

Bideford Rd

Cairnhill Rd

Saunders Rd

12

1
Hullet Rd Emerald Hill
Road

Ice Cold Beer ●

Que Pasa ●

Buyong Rd

4

17

Orchard Rd

23

Kramat Rd

Takashimaya
Food Village

10

24

11

Singapore
Visitors Centre
@ Orchard

Keok Rd

Kramat La

Orchard Link

Grange Rd

Penang
Rd

25

Somerset

Orchard Rd

Penang Rd

5

Edinburgh Rd

Exeter Rd

Killiney Rd

Eber Rd

Oxley Rd

Dhoby
Ghaut

St Thomas Walk

Devonshire Rd

Killiney Rd

Lloyd Rd

Oxley Rise

Clemenceau Ave

Penang La

6

8

E

F

G

H

Sights

Emerald Hill Road ARCHITECTURE

1 ⊙ MAP P84, F4

Take time out from your shopping to wander up frangipani-scented Emerald Hill Rd, graced with some of Singapore's finest terrace houses. Special mentions go to No 56 (one of the earliest buildings from 1902), Nos 39 to 45 (unusually wide frontages and a grand Chinese–style entrance gate), and Nos 120 to 130 (art-deco features dating from around 1925). At the Orchard Rd, there is a cluster of popular bars housed in fetching shophouse renovations. (Emerald Hill Rd; M Somerset)

Remède Spa SPA

2 ⊙ MAP P84, A3

Reputed to have the best massage therapists in town, the St Regis Hotel's in-house spa is also home to the award-winning Pedi:Mani:Cure Studio by renowned pedicurist Bastien Gonzalez. Remède's wet lounge – a marbled wonderland of steam room, sauna, ice fountains and spa baths – is a perfect prelude to standout treatments like the warm jade-stone massage ($310). (☎ 6506 6896; www.remedespasing apore.com; St Regis Hotel, 29 Tanglin Rd; massage from S$108; ☉ 10am-8pm Sun-Fri, 9am-10pm Sat; M Orchard)

Istana PALACE

3 ⊙ MAP P84, H3

The grand, whitewashed, neo-classical home of Singapore's president, set in 16 hectares of grounds, was built by the British between 1867 and 1869 as Government House, and is open to visitors just five times a year. Check the website to confirm exact dates. Only on these days will you get the chance to stroll past the nine-hole golf course, through the beautiful terraced gardens and into some of the reception rooms. Bring your passport and get here early; queues build quickly.

The rest of the time you can visit the **Istana Heritage Gallery** (☎ 6904 4289; www.istana.gov. sg; admission free; ☉ 10am-6pm, closed Wed) across Orchard Rd or glance through the heavily guarded gates. (www.istana.gov.sg; Orchard Rd; grounds/palace S$2/4; ☉ 8.30am-6pm Chinese New Year, Labour Day, National Day, Diwali & Hari Raya Puasa/Eid-ul Fitr; M Dhoby Ghaut)

Tomi Foot Reflexology MASSAGE

4 ⊙ MAP P84, D4

A no-frills massage joint lurking in the 1970s throwback Lucky Plaza. Head in for one of the best rubdowns in town, provided by the tactile team in matching pink polos. Techniques include acupressure and shiatsu, all approved by Jesus and Mary, hanging on the wall. (☎ 6736 4249; 01-94 Lucky Plaza, 304 Orchard Rd; 30min reflexology/massage S$30/50; ☉ 10am-10pm; M Orchard)

Eating

Iggy's

FUSION $$$

5 MAP P84, C3

Iggy's refined, sleek design promises something special, and with a large picture window drawing your eye to the magic happening in the kitchen, you can take a peek. Head chef Aitor Jeronimo Orive delivers with his ever-changing, highly seasonal, creative fusion dishes. Superlatives extend to the wine list, one of the city's finest. (☎6732 2234; www. iggys.com.sg; Level 3, Hilton Hotel, 581 Orchard Rd; set lunch/dinner from S$105/250; ☉7-9.30pm, plus noon-1.30pm Thu-Sat; 🖥; MOrchard)

Buona Terra

ITALIAN $$$

6 MAP P84, E2

This intimate, linen-lined Italian restaurant is one of Singapore's unsung glories. In the kitchen is young Lombard chef Denis Lucchi, who turns exceptional ingredients into elegant, modern dishes, like seared duck liver with poached peach, amaretti crumble and Vin Santo ice cream. Lucchi's right-hand man is Emilian sommelier Gabriele Rizzardi, whose wine list, though expensive, is extraordinary. (☎6733 0209; www.buonaterra.com. sg; 29 Scotts Rd; lunch S$68/128, dinner S$148; ☉noon-2.30pm & 6.30-10.30pm Mon-Fri, 6.30-10.30pm Sat; 🖥; MNewton)

Emerald Hill Rd

Black & Whites

Often seen peeking through the lush, forested corners of Singapore, these distinctive black-and-white bungalows are a reminder of Singapore's colonial past. Usually built by wealthy plantation owners between the late 19th century and WWII, these grand homes have retained the character and charm of days gone by. The design itself was greatly influenced by the Arts and Craft movement that originated in England in the 1860s and renewed value on craftsmanship, – a counter reaction to England's rapid industrialisation.

Once there were 10,000 of these beauties in Singapore, but after being left derelict post-WWII, approximately only 500 remain. The majority are now owned by the government and are regarded as National Monuments; however, some are rented to families and businesses. While they are incredibly popular with the expat community for their large gardens and airy interiors (rare to find in space-constrained Singapore), rental costs are hefty and hopeful tenants must bid to secure two-year leases.

Some Black & Whites are occasionally opened to the public, but the easiest way to see inside one is to join a tour with **Jane's SG Tours** (www.janestours.sg; group tours S$50-90), but be sure to book in advance. Alternatively, a number of restaurants call these properties home – you'll find several along Scotts Rd. If you're in the mood for a fancy Italian dinner, our pick is Buona Terra (p87).

Taste Paradise at ION Orchard
CHINESE $$

Preened staffers in headsets whisk you into this svelte dumpling den inside the ION mall (see 19 🔒 Map p84, D4), passing a glassed-in kitchen where Chinese chefs stretch their noodles and steam their buns. Skip the novelty-flavoured *xiao long bao* (soup dumplings) for the original version, which arguably beat those of legendary competitor Din Tai Fung (p93). Beyond these, standouts include *la mian* (hand-pulled noodles) with buttery, braised pork belly. No reservations taken. (☎6509 9660, www.paradisegp.com; 04-97 ION Orchard, 2 Orchard Turn; dishes S$5-20; ⏱11am-2.30pm, f6-10pm; Ⓜ Orchard)

Gordon Grill
INTERNATIONAL $$$

7 ❌ MAP P84, D2

With its old-world charm – complete with crisp linens – and its famed steaks, Gordon Grill, housed inside a colonial-era hotel, is a step back in time compared with ultramodern Orchard Rd. It's as much an experience as it is a meal, so this is perhaps the best place for splashing out on the wagyu beef, ordered by weight, cut at your table and cooked to your specifications. (📞6730 1744; www.goodwoodparkhotel.com; Goodwood Park Hotel, 22 Scotts Rd; mains S$44-62; ⏰noon-2.30pm & 7-10.30pm; 🛜; Ⓜ Orchard)

Killiney Kopitiam CAFE $

8 ❌ MAP P84, F6

Start the day the old-school way at this veteran coffee joint, adorned with endearingly lame laminated jokes. Order a strong *kopi* (coffee), a serve of *kaya* (coconut jam) toast and a side of soft-boiled egg. Crack open the egg, add a dash of soy sauce and white pepper, then dip your *kaya* toast in it. (📞6734 3910; www.killiney-kopitiam.com; 67 Killiney Rd; dishes S$1-7; ⏰6am-11pm, to 6pm Tue & Sun; Ⓜ Somerset)

Wasabi Tei JAPANESE $$

9 ❌ MAP P84, D3

Channelling 1972 with its Laminex countertop and wood-panelled walls, this tiny, cash-only sushi bar feels like a scrumptious local secret. Nab a spot at the counter and watch the masterful chef make raw fish sing with flavour. Note: the newer sibling restaurant next door is no substitute for the original. No reservations so make sure to arrive before the lunchtime rush. (05-70 Far East

Plaza, 14 Scotts Rd; mains S$10-35; ⏰noon-3pm & 5.30-9.30pm Mon-Sat; Ⓜ Orchard)

Providore CAFE $$

10 ❌ MAP P84, E4

Waiting at the top of Mandarin Gallery's outdoor escalator is Providore, a cool, upbeat cafe with white tiles, industrial details and shelves neatly stocked with gourmet pantry fillers. Sip a full-bodied latte or scan the menu for an all-bases list of options, from breakfast-friendly organic muesli and pancakes, to gourmet salads and sandwiches, to a carbalicious lobster mac and cheese. Weekend brunch is especially popular, so make sure you head in before 11am. (📞6732 1565; www.theprovidore.com; 02-05 Mandarin Gallery, 333A Orchard Rd; dishes S$12-29; ⏰9am-10pm; 🛜; Ⓜ Somerset)

Signs A Taste Of Vietnam Pho VIETNAMESE $

11 ❌ MAP P84, F5

Bowls of flavoursome broth and Vietnamese spring rolls bursting with freshness are the signature dishes at this no-frills eatery, and it's the owners, deaf couple Anthony and Angela, will be dishing up the goods. Enter with a smile and Anthony will quickly have you ticking boxes on the menu. Portions are generous. (B1-07 Midpoint Orchard, 220 Orchard Rd; dishes S$5-8; ⏰11am-9pm; Ⓜ Somerset)

Food Court Favourites

Burrow into the basement of most malls on Orchard Rd and you'll find a food court with stall upon stall selling cheap, freshly cooked dishes from all over the world. One of the best is heaving **Takashimaya Food Village** (Map p84, E4; ✆6506 0458; www.takashimaya. com.sg; B2 Takashimaya Department Store, Ngee Ann City, 391 Orchard Rd; dishes S$4-17; ◷10am-9.30pm; 🛜; MOrchard), which serves up a *Who's Who* of Japanese, Korean and other Asian culinary classics. Another top spot is **Food Republic** (Map p84, D4; www.foodrepublic. com.sg; Level 4, Wisma Atria, 435 Orchard Rd; dishes S$5-15; ◷10am-10pm; 🛜; MOrchard); OK, so this one is not actually in the basement, but the formula remains the same – lip-smacking food, a plethora of choices and democratic prices. The roving 'aunties' pushing around trolleys filled with drinks and dim sum complete the experience.

Tambuah Mas

INDONESIAN $$

12 🍴 MAP P84, E4

Hiding shyly in a corner of Paragon's food-packed basement, Tambuah Mas is where Indonesian expats head for a taste of home. Bright, modern and good value for Orchard Rd, it proudly makes much of what it serves from scratch, a fact evident in what could possibly be Singapore's best beef *rendang*. No reservations, so arrive early if dining Thursday to Saturday. (✆6733 2220; www. tambuahmas.com.sg; B1-44 Paragon, 290 Orchard Rd; mains S$8-29; ◷11am-10pm; 🛜; MSomerset)

Ice Cream Stand

ICE CREAM $

13 🍴 MAP P84, D4

Against the shiny facades of Orchard Rd's high-end malls, you'll spot a few out-of-place-looking, weather-beaten beach umbrellas.

Underneath each one of them, a favourite Singaporean snack (ice-cream sandwiches) are created. Pick your flavour and watch as a chunk is carved off the slab and popped between either two wafers or a slice of soft, rainbow bread. (Orchard Rd; S$1-1.50; ◷9am-9pm; MOrchard, Somerset)

Newton Food Centre

HAWKER $

14 🍴 MAP P84, F1

Opened in 1971 this famous hawker centre still has a great, at times smoky, atmosphere. You could eat here for a whole year and never get bored. Well-known stalls include Alliance seafood (01-27), Hup Kee fried oyster omelette (01-73) and Kwee Heng (01-13). Touts can be a problem for foreigners, but ignore them. The best stalls don't need to tout. (500 Clemenceau Ave Nth; dishes from S$2; ◷noon-2am; MNewton)

Drinking

Manhattan
BAR

Step back in time to the golden age of fine drinking at this handsome *Mad Men*–esque bar, where long-forgotten cocktails come back to life. Grouped by eras of New York, the drinks menu is ever-changing; however, waistcoated bartenders are only too happy to guide you. Sunday brings freshly shucked oysters, and an adults-only cocktail brunch (S$150) with make-your-own bloody Marys. Number 1 on Asia's 50 Best Bars 2017–18 list, this is not one to miss. (☏6725 3377; www.regenthotels.com/Singapore; Level 2 Regent, 1 Cuscaden Rd, ⊙5pm-1am, to 2am Fri & Sat, noon-3pm Sun; MOrchard)

Other Room
BAR

You'll find this hidden drinking house, a throwback to a bygone era, behind a secret door in the Singapore Marriott lobby – ring the doorbell for entry. Peruse the 50-page drinks menu and settle in for a night to remember. Award-winning mixologist Dario Knox takes spirits seriously; the American oak-barrel-aged spirits in different finishings are where you should begin. Night owls will rejoice at the late closing time by Singapore standards. (☏6100 7778; www.theotherroom.com.sg; 01-05 Singapore Marriott, 320 Orchard Rd; ⊙6pm-3am, to 4am Fri-Sun; MOrchard)

Newton Food Centre

Back-Alley Bars

It might not be a back alley as such, but Emerald Hill Rd feels like miles away from the frenetic energy of nearby Orchard Rd. Its cluster of bars – housed in century-old Peranakan shophouses – are popular with the after-work crowd. Top billing goes to neon-pimped **Ice Cold Beer** (Map p84, F4; 📞6735 9929; www.ice-cold-beer.com; 9 Emerald Hill Rd; 🕙5pm-2am, from 2pm Sat & Sun; Ⓜ Somerset), a boozy bar with dart boards, pool table, tongue-in-cheek soft-core wall pin-ups and daily happy-hour deals from 5pm to 9pm. For a slightly classier evening, head to **Que Pasa** (Map p84, F4; 📞6235 6626; www.quepasa. com.sg; 7 Emerald Hill Rd; 🕙1.30pm-2am, from 5.30pm Sun; Ⓜ Somerset), where you can work your way through the extensive wine list.

TWG Tea
TEAHOUSE

Posh tea purveyor TWG inside the ION mall (see 19 🟢 Map p84, D4) sells more than 800 single-estate teas and blends from around the world, from English breakfast to Rolls–Royce varieties like 24-carat-gold-coated Grand Golden Yin Zhen. Edibles include tea-infused macarons (the *bain de roses* is divine), ice cream and sorbet. Also available is an all-day dining menu. (📞6735 1837; www.twgtea. com; 02-21 ION Orchard, 2 Orchard Rd; 🕙10am-10pm; 📶; Ⓜ Orchard)

Bar Canary
BAR

17 🟢 MAP P84, E4

Canary-yellow sofas, artificial turf and the sound of humming traffic and screeching birds – this alfresco bar hovers high above frenetic Orchard Rd. It's fab for an evening tipple, with well-positioned fans. Book at least a week ahead for its Wednesday Girls' Night Out: S$55, plus tax, for free-flow champagne, house pours and selected cocktails from 7pm to 9pm. (📞6603 8855; www. parkhotelgroup.com/orchard; Level 4, Park Hotel Orchard, 270 Orchard Rd, entry on Bideford Rd; 🕙noon-1am, to 2am Fri & Sat; 📶; Ⓜ Somerset)

Privé
CAFE

18 🟢 MAP P84, C3

With its pedestrian pavement location and terraced seating, this Parisian–style cafe is the perfect ringside spot to watch the masses strutting up and down Orchard Rd. Serving decent cafe fare, plus soups, pastas and all-day breakfasts, Privé has a good cocktail and wine list and more than 15 whiskies. Happy hour is 5pm to 8pm; book for the best seats. (📞6776 0777; www.theprivegroup.com.sg; 01-K1 Wheelock Place, 501 Orchard Rd; 🕙9am-1am; Ⓜ Orchard)

Shopping

ION Orchard Mall

MALL

19 🔒 MAP P84, D4

Rising directly above Orchard MRT station, futuristic ION is the cream of Orchard Rd malls. Basement floors focus on mere-mortal high-street labels like Zara and Uniqlo, while upper-floor tenants read like the index of *Vogue*. Dining options range from food-court bites to posher nosh, and the attached 56-storey tower, **ION Sky** (admission free; ⏰2-8.30pm) has a top-floor viewing gallery. (📞6238 8228; www.ionorchard.com; 2 Orchard Turn; ⏰10am-10pm; 📶; Ⓜ️Orchard)

Tanglin Shopping Centre

MALL

20 🔒 MAP P84, B3

This retro mall specialises in Asian art and is the place to come for quality rugs, carvings, ornaments, jewellery, paintings, furniture and the like. Top billing goes to **Antiques of the Orient** (📞6734 9351; www.aoto.com.sg; ⏰10am-5.30pm Mon-Sat, 11am-3.30pm Sun), with original and reproduction prints, photographs, and maps of Singapore and Asia. Especially beautiful are the richly coloured botanical drawings commissioned by British colonist William Farquhar. (📞6737 0849; www.tanglinsc.com; 19 Tanglin Rd; ⏰10am-10pm; Ⓜ️Orchard)

Paragon

MALL

21 🔒 MAP P84, E4

Even if you don't have a Black Amex, strike a pose inside this Maserati of Orchard Rd malls. Status labels include Burberry, Prada, Jimmy Choo and Gucci. High-street brands include Ted Baker and G-Star Raw. In the basement you'll find dumpling king **Din Tai Fung** (📞6836 8336; www.dintaifung.com; buns S$2, dumplings S$5-16; ⏰11am-10pm, from 10am Sat & Sun) and a large Cold Storage supermarket. (📞6738 5535; www.paragon.com.sg; 290 Orchard Rd; ⏰10am-10pm; 📶; Ⓜ️Somerset)

Tangs

DEPARTMENT STORE

22 🔒 MAP P84, D3

Since opening its doors more than 85 years ago, Tangs has become a Singaporean institution. This five-floor department store is popular with all generations, selling business suits, formal evening attire and streetwear in the huge clothes section, as well as electronics, shoes and some of the best homewares in town. (📞6737 5500; www.tangs.com; 310 Orchard Rd; ⏰10.30am-9.30pm, to 8.30pm Sun; 📶; Ⓜ️Orchard)

Ngee Ann City

MALL

23 🔒 MAP P84, E4

It might look like a forbidding mausoleum, but this marble-and-granite behemoth promises retail giddiness on its seven floors. International luxury brands compete for space with sprawling bookworm nirvana **Kinokuniya** (☏ 6737 5021; www.kinokuniya.com. sg; ☻ 10am-9.30pm) and up-market Japanese department store **Takashimaya** (☏ 6738 1111; www. takashimaya.com.sg; ☻ 10am-9.30pm; ☏), home to Takashimaya Food Village (p90), one of the strip's best food courts. (☏ 6506 0461; www.ngeeanncity.com.sg; 391 Orchard Rd; ☻ 10am-9.30pm; Ⓜ Somerset)

Beyond the Vines   CLOTHING

24 🔒 MAP P84, E4

Singaporean womenswear label Beyond the Vines offers functional and luxurious basics in soothing, pastel hues. Browse the modern brass racks that surround the central ottoman, complete with a real tree in the middle, and be surprised by the very reasonable price tags on these mix-and-match separates in fabrics such as jersey, cotton and silk blends. (☏ 8157 0577; www.beyondthevines.com; 02-21 Mandarin Gallery, 333A Orchard Rd; ☻ 10am-9pm; Ⓜ Somerset)

In Good Company   CLOTHING

One of Singapore's most lauded home-grown fashion labels has experienced a spectacular rise, just three years since the design house opened its flagship store in Orchard Rd's swanky ION mall (see 19 🔒 Map p84, D4)). All-white interiors with industrial black racks, light woods, granite and polished concrete create a serene canvas to display the label's geometric modern aesthetic that also includes lust-worthy statement necklaces.

Wheelock Place

Hidden in the back is an outpost of the Plain Vanilla Bakery (p159), a heaven for cupcake lovers. (📞6509 4786; www.ingoodcompany.asia; B1-06 ION Orchard, 2 Orchard Turn; ⏱10am-9.30pm; ⓂOrchard)

Orchardgateway   MALL

25 🔒 MAP P84, F5

Occupying a position on both sides of Orchard Rd, conveniently linked by an underground and above-ground walkway, this mall is home to boundary-pushing fashion stores **Sects Shop** (📞9889 2179; www.sectsshop.com; ⏱noon-10pm) and **i.t** (📞6702 7186; www.itlabels.com.sg; ⏱11am-9pm, to 10pm Fri & Sat).

Head to level four, for unique fashion and accessories tailored to discerning gentlemen. (📞6513 4633; www.orchardgateway.sg; 277 & 218 Orchard Rd; ⏱10.30am-10.30pm; ⓂSomerset)

Wheelock Place   MALL

26 🔒 MAP P84, C3

Linked to ION Orchard and the MRT by an underground walkway,

Orchard Rd's Last Building Block

With new shopping malls being shoehorned into every available space on Orchard Rd, why, many visitors ask, does the Thai embassy occupy such large, prominent grounds in an area of staggeringly expensive real estate? Back in the 1990s the Thai government was reportedly offered S$139 million for the site, but they turned it down because selling the land, bought by Thailand for S$9000 in 1983 by the revered King Chulalongkorn (Rama V), would be seen as an affront to his memory. And so, it remains, coveted by frustrated developers.

Wheelock Place is more than just spas and laser clinics. Dapper gents head to Benjamin Barker for sharp shirts, suits and accessories. (www.wheelockplace.com; 501 Orchard Rd; ⏱10am-10pm; ⓂOrchard)

Worth a Trip 👀

Walk With the Animals at Singapore Zoo

Singapore Zoo is a verdant, tropical wonderland of freely roaming animals and interactive attractions. Breakfast with orang-utans, dodge flying foxes, mosey up to tree-hugging sloths, even snoop around a replica African village. Then there's the setting: 26 soothing hectares on a lush peninsula jutting out onto the waters of the Upper Seletar Reservoir. It's a Singapore must-do.

📞 6269 3411

www.wrs.com.sg

80 Mandai Lake Rd

adult/child under 13yr/3yr
S$33/22/free

🕗 8.30am-6pm

Jungle Breakfast with Wildlife

Orang-utans are the zoo's celebrity residents and you can devour a scrumptious breakfast buffet in their company at **Jungle Breakfast with Wildlife** (Ah Meng Restaurant; adult/child under 12yr/6yr S$35/25/free; ☉9-10.30am). If you miss out, get your photo taken with them at the neighbouring Free Ranging Orang-utan Island (11am, 3.30pm and 4.30pm). Best of all, you're free to use your own camera.

Fragile Forest

Close encounters await at the Fragile Forest, a giant biodome that replicates the stratas of a rainforest. Cross paths with free-roaming butterflies and colourful lories, swooping Malayan flying foxes and unperturbed ring-tailed lemurs. The pathway leads up to the forest canopy and the dome's most chilled-out locals, the two-toed sloths.

Great Rift Valley of Ethiopia

Featuring cliffs, a waterfall and a stream fashioned to look like the Ethiopian hinterland, the evocative Great Rift Valley exhibit is home to Hamadryas baboons, Nubian ibexes, banded mongooses, black-backed jackals and rock hyraxes. You'll also find replica Ethiopian villages, complete with dwelling huts and an insight into the area's harsh living conditions.

Rainforest Kidzworld

Let your own little critters go wild at **Rainforest Kidzworld** (carousel/pony rides per person S$4/6; ☉9am-6pm; 🚌138), a Technicolor play area complete with slides, swings and a carousel. Kids can also ride ponies, feed farmyard animals and squeal to their heart's content in the wet-play area. Swimwear is available for purchase if you haven't brought your own.

★ Top Tips

o Try to arrive as the gates open (8.30am) – not only is it cooler for you, but the animals tend to be more active in the early morning.

o Consider combining your trip with a visit to the neighbouring Night Safari (p98).

o Feeding times are staggered. Check the website for details.

o Tickets bought online receive a 5% discount. If you're planning on visiting Singapore Zoo, Night Safari, River Safari or Jurong Bird Park, check out the combined park tickets and save up to 50%.

✖ Take a Break

There's no shortage of eateries on-site, serving everything from American fast food to local staples.

★ Getting There

Catch the train to Ang Mo Kio MRT and then bus 138. It will cost about S$25 for a taxi from the CBD.

Worth a Trip Walk with the Animals at Singapore Zoo

Worth a Trip 👀
Spot Leopards at the Night Safari

Singapore's acclaimed Night Safari offers a different type of nightlife. Home to over 130 species of animals, the park's barriers seem to melt away in the darkness, giving you the feeling of being up close with the likes of lions, leopards and elephants. The atmosphere is heightened by strolling antelopes, often passing within inches of the trams you're travelling in.

📞 6269 3411

www.wrs.com.sg

80 Mandai Lake Rd

adult/child under 13yr/3yr
S$47/31/free

🕐 7.15pm-midnight

Electric Tram Tour

Almost everyone heads to the tram queue as they enter, and you should too. These near-silent, open-sided vehicles come with a guide whose commentary is a good introduction to the park's animals and different habitats. The journey lasts 45 minutes, though we highly recommend that you alight at the designated stops to explore more of the park on foot. If possible, opt for the second or third cars as they offer the best views.

Walking Trails

The grounds offer four interlinked walking trails, each taking between 20 and 30 minutes to explore. Get centimetres away from wild spotted felines on the Leopard Trail, also home to the thrilling Giant Flying Squirrel aviary. Peer at splash-happy cats and the world's largest bat, the Malayan flying fox, on the Fishing Cat Trail. The Wallaby Trail is home to a walk-through wallaby habitat, while the outstanding East Lodge Trail awaits with highly endangered babirusas and elegant Malayan tigers. Make sure you wear comfortable shoes and bring insect repellent and an umbrella, just in case.

Creatures of the Night

If you have kids in tow, consider checking out **Creatures of the Night** (⊙7.15pm, 8.30pm, 9.30pm, plus 10.30pm Fri & Sat), an interactive 25-minute show with stars that include binturongs, civets and a hyena. Seating is unassigned, so it's a good idea to arrive a little early to secure a good vantage point. Shows may be cancelled in case of wet weather.

We must note that animal performances have been criticised by animal-welfare groups, who say that captivity is debilitating and stressful for animals, and that this is exacerbated by human interaction.

★ **Top Tips**

● When returning from the safari, catch a bus at around 10.45pm as the last MRT train leaves Ang Mo Kio at 11.30pm.

● Make sure your camera flash is off. Safari personnel take this very seriously and have been known to stop rides because of flashers.

✗ **Take a Break**

Food and drink options abound outside the entrance. **Jungle Rotisserie** (Entrance Plaza; mains S$15-25; ⊙5.30-11pm; 🛜) serves fresh-from-the-oven roast chicken.

For local specialities, try **Ulu Ulu Safari Restaurant** (☎6360 8560; Entrance Plaza; buffet adult/child under 13 yr from S$29/19, mains S$17-36; ⊙5.30-10.30pm), with both à la carte options and a buffet.

★ **Getting There**

Catch the train to Ang Mo Kio MRT and then bus 138. It will cost about S$25 for a taxi from the CBD.

Explore

Holland Village, Dempsey Hill & the Botanic Gardens

Chic, salubrious Holland Village may not be a must for visitors, but its boutiques, cafes and 'lunching ladies' offer a revealing slice of expat life. Even leafier is historic Dempsey Hill, a converted barracks laced with antiques dealers, cafes and languid bistros. Upstaging them both is the Botanic Gardens, an invigorating blend of rare orchids and precious rainforest.

The Short List

◦ *Singapore Botanic Gardens (p102)* Taking deep, blissful breaths of air in Singapore's lush retreat.

◦ *National Orchid Garden (p103)* Marvelling at the beauty, diversity and sheer quantity of varieties on display at this orchid showcase.

◦ *Dempsey Hill (p112)* Shopping for unique home-wares in the area's antique shops and galleries.

◦ *Candlenut (p106)* Savouring Michelin-starred Peranakan cuisine in colonial Dempsey Hill.

Getting There & Around

Ⓜ Singapore Botanic Gardens and Holland Village both have their own MRT stations.

🚌 To reach Dempsey Hill catch bus 7, 75, 77, 105, 106, 123 or 174 from behind Orchard MRT, on Orchard Blvd. Get off two stops after the Singapore Botanic Gardens, then walk up to your left. Buses 75 and 106 are two of several linking Holland Village with Dempsey Hill.

Neighbourhood Map on p104

Singapore Botanic Gardens (p102) SIMONLONG/GETTY IMAGES ©

Top Experience 📷

Relax in Singapore Botanic Gardens

For instant stress relief, take a dose of the Singapore Botanic Gardens. At the tail end of Orchard Rd, Singapore's most famous sprawl of greenery offers more than just picnic-friendly lawns and lakes. It's home to ancient rainforest, themed gardens, rare orchids, free concerts and one of Singapore's most romantic nosh spots. Breathe in, breathe out.

◉ MAP P104, H5

📞 1800 471 7300

www.nparks.gov.sg/sbg

1 Cluny Rd

admission free

⏱ 5am-midnight

🅿️; 🚌 7, 75, 77, 105, 106, 123, 174; Ⓜ️ Botanic Gardens

National Orchid Garden

The Botanic Gardens' now famous orchid breeding began in 1928 and you can get the historical low-down at the **National Orchid Garden** (adult/child under 12yr S\$5/free; ⏱8.30am-7pm, last entry 6pm). To date, its 3 hectares are home to over 1000 species and 2000 hybrids, – the largest showcase of tropical orchids on Earth.

Learning Forest

The newest addition to the gardens gives visitors even more forest habitat to explore. With its elevated walkways and plenty of boardwalks, you can practically walk on the swamp wetland's water or touch the leaves in the forest canopy. If you need a break, lay back in the canopy web, a spider-like web built into the elevated walkway, and relax to the sounds of the forest.

Ginger Garden

If you thought there was only one type of ginger, the compact **Ginger Garden** (admission free; ⏱5am-midnight) will set you straight. Located next to the National Orchid Garden, this 1-hectare space contains over 250 members of the Zingiberaceae family. It's also where you'll find ginger-centric restaurant Halia (p107). A supporting cast of plants include the little-known Lowiaceae, with their orchid-like flowers.

Jacob Ballas Children's Garden

A great place for kids to interact with the natural world around us. The interactive zones, including a sensory garden and 'Magic of Photosynthesis' (process in which plants make food), are super fun, There's lots of enjoyment to be had traversing the suspension and log bridges, discovering the forest adventure playground, and cooling off in the water-play feature.

★ Top Tips

o Excellent, volunteer-run guided tours of the Botanic Gardens take place every Saturday. See the website for times and themes.

o Check the website for free opera concerts, occasionally held at the Botanic Gardens' Symphony Lake.

o Buy water when you see it, not when you need it: signage in the Botanic Gardens is not always consistent and back-tracking is hardly fun, especially when you're thirsty.

✕ Take a Break

For a romantic meal among the Botanic Garden's ginger plants, grab a table at Halia (p107). Or for true alfresco dining order a picnic set from **Casa Verde** (Map p104, H3; ☎6467 7326; www.casaverde. com.sg; dishes S\$8-20, pizza S\$24; ⏱7.30am-7.30pm, to 8.30pm Sat & Sun; 👫🐾) and set up in a spot of your choosing.

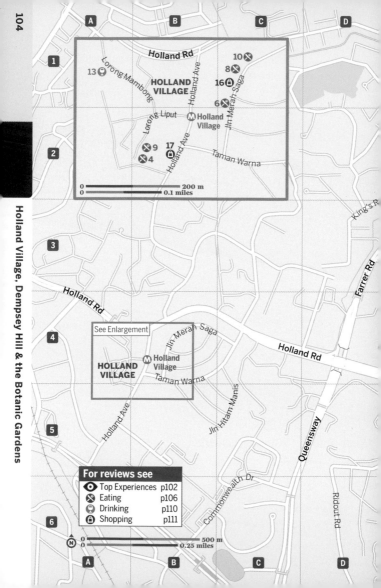

A B C D

1

Holland Rd

13 Lorong Mambong

HOLLAND VILLAGE

Lorong Liput

10
8
16
6

Jln Merah Saga

Holland Ave

Ⓜ Holland Village

2

9
4

17

Holland Ave

Taman Warna

0 ————— 200 m
0 ————— 0.1 miles

King's R

3

Holland Rd

4

See Enlargement

HOLLAND VILLAGE

Ⓜ Holland Village

Jln Merah Saga

Taman Warna

Holland Rd

Farrer Rd

5

Holland Ave

Jln Hitam Manis

Queensway

Ridout Rd

6

Ⓝ 0 ————— 500 m
0 ————— 0.25 miles

Commonwealth Dr

For reviews see

◉ Top Experiences   p102
✖ Eating   p106
🍷 Drinking   p110
🔒 Shopping   p111

A B C D

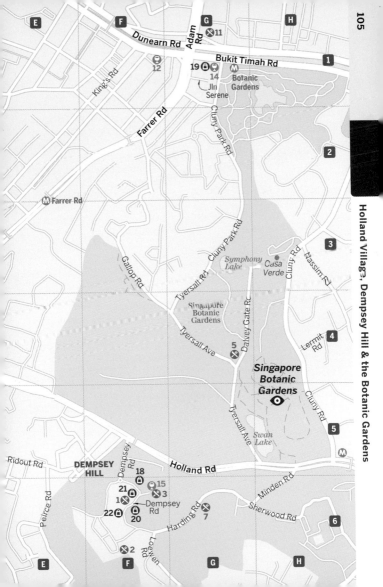

E
F
G
Adam Rd
11
H

Dunearn Rd

12

Bukit Timah Rd

1

19
14
Jln Serene
M
Botanic Gardens

King's Rd

Farrer Rd

2

M Farrer Rd

3

Cluny Park Rd

Symphony Lake
Casa Verde

Gallop Rd

Tyersall Rd

Cluny Park Rd

Cluny Rd

Nassim Rd

Singapore Botanic Gardens

Dalvey Gate Rd

5

Tyersall Ave

Lermit Rd

4

Singapore Botanic Gardens

5

Cluny Rd

Tyersall Ave

Swan Lake

M

Ridout Rd

DEMPSEY HILL

Dempsey Rd

Holland Rd

Minden Rd

18
21
1
3
15
22
20
Dempsey Rd
7
Harding Rd
Sherwood Rd

6

Peirce Rd

2

Loewen Rd

E
F
G
H

Eating

Candlenut
PERANAKAN $$

1 ❌ MAP P104, F6

The first and only Peranakan restaurant with a Michelin star, Candlenut is where Singaporeans head to impress out-of-towners. Chef Malcolm Lee does not churn out any old Straits Chinese dishes, instead he elevates them to new culinary heights. Most are amazing, but some are a little lost in translation. The jury is still out on whether Nonya would approve. (✆ 1800 304 2288; www.comodempsey. sg; Block 17A, Dempsey Rd; mains S$20-32; ⏲ noon-2.30pm & 6-9.30pm, to 10.30pm Fri & Sat; 🚌 7, 75, 77, 105, 106, 123, 174)

Chopsuey
CHINESE $$$

2 ❌ MAP P104, F6

Swirling ceiling fans, crackly 1930s tunes and ladies on rattan chairs – Chopsuey has colonial chic down pat. It serves revamped versions of retro American-Chinese dishes, but the real highlight is the lunchtime yum cha; standouts include grilled pork and coconut salad, crispy lobster wontons, and *san choy pau* (minced meat in lettuce cups). The marble bar is perfect for solo diners. (✆ 6708 9288; www. chopsueycafe.com; 01-23, Block 10, Dempsey Rd; dumplings S$7-15, mains S$12-46; ⏲ 11.30am-10.30pm, from 10.30am Sat & Sun; 🚌 7, 75, 77, 105, 106, 123, 174)

Long Beach Seafood
SEAFOOD $$

3 ❌ MAP P104, F6

One of Singapore's top seafood restaurant chains. Settle in on the verandah, gaze out at the tropical greenery and tackle the cult-status black-pepper crab. The original Long Beach lays claim to inventing the iconic dish, and the version here is fantastically peppery and earthy. Best of all, the kitchen is open later than those of many restaurants in town. (✆ 6323 2222; www.longbeachseafood.com.sg; 01-01, Block 25, Dempsey Rd; mains S$12-22, crab per kg from S$78; ⏲ 11am-3pm & 5pm-1am; 🚌 7, 75, 77, 105, 106, 123, 174)

Dempsey Cookhouse & Bar
BISTRO $$$

Visually stunning with a white-and-black colour scheme, a soaring ceiling dotted with oversized lantern lights, and touches of tropical greenery, there is a definite buzz in this restaurant (see 1 ❌ Map p 104, F6) opened by one of New York's most celebrated chefs, Jean-Georges Vongerichten. Skip the signature egg caviar and opt for the creamy burrata (Italian semi-soft cheese) with lemon jam, followed by the spice-crusted snapper. (✆ 1800 304 5588; www.comodempsey. sg; Block 17D, Dempsey Rd; mains S$19-67; ⏲ noon-2.30pm & 6-10pm, to 11pm Fri & Sat; 🚌 7, 75, 77, 105, 106, 123, 174)

Halia

Blu Kouzina
GREEK $$$

Opa! Stepping into this large, bustling restaurant (see 2 ❌ Map p104 F6) is like joining a large and very festive gathering. Plates of succulent meats, grilled seafood and flavourful salads are shared among guests at cosy and family-sized tables. Take a seat and get ordering – don't miss the *saganaki* (cheese) with figs, which you can wash down with decent Greek wine. (📞6875 0872; www.blukouzina.com; 01-21, Block 10, Dempsey Rd; dishes S$15-49, sharing platters from S$51; ⏰noon-2.30pm & 6-10pm; 🚌7, 75, 77, 105, 106, 123, 174)

2am: dessertbar
DESSERTS $$

4 ❌ MAP P104, B2

Posh desserts with wine and cocktail pairings is the deal at this swanky hideout. The menu includes savoury grub like pork sliders and mac and cheese, but everyone comes here for Janice Wong's sweet show-stoppers, from chocolate tart to cassis plum bombe with elderflower yoghurt foam. Book ahead for Thursday to Saturday night. (📞6291 9727; www.2amdessertbar. com; 21A Lorong Liput; dishes S$15-24; ⏰3pm-2am Tue-Fri, from 2pm Sat & Sun; Ⓜ Holland Village)

Halia
FUSION $$$

5 ❌ MAP P104, G4

Atmospheric Halia is surrounded by the Botanic Gardens' ginger plants, a fact echoed in several unusual ginger-based dishes. Menus are a competent, fusion affair (think chilli-crab spaghettini), and the weekday set lunch (two/three courses S$28/34) is especially good value. There's a vegetarian and a kids' menu, and at weekends you can also do brunch (10am to 5pm); no reservations taken.

No alcohol is served, but it does refreshing fruit mocktails. (📞8444 1148; www.thehalia.com; 1 Cluny Rd, Singapore Botanic Gardens; mains S$22-62; ⏱noon-9.30pm, from 5pm Sat & Sun; 🍴👶; 🚌7, 75, 77, 105, 106, 123, 174, Ⓜ Botanic Gardens)

Original Sin   VEGETARIAN $$

 6 🍴 MAP P104, C1

Vibrant textiles, crisp linen and beautiful stemware set a smart, upbeat scene for sophisticated, flesh-free dishes like spicy, quinoa-stuffed roasted capsicum, and Middle Eastern eggplant moussaka. The restaurant is on a residential street dotted with eating options; book an outdoor table if possible. (📞6475 5605; www.originalsin.com.sg; 01-62, 43 Jln Merah Saga; mains S$24-29; ⏱11.30am-2.30pm & 6-10pm; 🍴; Ⓜ Holland Village)

White Rabbit   INTERNATIONAL $$$

7 🍴 MAP P104, G6

Dempsey Hill's 1930s Ebenezer chapel has been reborn as a sophisticated, whitewashed dining room and bar. Find the light in tweaked Euro comforters like tagliatelle with Alaskan king crab and 36-hour short ribs with ruby port glaze. Weekend brunch (10.30am to 3pm) includes breakfast staples like eggs and waffles but mixes things up with oysters and wagyu burgers.

Hop on outside to the Rabbit Hole garden bar to enjoy a refreshing craft gin and homemade tonic. (📞6473 9965; www.thewhiterabbit.com.sg; 39C Harding Rd; 2-/3-course set lunch S$38/42, mains S$28-65;

Tanglin Barracks

The area now known as Dempsey Hill was the site of Tanglin Barracks, one of the first barracks constructed in Singapore. Opened in 1861 the original buildings were spacious, elevated wooden structures topped with thatched *attap* (sugar-palm) roofs and able to house 50 men. Among the barracks' amenities were hospital wards, wash houses, kitchens, a library, a reading room and a school, as well as office quarters. Extensive renovation between 1934 and 1936 saw the airy verandahs make way for more interior space, though the French-tiled roofs – which had replaced the original thatched ones – were, thankfully, preserved. Home to the British military for over a century, the barracks served as the headquarters of the Ministry of Defence between 1972 and 1989, before their current reinvention as an upmarket lunch hang-out.

⏱ noon-2.30pm & 6.30-10.30pm Tue-Fri, from 10.30am Sat & Sun; 🚌 7, 75, 77, 105, 106, 123, 174)

Sunday Folks

DESSERTS $$

8 ✖ MAP P104, C1

A sugar rush is a given at this airy, industrial-style dessert cafe where every delectable treat is hand-made. Folks flock here for the fluffy waffles crowned with a towering swirl of decadent soft-serve ice cream. Choose one of four ice-cream flavours – our pick is the sweet-and-savoury sea-salt *gula melaka* (palm sugar) – and then go nuts with toppings. (📞 6479 9166; www.sundayfolks.com; 01-52, 44 Jln Merah Saga; waffles S$10-20; ⏱ 1-10pm Tue-Thu, from noon Fri-Sun; Ⓜ Holland Village)

Island Creamery

ICE CREAM $

9 ✖ MAP P104, B2

A calorific shrine for many Singaporeans, who don't mind queuing at this tiny shop for its freshly made ice creams, sorbets and pies. Keep it local with flavours including *teh tarik* (sweet spiced Indian tea) and the wonderful Tiger beer sorbet, or get nostalgic over the Milo or Horlicks concoctions. (📞 6468 8859; www.islandcreamery.com; 19 Lorong Liput; ⏱ noon-10pm, to 11pm Fri & Sat; Ⓜ Holland Village)

Da Paolo Pizza Bar

ITALIAN $$

10 ✖ MAP P104, C1

The successful Da Paolo chain has two outlets in Holland Village alone:

Chicken satay, Candlenut (p106)

YVETTE CARDOZO/ALAMY STOCK PHOTO ©

a deli cafe (at 118 Holland Ave) and this polished bistro with terrace seating. Under a cowhide ceiling, svelte expats dine on delicious thin-crust pizzas, competent pastas and warm chocolate brownies. There's a good-value weekday set lunch (S$23) and one-for-one happy hour noon to 2.30pm and 5.30pm to 7.30pm. (📞 6479 6059; www.dapaolo.com.sg; 01-46, 44 Jln Merah Saga; pizzas S$20-31, pasta S$22-28; ⏱ noon-2.30pm & 5.30-10.30pm Mon-Fri, 11am-10.30pm Sat & Sun; Ⓜ Holland Village)

Adam Road Food Centre

HAWKER $

11 ✖ MAP P104, G1

Locals tout this hawker centre as home to the best *nasi lemak* (coconut rice served with fried anchovies, peanuts and a curry dish) in town.

Join the line at Selera Rasa Nasi Lemak (stall 01-02) to taste the dish rumoured to have been served to Indonesian president Joko Widodo by Singapore's prime minister, Lee Hsien Loong, in 2014. (cnr Adam & Dunearn Rds; dishes from S$2.50; ⊙7am-2am; Ⓜ Botanic Gardens)

Drinking

Atlas Coffeehouse COFFEE

12 Ⓠ MAP P104, F1

This airy industrial-styled coffeehouse has caffeine lovers lining up for the in-house Guatemalan and Brazilian bean blend by Two Degrees North Coffee Co. Like your coffee served cold? Try the Black Bird, a taste flight of cold brew, nitro brew and iced black

– perfect on a hot day. (✆6314 2674; www.atlascoffeehouse.com.sg; 6 Duke's Rd; ⊙8am-6.30pm Tue-Sun; Ⓜ Botanic Gardens)

Wala Wala Café Bar BAR

13 Ⓠ MAP P104, A1

Perennially packed at weekends (and most evenings, too), Wala Wala has live music on the 2nd floor, with warm-up acts Monday to Friday from 7pm and main acts nightly from 9.30pm. Downstairs it pulls in football fans with its large sports screens. As at most nearby places, tables spill out onto the street in the evenings. (✆6462 4288; www.wala wala.sg; 31 Lorong Mambong; ⊙4pm-1am Mon-Thu, to 2am Fri, 3pm-2am Sat, 3pm-1am Sun; Ⓜ Holland Village)

Gastronomia CAFE

14 Ⓠ MAP P104, G1

Across the road from the Botanic Gardens MRT station, this casual coffeeshop is a perfect pit stop before or after your garden visit. Pull up a chair on the breezy verandah or grab a coffee to go and head upstairs to explore the trendy fashion and homewares boutiques geared towards the local expat community. (✆6468 7010; www.dapaolo.com.sg; 01-01 Cluny Ct, 501 Bukit Timah Rd; ⊙7.30am-10pm; Ⓜ Botanic Gardens)

RedDot Brewhouse MICROBREWERY

15 Ⓠ MAP P104, F6

In a quiet spot in Dempsey Hill, RedDot has been pouring its

Gastronomia

RIA DE JONG/LONELY PLANET ©

A Virtuous Morning

If you feel like stretching your limbs, join the early morning fitness fanatics who descend on the Botanic Gardens (p102) from sunrise to stroll, run, roll out yoga mats and submit to bootcamp instructors. Keep an eye out for the mesmerising tai chi classes; the ones using fans or swords are the best. You'll find plenty of shelters in case the heavens open, but water fountains are hard to locate, so bring your own water bottle. Workout done, reward yourself with breakfast at Casa Verde (p103) at the Nassim Gate Visitors Centre, or Gastronomia just outside the Bukit Timah gate, the latter conveniently situated next to the Botanic Gardens MRT.

own microbrews for years. Ditch the average food and focus on the suds, sipped to the sound of screeching parrots. There are eight beers on tap (S$12 for a pint), including an eye-catching, spirulina-spiked green lager. Happy hour runs from noon to 7pm, with S$9 pints. (✆6475 0500; www.reddotbrewhouse.com.sg; 01-01, Block 25A, Dempsey Rd; ⏰noon-midnight, to 2am Fri & Sat, 10am-midnight Sun; 🚌7, 75, 77, 105, 106, 123, 174)

Shopping

Bynd Artisan ARTS & CRAFTS

16 📍 MAP P104, C1

Connoisseurs of bespoke stationery and leather will love this sublime store that prides itself on artisanal excellence. Select from the range of handmade journals or spend time customising your own; don't forget to deboss your name. Other items include leather travel accessories and jewellery

pieces. For the complete artist experience, sign up for a course (from S$78) in leather crafting or bookbinding. (✆6475 1680; www.byndartisan.com; 01-54, 44 Jln Merah Saga; ⏰noon-9pm, from 10am Sat & Sun; MHolland Village)

Holland Road Shopping Centre MALL

17 📍 MAP P104, B2

Holland Road Shopping Centre remains a magnet for expats seeking art, handicrafts, homewares and offbeat fashion. Dive into **Lim's** (✆6466 3188; www.facebook.com/limshollandvillage; ⏰10am-8pm) for some good Asian–inspired finds or scour the shelves of **Independent Market** (✆6466 5534; www.independentmarket.sg; ⏰noon-7pm Mon-Sat, 1-6pm Sun) for a quirky Singaporean souvenir. Shopped out? Hit the nail spas or massage parlours, which are dotted over the two levels. (211 Holland Ave; ⏰10am-8.30pm; MHolland Village)

Shang Antique

ANTIQUES

18 🔒 MAP P104, F6

Specialising in antique religious artefacts from Cambodia, Laos, Thailand, India and Myanmar (Burma), as well as reproductions, Shang Antique has items dating back nearly 2000 years – with price tags to match. Those with more style than savings can pick up old bronze gongs, beautiful Thai silk scarves or Burmese ornamental rice baskets for under S$50. (📞6388 8838; www.shangantique.com.sg; 01-03, Block 26, Dempsey Rd; 🕙10am-7pm; 🚌7, 75, 77, 105, 106, 123, 174)

Bungalow 55

HOMEWARES

19 🔒 MAP P104, G1

Colonial chic hits overdrive in this beautifully curated store brimming with chinoiserie lamps, tropical-scented candles, overstuffed cushions and everything a Singapore–based host-with-the-most would need in their life. Wander around and imagine relaxing on the verandah sipping G&Ts from your well-stocked cane bar cart – don't forget a Panama hat for the complete experience. (📞6463 3831; www.thebungalow55.com; 01-05A, Cluny Court, 501 Bukit Timah Rd; 🕙10am-7pm, to 5pm Sun; Ⓜ Botanic Gardens)

Expat Heavy Holland Village

Nonpermanent residents make up just under 30% of Singapore's population of 5.6 million residents, up from around 25% in 2000.

While many are low-paid construction and service-industry workers from China and South and Southeast Asia, a huge number are highly skilled professionals working in areas as diverse as finance, oil and gas, IT, biomedical science and academia, as well as tourism and hospitality. Indeed, one in four skilled workers in Singapore is foreign.

There are over 40,000 British nationals in Singapore alone, with other large communities including Australians, Americans, French and Japanese. Popular expat neighbourhoods include Orchard, Tanglin, Novena, Holland Village, Bukit Timah and the East Coast.

It's a thriving, vibrant scene, with no shortage of social and sporting clubs, international schools and expat magazines and websites. For many, Singapore's appeal is obvious: low crime, lower taxes, world-class healthcare and education, affordable domestic help and superlative international connections. Increasingly less appealing, however, is the soaring cost of living, made worse by the increasing number of companies moving away from all-inclusive expat packages to less-lucrative local contracts.

Em Gallery

FASHION, HOMEWARES

20 🔒 MAP P104, F6

Singapore-based Japanese designer Emiko Nakamura keeps Dempsey's society women looking whimsically chic in her light, sculptural creations. Emiko also collaborates with hill tribes in Laos to create naturally dyed hand-woven handicrafts, such as bags and cushions. Other homewares might include limited-edition (and reasonably priced) pottery from Cambodia. (📞6475 6941; www.emtradedesign.com; 01-03A Block 26, Dempsey Rd; ⏲10am-7pm, from 11am Sat & Sun; 🚌7, 75, 77, 105, 106, 123, 174)

Dover Street Market

FASHION & ACCESSORIES

21 🔒 MAP P104, F6

Singapore's fashion elite, with the very deepest of pockets, peruse the racks of this outpost of famous London fashion retailer. The ginormous warehouse space has been sectioned off with metal cage-like dividers, which make it feel like you're getting lost in a maze of high fashion. Labels include Gucci, Balenciaga, Comme des Garçons, Sara Lanzi and Sacai. (📞6304 1388; https://singapore.doverstreetmarket.com; Block 18, Dempsey Rd; ⏲11am-8pm; 🚌7, 75, 77, 105, 106, 123, 174)

Pasardina Fine Living

ANTIQUES, HOMEWARES

22 🔒 MAP P104, F6

If you plan on giving your home a tropical Asian makeover, this rambling treasure trove is a good starting point. Inspired by traditional Indonesian design, its collection includes beautiful teak furniture, ceramic and wooden statues, bark lampshades and the odd wooden archway. (📞6472 0228; www.facebook.com/pasardina fineliving; 01-01, Block 13, Demspey Rd; ⏲noon-6.30pm, to 7.30pm Sat & Sun; 🚌7, 75, 77, 105, 106, 123, 174)

Explore ◈
West & Southwest Singapore

From walking the stunning Southern Ridges to meandering through fabulous, and free, art galleries at colonial Gillman Barracks, there's plenty to keep you busy west of the CBD.

The Short List

○ Southern Ridges (p116) *Stretching your legs for a park-to-park walk along the lush Southern Ridges to Mt Faber, then hopping onto the cable car for sensational views.*

○ Gillman Barracks (p120) *Immersing yourself in culture, art and food while wandering around colonial gem Gillman Barracks.*

○ Haw Par Villa (p121) *Reliving a little 1950s tourism at this wonderfully quirky, more than slightly scary, theme park.*

Getting There & Around

Ⓜ HarbourFront, Jurong East, Boon Lay, Chinese Garden, Pioneer and Kranji are all useful stations within walking distance of sights or with bus connections to them.

Neighbourhood Map on p118

Haw Par Villa (p121) SIRAPHAT/SHUTTERSTOCK ©

Top Experience 📷

Take in Stunning Vistas at Southern Ridges

A series of parks and hills connecting Mt Faber to West Coast Park, the Southern Ridges brings the jungle to the heart of the city. The best stretch of the 10km route is from Kent Ridge Park to Mt Faber. It's relatively easy, and serves up some stunning sights, from skyline and jungle vistas to a seriously striking, wave-like walkway.

◎ MAP P118, D4

📞 1800 471 7300

www.nparks.gov.sg

🕐 24hr

🅿

Ⓜ Pasir Panjang

Reflections at Bukit Chandu

Commemorating the last stand of the Malay Regiment against the Japanese in 1942, **Reflections at Bukit Chandu** (6375 2510; www.nhb. gov.sg; 31K Pepys Rd; admission free; 9am-5.30pm Tue-Sun) combines firsthand accounts, personal artefacts and films to describe the fierce battle that almost wiped out the regiment.

Kent Ridge Park

Behind Reflections at Bukit Chandu you'll find **Kent Ridge Park** (Vigilante Dr; 24hr). It's strangely deserted so you'll have its short, yet wonderful, canopy walk pretty much to yourself. From here, stroll downhill to **HortPark** (33 Hyderabad Rd; 6am-10pm;).

Forest Walk

A leaf-like bridge crosses over Alexandra Rd from HortPark, leading to the superb Forest Walk. While you can opt for the Earth trail, the Elevated Walkway is more appealing, offering eye-level views of the jungle canopy covering **Telok Blangah Hill** (Telok Blangah Green; 24hr).

Henderson Waves

The remarkable Henderson Waves, a rippling walkway soaring high above the forest floor, sits between Telok Blangah Hill Park and Mt Faber Park. The towers that seem to rise straight out of the jungle are part of Reflections at Keppel Bay – a residential development designed by world-renowned architect Daniel Libeskind.

Mt Faber

Rising 105m above the southern fringe of the city, Mt Faber's terraced trails wind past strategically positioned viewpoints. It's here you'll find the **cable-car service** (6377 9688; www.onefabergroup.com; adult/child return S$33/22; 8.45am-9.30pm) to HarbourFront and Sentosa.

★ Top Tips

o The best time to hit the trail is late afternoon. This way you can avoid the worst of the midday heat and make it to Mt Faber in time for sunset drinks or dinner.

o Wear comfortable shoes, sunglasses and a hat. Always bring plenty of water, and don't forget to pack an umbrella.

o Bring your camera. The walk delivers beautiful views of the city, jungle and South China Sea.

o If you encounter monkeys, do not feed them. This only encourages them to pester humans.

✕ Take a Break

For drinks and bistro fare with breathtaking city views, head to **Dusk** (p124). For more casual bites, opt for **Spuds & Aprons** (6377 9688; www. onefabergroup. com; 109 Mt Faber Rd; mains S$14-40; 11am-10pm; Mt Faber). Both are atop Mt Faber.

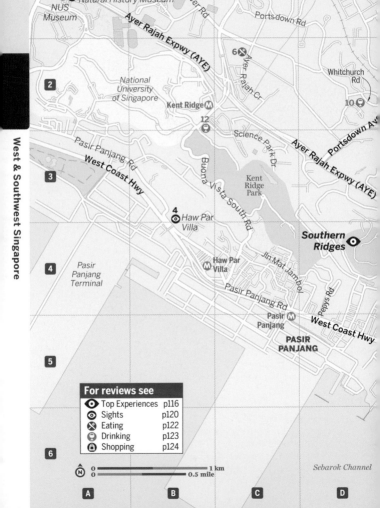

West & Southwest Singapore

E F G H

1

2

DEMPSEY HILL

Loewen Rd

Grange Rd

Chatsworth Rd

Queensway

Commonwealth Ave

QUEENSTOWN

Tanglin Rd

Jervois Rd

Bishopgate

Queensway

Singapore River

Tiong Bahru Rd

Alexandra Rd

Redhill

Delta Stadium

Tiong Bahru Rd

3

Jln Tiong

Henderson Rd

Lower Delta Rd

Alexandra Rd

Jln Bukit Merah

Ayer Rajah Expwy (AYE)

Depot Rd

4

Lock Rd

11

1 Gillman Barracks

Telok Blangah Hill Park

Alexandra Rd

8

Telok Blangah Dr

Henderson Rd

Mt Faber Cable Car Station

15

Labrador Park

Labrador Villa Rd

Telok Blangah

Mt Faber Park

▲Mt Faber

5

13

7

Port Rd

9

West Coast Hwy

5 Labrador Nature Reserve

Keppel Harbour

14 Pulau Keppel

HarbourFront Cable Car Station

HarbourFront

16

VivoCity

6

Sentosa Gateway

E F G H

Sights

Gillman Barracks GALLERY

1 ◉ MAP P118, E4

A former British military encampment, Gillman Barracks now houses a contemporary arts hub set in a lush landscape. Among its 11 galleries is New York's **Sundaram Tagore** (☎6694 3378; www.sundaramtagore.com; 01-05, 5 Lock Rd; admission free; ⊙11am-7pm Tue-Sat), which represents big names such as Annie Leibovitz. Also on-site is the **NTU Centre for Contemporary Art** (☎6339 6503; www.ntu.ccasingapore.org; Block 43, Malan Rd; admission free; ⊙noon-7pm Tue-Thu, Sat & Sun, to 9pm Fri), a forward-thinking art-research centre hosting art talks, lectures and contemporary exhibitions from dynamic regional and international artists working in a variety of media. Individual gallery hours vary.

To reach Gillman Barracks, catch the MRT to Labrador Park station and walk north up Alexandra Rd for 800m; the entry to Gillman Barracks is on your right. A one-way taxi fare from the CBD will set you back around S$12. (www.gillmanbarracks.com; 9 Lock Rd; admission free; ⊙11am-7pm Tue-Sun; P; MLabrador Park)

Lee Kong Chian Natural History Museum MUSEUM

2 ◉ MAP P118, A1

What looks like a giant rock bursting with greenery is actually Singapore's high-tech, child-friendly natural history museum. The main Biodiversity Gallery delves into the origin of life using a stimulating combo of fossils, taxidermy and interactive displays. Hard to miss are Prince, Apollonia and Twinky: three 150-million-year-old Diplodocid sauropod dinosaur skeletons, two with their original skulls. Upstairs, the Heritage Gallery explores the collection's 19th-century origins, with an interesting section on Singapore's geology to boot. (☎6601 3333; http://lkcnhm.nus.edu.sg; 2 Conservatory Dr; adult/child under 13yr S$21/13; ⊙10am-7pm Tue-Sun; P; ⬜96)

NUS Museum MUSEUM

3 ◉ MAP P118, A1

Located on the verdant campus of the National University of Singapre (NUS), this museum is one of the city's lesser-known cultural delights. Ancient Chinese ceramics and bronzes, as well as archaeological fragments found in Singapore, dominate the ground-floor Lee Kong Chian Collection; one floor up, the South and Southeast Asian Gallery showcases paintings, sculpture and textiles from the region. The Ng Eng Teng Collection is dedicated to Ng Eng Teng (1934–2001), Singapore's foremost modern artist, best known for his figurative sculptures. (☎6516 8817; www.museum.nus.edu.sg; National University of Singapore, 50 Kent Ridge Cres; admission free; ⊙10am-6pm Tue-Sat; P; ⬜96)

Haw Par Villa

MUSEUM, PARK

4 ⊙ MAP P118, B3

The refreshingly weird and kitsch Haw Par Villa was the brainchild of Aw Boon Haw, the creator of the medicinal salve Tiger balm. After Aw Boon Haw built a villa here in 1937 for his beloved brother and business partner, Aw Boon Par, the siblings began building a Chinese-mythology theme park within the grounds. Top billing goes to the Ten Courts of Hell (closes at 5.45pm), a walk-through exhibit depicting the gruesome torments awaiting sinners in the underworld. (☑6773 0103; www.hawparvilla. sg; 262 Pasir Panjang Rd; admission free; ⊙9am-7pm, last entry 6pm; P; MHaw Par Villa)

Labrador Nature Reserve

PARK

5 ⊙ MAP P118, E6

Combining forest trails rich in birdlife and a beachfront park, Labrador Park is also scattered with evocative British war relics, only rediscovered in the 1980s. Look out for old gun emplacements mounted on moss-covered concrete casements, as well as for the remains of the entrance to the old fort that once stood guard on this hill. The reserve's hilly terrain sweeps down to the shore, where expansive lawns, shade and the sound of lapping waves invite a lazy picnic. (☑1800 471 7300; www.nparks.gov.sg; Labrador Villa Rd; ⊙24hr; P; MLabrador Park)

West & Southwest Singapore Sights

NUS Museum

Eating

Timbre+ HAWKER $

6 MAP P118, C2

Welcome to the new generation of hawker centres. With over 30 food outlets, Timbre+ has it all: artwork-covered shipping containers, Airstream trailer food trucks, craft beer and live music nightly. But it's the food that draws the crowds: a mixture of traditional and New Age. Head here in the late afternoon before the old-school hawker stalls shut at 6pm. (☑6252 2545; www.timbre plus.sg; JTC LaunchPad@one-north, 73A Ayer Rajah Cres; dishes from S$3; ☺6am-midnight Mon-Thu, to 1am Fri & Sat, 11am-10pm Sun, stall hours vary; ⓂOne North)

Tamarind Hill THAI $$$

7 MAP P118, E6

In a colonial bungalow in Labrador Park, Tamarind Hill sets an elegant scene for exceptional Thai. The highlight is the Sunday brunch (S$60; noon to 3pm), a buffet of beautiful cold dishes and salads plus as many dishes from the à la carte menu as you like. Book ahead. (☑6278 6364; www.tamarindrestaurants.com; 30 Labrador Villa Rd; mains S$18-59; ☺noon-2.30pm Mon-Sat, 11.30am-3pm Sun, 6.30-9.45pm Sun-Thu, to 10.30pm Fri & Sat; 🛜; ⓂLabrador Park)

Naked Finn SEAFOOD $$$

8 MAP P118, E5

You'll find this slinky pocket rocket at the commercial gallery hub,

Timbre+

Gillman Barracks. It's located in a glass-like box, with lush greenery wall, and serves up super-fresh seafood dishes in pared-down style. If you're there for lunch be sure to order the lobster roll, raved about all over Singapore – sadly it's not available at dinner. (☎6694 0807; www.nakedfinn.com; 39 Malan Rd, Gillman Barracks; mains S$30-78; ⏱noon-2.30pm Tue-Sat, 6-9pm Tue-Thu, to 9.30pm Fri & Sat; Ⓜ Labrador Park)

Masons INTERNATIONAL $$

Located on the grounds of Gillman Barracks (see 1 ⓞ Map p118, E4), this cafe-bistro comes with high ceilings, elegant verandah seating and a marble bar with black leather sofas for a post-gallery cocktail (happy hour 4pm to 7pm). Italian flavours dominate the menu, accompanied by American staples including bourbon-smoked ribs and juicy beef burgers. Herbivores will appreciate the dedicated vegetarian options. (☎6694 2216; www.masons.sg; 8 Lock Rd, Gillman Barracks; mains S$18-38; ⏱noon-11pm; 🍴; Ⓜ Labrador Park)

PeraMakan PERANAKAN $$

9 ❌ MAP P118, F6

Run by a genial couple of cooking enthusiasts, this paragon of homestyle Baba-Nonya cuisine migrated from its spiritual Joo Chiat home. Thankfully, classics such as sambal squid and *rendang* remain as plate-lickingly good as ever. One dish you don't

Worth a Trip

Visits to the **Tiger Brewery** (☎6860 3005; www.tigerbrewerytour.com.sg; 459 Jln Ahmad Ibrahim; adult/child S$18/12; ⏱1-6.30pm Tue-Sun; Ⓟ; Ⓜ Tuas West Rd) are divided into two parts: a 45- minute tour of the place followed by 45 minutes of free beer tasting in the wood-and-leather Tiger Tavern. Tours run on the hour from 1pm to 5pm and must be booked in advance. Under 18s will only be admitted with an adult and are not allowed alcoholic drinks.

want to miss is the ayam buah keluak (chicken in a rich spicy sauce served with Indonesian black-nut pulp). (☎6377 2829; www.peramakan.com; Level 3, Keppel Club, 10 Bukit Chermin Rd; mains S$14-25; ⏱11.30am-2pm & 6-9pm; Ⓟ 🍴; Ⓜ Telok Blangah)

Drinking

Colbar BAR

10 🍺 MAP P118, D2

Raffish Colbar is an evocative colonial throwback, a former British officers' mess turned languid drinking spot. It's still 1950-something here, a place where money is kept in a drawer, football team photos hang on the wall and locals linger over beers and well-priced ciders on the spacious verandah. (☏ 6779 4859; 9A Whitchurch Rd; ⏰ 11am-10pm Tue-Sun; 🚌 191)

Handlebar

PUB

11 🚇 MAP P118, E4

You might not expect to find a biker bar sitting alongside fancy art galleries and top-notch restaurants, but here Handlebar is. There are usually more families here than motorheads, and it makes a lovely place for a few drinks in the cool of the afternoon. The daiquiris made in blenders fashioned out of petrol engines go down a treat. (☏ 6268 5550; www.handlebaroriginal.com; Block 10, Lock Rd, Gillman Barracks; ⏰ noon-midnight Tue-Thu & Sun, to 1am Fri & 2am Sat; Ⓜ Labrador Park)

Good Beer Company

CRAFT BEER

12 🚇 MAP P118, B2

After injecting Chinatown Complex (p148) with a dose of new-school cool, this hawker-centre beer stall made the move in September 2017 to much bigger digs, just minutes from the National University of Singapore. With eight craft beers on tap and an impressive booty of bottled craft suds, sourced from far-flung corners of the world, it's a brew enthusiast's paradise. (☏ 9430 2750; www.facebook.com/goodbeersg; 01-23 Savourworld, 2 Science Park Dr; ⏰ 4-11pm Mon-Thu, to 11.45pm Fri & Sat; Ⓜ Kent Ridge)

Dusk

BAR

13 🚇 MAP P118, H5

Perched atop Mt Faber, Dusk has a sweeping view over Harbour-Front to Sentosa Island and the Strait of Singapore beyond. Sunset is the perfect time to enjoy the sky's changing hues as you sit, cocktail in hand. (☏ 6377 9688; www.onefabergroup.com; 109 Mt Faber Rd; ⏰ 4-11pm Mon-Thu, to 2am Fri & Sat, 11am-11pm Sun; 🚠 Mt Faber)

Privé Keppel Bay

BAR

14 🚇 MAP P118, F6

You couldn't ask for a better setting for morning coffee or evening drinks: this bar is located on an island out in the middle of Keppel Harbour, with the city on one side and Sentosa Island on the other. Happy hour runs from 5pm to 8pm daily. Attracts an affluent, well-dressed crowd looking to unwind by the water. (☏ 6776 0777; www.theprivegroup.com.sg; Marina at Keppel Bay, 2 Keppel Bay Vista; ⏰ 9am-midnight Mon-Fri, from 8am Sat & Sun; Ⓜ HarbourFront)

Shopping

Dustbunny Vintage

VINTAGE

15 🔒 MAP P118, H5

This vintage veteran is not in the most convenient location, tucked away on a HDB (Housing and Development Board) estate, but the well-curated collection of dresses, handbags and accessories has made it a must-shop if you're

VivoCity

on the lookout for great-value designer finds. Boutique owner Pia revels in helping shoppers find the perfect pieces to add to their collections. (☎ 6274 4200; 01-203, Block 112, Bukit Purmei Rd; ⏰ 12.30-8.30pm Mon-Fri, 1-7pm Sat, 1-5pm Sun by appointment; 🚌 123, 131)

VivoCity
MALL

16 🔒 MAP P118, H6

More than just Singapore's largest shopping mall, VivoCity offers that rare commodity: open space. There's an outdoor kids' playground on level two and a rooftop 'skypark' where little ones can splash about in free-to-use paddling pools. The retail mix is predominantly mid-range, and there's a large Golden Village cineplex. (☎ 6377 6860; www. vivocity.com.sg; 1 HarbourFront Walk; ⏰ 10am-10pm; 🛜 👫; Ⓜ HarbourFront, 🚈 Sentosa Express)

Explore

Sentosa Island

*Epitomised by its star attraction, Universal Studios,
Sentosa is essentially one giant Pleasure Island. The
choices are head-spinning, from duelling roller coasters
and indoor skydiving to fake surf and luge racing. Add
to this a historic fort, state-of-the-art aquarium and
Ibiza-inspired beachside bars and restaurants and it's
clear why locals head here to live a little*

The Short List

○ **Universal Studios (p128)** Indulging your inner
child at Singapore's blockbuster theme park, home to
warrior mummies, bad-tempered dinosaurs and the
world's tallest duelling roller coasters.

○ **SEA Aquarium (p131)** Visiting the adorable, the
curious and the deadly at the world's largest aquarium.

○ **Tanjong Beach Club (p134)** Feeling the sand
between your toes and the breeze on your face as you
toast the sunset with the party set.

○ **Knolls (p134)** Popping the champagne and eating till
your heart's content at the free-flow Sunday brunch.

Getting There & Around

🚠 Ride to/from Mt Faber or the HarbourFront Centre to
Sentosa Station on the island. On Sentosa, a separate cable-
car line, the Sentosa Line, stops at Imbiah Lookout, Merlion
and Siloso Point.

🚝 The Sentosa Express monorail goes from VivoCity to three
stations on Sentosa: Waterfront, Imbiah and Beach.

🚶 Simply walk across the Sentosa Boardwalk from VivoCity.

🚌 Sentosa is serviced by free 'beach tram' (an electric bus)
shuttles, and buses.

Neighbourhood Map on p130

Sentosa Island LEUNGCHOPAN/GETTY IMAGES ©

Top Experience 📷
Get Your Thrills at Universal Studios

The top draw in sprawling Resorts World (an integrated resort on Sentosa Island) is Universal Studios. It offers a booty of rides, roller coasters, shows, shops and restaurants, all neatly packaged into fantasy-world themes based on your favourite Hollywood films. Attractions span both the toddler-friendly and the seriously gut-wrenching.

◎ MAP P130, E2

📞 6577 8888

www.rwsentosa.com

Resorts World, 8 Sentosa Gateway

adult/child under 13yr S$76/56

🕙 10am-7pm

🚇 Waterfront

Battlestar Galactica

If you're a hard-core thrill seeker, strap yourself into Battlestar Galactica, which consists of the world's tallest duelling roller coasters. Choose between the sit-down HUMAN roller coaster and the CYLON, an inverted roller coaster with multiple loops and flips. If you can pull your attention away from the screaming (yours and others'), be sure to enjoy the bird's-eye view.

Revenge of the Mummy

The main attraction of the park's Ancient Egypt section, Revenge of the Mummy will have you twisting, dipping and hopping in darkness in your search for the Book of the Living. Contrary to Hollywood convention, your journey will end with a surprising, fiery twist.

Transformers: The Ride

This exhilarating, next-generation motion thrill ride deploys high-definition 3D animation to transport you to a dark, urban other-world where you'll be battling giant robots, engaging in high-speed chases, and even plunging off the edge of a soaring skyscraper. It's incredibly realistic, adrenaline-pumping experience.

Puss in Boots' Giant Journey

Perfect for little kids, this suspended roller coaster takes you on a fairly tame ride with Puss in Boots and his girlfriend, Kitty Softpaws, in search of Mother Goose's precious golden egg. The attention to detail is wonderful; sit in the last row for more of a thrill.

WaterWorld

Gripping stunts and fiery explosions are what you get at WaterWorld, a spectacular live show based on the Kevin Costner flick. Head here at least 20 minutes before show time if you want a decent seat. Those wanting a drenching should sit in the soak zone, right at the front.

★ Top Tips

o If lining up isn't your thing, it may be worth investing in an express pass (from S$30), which lets you jump in the fast lane once for each participating ride.

o Lockers are available around the park, so you don't have to lug everything around with you all day. A small locker (S$15) is the perfect size for a backpack.

✕ Take a Break

For those travelling with a tribe, head to **Loui's NY Pizza Parlor** (New York Zone; large pizza S$50; ⊙10am-7pm) for a humongous, tasty pizza.

Want to leave Universal Studios? Head just outside the main entrance to Malaysian Food Street (p133). Make sure to get a stamp on your hand if you want to re-enter the theme park.

Sentosa Island

1
2
3
4

A **B** **C** **D** **E** **F**

Fort Siloso **1**

Pulau Brani

Brani Terminal Ave

Sedat Sengkir

Causeway Bridge

Sentosa Gateway

Keppel Harbour

Siloso Rd

Siloso Point **1**

Siloso Beach **10**

AJ Hackett Bungy **4**

Mt Imbiah

Imbiah Walk

Adventure Cove Waterpark **5**

Sentosa Cable Car Station

Imbiah Lookout

Images of **3** Singapore

Siloso Beach **13**

Skyline Luge Sentosa **7**

6 Merlion

9 iFly

Beach View

Beach

Sentosa **14**

SEA Aquarium **2**

Waterfront **1**

Resorts World

Merlion Plaza

Imbiah

Universal Studios

Gateway Ave

Artillery Ave

The Knolls

Knolls

Serapong Golf Course

Allanbrooke Rd

Bukit Manis Rd

Palawan Beach

Palawan Beach

Sebarok Channel

Tanjong Golf Course

Tanjong Beach

Tanjong Beach

8

11

12

9 3

For reviews see	
◉ Top Experiences	p128
◉ Sights	p131
⊗ Eating	p133
🍷 Drinking	p134
★ Entertainment	p135

0 500 m
0 0.25 miles

Ⓝ

Sights

Fort Siloso
MUSEUM

1 ◎ MAP P130, A1

Dating from the 1880s, when Sentosa was called Pulau Blakang Mati (Malay for 'the island behind which lies death'), this British coastal fort was famously useless during the Japanese invasion of 1942. Documentaries, artefacts, animatronics and re-created historical scenes take visitors through the fort's history, and the underground tunnels are fun to explore. The Surrender Chambers bring to life two pivotal moments in Singapore's history: the surrender of the British to the Japanese in 1942, and then the reverse in 1945. (☑6736 8672; www.sentosa.com.sg; Siloso Point, Siloso Rd; admission free; ◎10am-6pm; 👪; 🚋Siloso Point; 🚌Siloso Point)

SEA Aquarium
AQUARIUM

2 ◎ MAP P130, D1

You'll be gawking at more than 800 species of aquatic creature at Singapore's impressive, sprawling aquarium. The state-of-the-art complex re-creates 49 aquatic habitats found between Southeast Asia, Australia and Africa. The Open Ocean habitat is especially spectacular, its 36m-long, 8.3m-high viewing panel is one of the world's largest. The complex is also home to an interactive, family-friendly exhibition exploring the history of the maritime Silk Route. (☑6577 8888; www.rwsentosa.com; Resorts World, 8 Sentosa Gateway; adult/child under 13yr S$39/29; ◎10am-7pm; 🅿; 🚋Waterfront)

Images of Singapore Live
MUSEUM

3 ◎ MAP P130, C2

Using dramatic light-and-sound effects, actors and immersive exhibitions, Images of Singapore Live resuscitates the nation's history, from humble Malay fishing village to bustling colonial port and beyond. Kids will especially love the Spirit of Singapore Boat Ride, a trippy, high-tech journey that feels just a little *Avatar*. Tickets include entry to Madame Tussauds and are S$10 cheaper when purchased online. (☑6715 1000, www.imagesofsingaporelive.com; 40 Imbiah Rd, adult/child under 13yr S$42/32; ◎10am-6pm, to 7.30pm Sat & Sun; 🚋Imbiah)

From Here to There

Electric 'beach trams' (buses) run the length of Sentosa's three beaches – Siloso, Palawan and Tanjong – from 9am to 10.30pm Sunday to Friday, and from 9am to midnight Saturday. Two bus routes link the main attractions. Bus A (westbound) and bus B (eastbound) runs 7am to midnight daily. Both routes depart from the bus stop just east of Beach monorail station. The monorail, tram and buses are free.

AJ Hackett Bungy

BUNGEE JUMPING

4 ◉ MAP P130, C2

The famous New Zealand bungee company has now set up shop on Palawan Beach on Sentosa, complete with a 47m platform to hurtle yourself off should the desire grab you. There's also a giant swing, and a sky bridge for those who'd just like to look. (☏6911 3070; www.ajhackett.com; 30 Siloso Beach Walk; bungee S$199, swing S$79, skybridge S$16; ⊙1-7pm, to 8pm Fri-Sun; ☐Siloso Beach)

Adventure Cove Waterpark

WATER PARK

5 ◉ MAP P130, D1

Despite the rides being better suited to kids and families, adult thrill-seekers will appreciate the

Riptide Rocket (Southeast Asia's first hydro-magnetic coaster), Pipeline Plunge and Bluwater Bay, a wave pool with serious gusto. (☏6577 8888; www.rwsentosa.com; Resorts World, 8 Sentosa Gateway; adult/child under 13yr S$38/30; ⊙10am-6pm; ☐Waterfront)

iFly

ADVENTURE SPORTS

6 ◉ MAP P130, C2

If you fancy free-falling from 3660m to 914m without jumping out of a plane, leap into this indoor-skydiving centre. The price includes an hour's instruction followed by a short but thrilling skydive in a vertical wind chamber. Divers must be at least seven years old. Tickets purchased two days in advance for off-peak times are significantly cheaper. See the

Fort Siloso (p131)

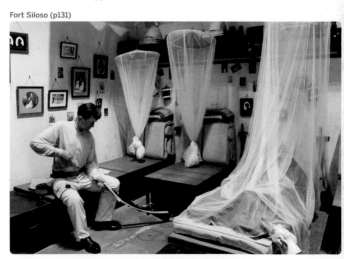

website for details. (📞6571 0000;
www.iflysingapore.com; 43 Siloso Beach
Walk; 1/2 skydives S\$89/119; ⏱9am-
9.30pm, from 11am Wed; 🖳Beach)

Skyline Luge
Sentosa
ADVENTURE SPORTS

 ◎ MAP P130, C2

In the need for speed? Hop onto
your luge (think go-cart meets
toboggan) and race family and
friends around hairpin bends and
along bone-shaking straights
carved through the forest (manda-
tory helmets are provided). Young
kids will love this. Those with heart
conditions or bad backs won't.
You'll find entrances at Imbiah
Lookout and Siloso. (📞6274 0472;
www.skylineluge.com; 45 Siloso Beach
Walk; luge & skyride combo from S\$24;
⏱10am-9.30pm; 🖳Beach, Imbiah;
🖳 Siloso Beach; 🖳 Imbiah Lookout,
Sentosa Cable Car Station)

Eating
Panamericana
GRILL \$\$

 ❌ MAP P130, E4

The perfect mix of island casual
(minus the sand) and refined
service, this bar and grill offers
colonial-chic surroundings and
sweeping views of the Strait of Singapore. The menu offers a mixture
of cuisines found along the Pan-
American Hwy, from North America
down to Argentina. The empanadas
are a must, as is the salt-baked
trout with tomatillo verde. (📞6253
3182; www.panamericana.sg; Sentosa
Gold Course, 27 Bukit Manis Rd; dishes

Millionaire's
Playground

Head down to sleek and
sparkly Sentosa Cove in the
east of the island and join
clued-up locals and expats
in this upmarket residential
and restaurant precinct. Enjoy
your waterside nosh while
admiring the stunning marina,
jam packed with floating
million-dollar play toys of the
seriously rich.

S\$12-50; ⏱noon-11pm Wed-Fri, from
9am Sat & Sun; 🖳B)

Mykonos on the Bay
GREEK \$\$

9 ❌ MAP P130, F3

At Sentosa Cove, this slick, marina-
flanking taverna serves up Hellenic
flavours that could make your
papou weep. Sit alfresco and tuck
into perfectly charred, marinated
octopus, pan-fried Graviera cheese
and house-made *giaourtlou* (spicy
lamb sausage). Book ahead if you
plan to come later in the week.
(📞6334 3818; www.mykonosonthebay.
com; 01-10 Quayside Isle, 31 Ocean
Way; tapas S\$9-26, mains S\$26-43;
⏱6-10.30pm Mon-Wed, noon-2.30pm &
6-10.30pm Thu & Fri, noon-10.30pm Sat
& Sun; 🖋; 🖳B)

Malaysian
Food Street
HAWKER \$

With its faux-Malaysian
streetscape, this indoor hawker
centre near the rotating globe at
the entrance to Universal Studios

(see **2** 👁 Map p130, D1) feels a bit Disney. Thankfully, there's nothing fake about the food, cooked by some of Malaysia's best hawker vendors. (www.rwsentosa.com; Level 1, Waterfront, Resorts World, 8 Sentosa Gateway; dishes S$2-11; ⊙11am-9pm, 9am-10pm Fri-Sun; 🚊Waterfront)

Trapizza

PIZZA $$

10 🍴 MAP P130, B1

At the quieter end of Siloso Beach, Trapizza is the place to head if you're after a great beach vista coupled with yummy thin-crust pizzas straight from the wood-fire oven. There's also a decent wine and cocktail list, but you may want to stay clear of the pizza-inspired cocktails – pepperoni 'pizzatini', anyone? (📞6376 2662; www.shangri-la.com; Siloso Beach; pizzas S$20-26; ⊙11am-10pm; 🚊Siloso Point)

Brunch at Knolls

Free-flowing-alcohol Sunday brunch is huge in Singapore, and posh, secluded **Knolls** (Map p130, E3; 📞6591 5046; www.capellahotels.com; Capella, 1 The Knolls; mains S$24-59, Sun brunch from S$148; ⊙7am-11pm; 🚊Imbiah) serves one of the best. Style up and join the see-and-be-seen crowd for scrumptious buffet fare like freshly shucked oysters, sizzling skewers straight from the live grills, fine-cut meats and mountains of cheese.

Drinking

Tanjong Beach Club

BAR

11 🍺 MAP P130, E4

Generally cooler than the bars on Siloso Beach, Tanjong Beach Club is an evocative spot, with loungers on the sand, a small, stylish pool for guests, and a sultry, lounge-and-funk soundtrack. The restaurant serves trendy beachside fare, and a kick-ass weekend-brunch menu. Some of the island's hottest parties happen on this shore; check the website for details. (📞6270 1355; www.tanjongbeachclub.com; 120 Tanjong Beach Walk; ⊙11am-10pm, from 10am Sat, from 9am Sun; 🐾; 🚊Tanjong Beach)

FOC Sentosa

BAR

12 🍺 MAP P130, E3

A tiny slice of Barcelona on Palawan Beach, this vibrantly striped hang-out is perfect for lazing the afternoon away either by the compact infinity pool or ensconced on a lounger on the sand. Tummy rumbling? Pick a few bites from the menu of seafood-heavy tapas, and wash it down with a refreshing cocktail – our pick is the 'never ending summer', made with vodka, strawberry and watermelon. (📞6100 1102; www.focsentosa.com; 110 Tanjong Beach Walk; ⊙11.30am-11pm Tue-Sun; 🚊Palawan Beach)

Tanjong Beach Club

Coastes

BAR

13 MAP P130, C2

More family-friendly than many of the other beach venues, Coastes has picnic tables on the palm-studded sand and sun loungers (S$22) by the water. Feeling peckish? There's a comprehensive menu of standard offerings, including burgers, pastas, pizzas and salads. (6631 8938; www.coastes.com; 01-05, 50 Siloso Beach Walk; 9am-11pm, to 1am Fri & Sat; Beach; Siloso Beach)

Entertainment

Wings of Time

THEATRE

14 MAP P130, C2

This ambitious show set above the ocean, fuses Lloyd Webber–esque theatricality with an awe-inspiring sound, light and laser extravaganza. Prepare to gasp, swoon and (occasionally) cringe. (6377 9688; www.wingsoftime.com.sg; Siloso Beach; standard/premium seats S$18/23; shows 7.40pm & 8.40pm; Beach)

Explore ⊕
Chinatown
& the CBD

While Singapore's Chinatown may be a tamer version of its former self, its temples, heritage centre, and booming restaurant and bar scene make the trip there worthwhile. The CBD is best known for its stunning, ever-evolving skyline: rooftop bars jostle with old-school temples, all set against the financial heart that funds Singapore.

The Short List

o **Chinatown Heritage Centre (p138)** Delving into the unspeakable hardships, destructive temptations and ultimate resilience of the immigrants who gave this part of town its name.

o **Chinese Theatre Circle (p155)** Meeting the stars of the show in the unusually informal teahouse.

o **Ya Kun Kaya Toast (p150)** Skipping your hotel brekkie for an old-school traditional morning slap-up.

o **Burnt Ends (p147)** Giving the chopsticks a rest to savour show-stopping grilled meats at this mod-Oz favourite.

o **Operation Dagger (p152)** Chatting and flirting the night away in this basement bar before coming up for air at Club St, the city's bar-scene heartland.

Getting There & Around

Ⓜ The heart of Chinatown is served by Chinatown MRT station, which spits you out onto Pagoda St. Telok Ayer station is handy for eateries and bars around Amoy St and Club St. Further south, Outram Park and Tanjong Pagar stations are best for Duxton Hill. Raffles Place station is best for the CBD.

Neighbourhood Map on p142

Chinatown market PETER ADAMS/GETTY IMAGES ©

Top Experience 📷

Time Travel at the Chinatown Heritage Centre

The Chinatown Heritage Centre lifts the lid off Chinatown's chaotic and colourful past. Its endearing jumble of old photographs, personal anecdotes and re-created environments delivers an evocative stroll through the neighbourhood's highs and lows. It will help you see Chinatown's now tourist-conscious streets in a much more intriguing light.

◎ MAP P142, D2

📞 6224 3928; 48 Pagoda St

www.chinatownheritage centre.com.sg

adult/child under 13yr/7yr S$15/11/free

🕘 9am-8pm, closed 1st Mon of month

Ⓜ Chinatown

Tailor Shop & Living Cubicles

The journey back to old Singapore begins on the ground floor with a re-created tailor shop-front, workshop and cramped living quarters of the tailor's family and apprentices. By the early 1950s, Pagoda St was heaving with tailor shops and this is an incredibly detailed replica of what was once a common neighbourhood fixture.

Re-Created Cubicles

Time travel continues on the 1st floor. Faithfully designed according to the memories and stories of former residents, a row of cubicles will have you peering into the ramshackle living quarters of opium-addicted coolies, stoic Samsui women and even a family of eight! It's a powerful sight, vividly evoking the tough, grim lives that many of the area's residents endured right up to the mid-20th century. Keep your eyes peeled for the vermin (don't worry, they're fake) in every cubicle.

Early Pioneers

The flashy top floor invites you to join the perilous journey Chinese immigrants undertook to reach Singapore, and to discover the customs, cuisine and importance of family networks when they arrived, via a range of sensory exhibits. Many new arrivals fell victim to gambling rings and opium dealers; see the pipes and tiles that they used to lose their minds and their money. One street you won't want to go down is Sago Lane ('Street of the Dead'), where many of Chinatown's poor spent their final days in 'death houses'.

★ **Top Tips**

o Aim to arrive just after opening – the museum is physically very small so it's best to beat the crowds.

o Allow at least 1½ hours to see and experience all the exhibits, more if you're a history buff.

o Keep your nostrils on alert – you may get a whiff of some old Chinatown smells.

✕ **Take a Break**

If you arrive before opening time, join the locals at **Nanyang Old Coffee** (☑ 6100 3450; www.nanyangoldcoffee.com; 268 South Bridge Rd; toast sets S$4.30, kopi from S$1.70; ⊙7am-10pm) for a traditional breakfast set of *kaya* (coconut jam) toast, runny eggs and *kopi*.

For tasty local fare, head to Chinatown Complex (p148), a labyrinth of hawker stalls. Check the queue at Michelin-starred Hong Kong Soya Sauce Chicken Rice & Noodle (p148) and decide if you can wait.

Walking Tour 🥾

Chinatown Taste Buds & Temples

Given its past as a hotpot of opium dens, death houses and brothels, it's easy to write off today's Chinatown as a paler version of its former self. Yet beyond the tourist tack that chokes Pagoda, Temple and Trengganu Sts lies a still-engrossing neighbourhood where life goes on as it has for generations.

Walk Facts

Start Chinatown Wet Market (Ⓜ Chinatown)

Finish Telok Ayer St (Ⓜ Telok Ayer)

Length 1.3km; one to two hours with stops

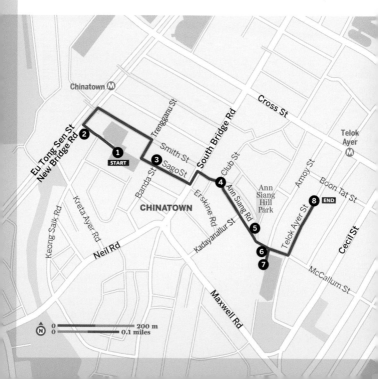

❶ Chinatown Wet Market

Elbow aunties at **Chinatown Wet Market** (Chinatown Complex, 335 Smith St; ⏰5am-noon, stall hours vary), in the basement of the Chinatown Complex. It's a rumble-inducing feast of wriggling seafood, exotic fruits and vegetables, Chinese spices and preserved goods.

❷ Tiong Shian Porridge Centre

Appetite piqued, pull up a plastic stool at **Tiong Shian Porridge Centre** (📞6222 3911; 265 New Bridge Rd; porridge S$3.80-22; ⏰8am-4am), an old-school *kopitiam*. Winners here include delicious porridge with century egg and pork, and the speciality claypot frog-leg porridge.

❸ Chop Tai Chong Kok

Pick up lotus-paste mooncakes at **Chop Tai Chong Kok** (📞6227 5701; www.taichongkok.com; 34 Sago St; pastries from S$1; ⏰9.30am-6pm Mon, to 8pm Tue-Sun), a super-traditional pastry shop in business since 1938. Once known for its sago factories and brothels, Sago St itself now sells everything from barbecued meat to pottery.

❹ Ann Siang Rd & Club St

A quick walk away is trendy Ann Siang Rd, known for its restored heritage terraces and fashionable restaurants, bars and boutiques. Architecture buffs will appreciate the art deco buildings at Nos 15, 17 and 21. Mosey along it and adjacent Club St, also famed for its old shophouses and hip establishments.

❺ Ann Siang Hill Park

At the top of Ann Siang Rd is the entrance to Ann Siang Hill Park. Not only is this Chinatown's highest point, it's a surprising oasis of green. Follow the walkways downward to Amoy St.

❻ Siang Cho Keong Temple

Small Taoist **Siang Cho Keong Temple** (📞6324 4171; 66 Amoy St; admission free; ⏰8am-5pm) was built by the Hokkien community in 1867–69. Left of the temple entrance you'll see a small 'dragon well': drop a coin and make a wish.

❼ Coffee Break

Time for a pit stop at **Coffee Break** (www.facebook.com/coffeebreak amoystreet; 02-78 Amoy Street Food Centre; ⏰7.30am-2.30pm Mon-Fri), a humble drink stall with options like sea-salt caramel lattes and melon milk tea. Make no mistake though, it's still good old Singaporean *kopi* (coffee) – just with a twist.

❽ Telok Ayer St

In Malay, Telok Ayer means 'Water Bay', and Telok Ayer St was a coastal road until land reclamation efforts in the 19th century. Seek out Al-Abrar Mosque, built in the 1850s; Thian Hock Keng Temple, the oldest Hokkien temple in Singapore with a stunning heritage mural on its outside back wall; and Nagore Durgha Shrine, a mosque built between 1828 and 1830 by Chulia Muslims from South India.

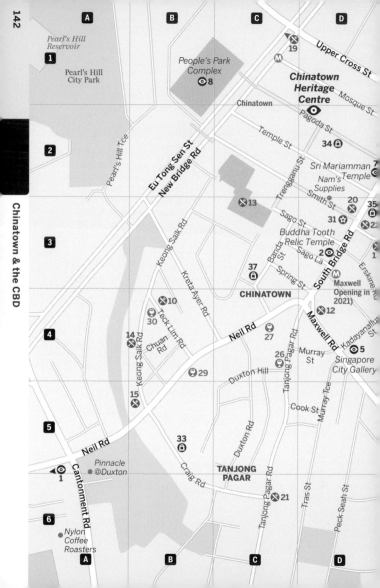

A

Pearl's Hill
Reservoir

1

Pearl's Hill
City Park

Pearl's Hill Tce

2

Eu Tong Sen St
New Bridge Rd

3

Keong Saik Rd

Kreta Ayer Rd

4

14

Keong Saik Rd

Teck Lim Rd

30

Chuan
Rd

15

5

Neil Rd

Cantonment Rd

1

Pinnacle
@Duxton

6

Nylon
Coffee
Roasters

B

People's Park
Complex

8

Chinatown

Temple St

13

37

10

29

Craig Rd

33

TANJONG
PAGAR

C

19

Chinatown
Heritage
Centre

Pagoda St

Smith St

Nam's
Supplies

Sago St

Buddha Tooth
Relic Temple

2

Banda St

Sago La

Spring St

CHINATOWN

Maxwell
(Opening in
2021)

12

Neil Rd

27

26

Murray
St

Duxton Hill

Murray Tce

Cook St

Duxton Rd

Tanjong Pagar Rd

21

D

Upper Cross St

Mosque St

34

Sri Mariamman
Temple

Trengganu St

20

35

31

South Bridge Rd

Erskine Rd

Maxwell Rd

Kadayanallur St

5

Singapore
City Gallery

Tras St

Peck Seah St

7

22

1

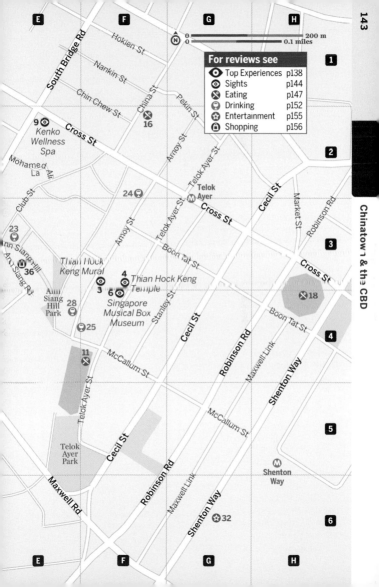

Chinatown & the CBD

For reviews see

◉	Top Experiences	p138
◎	Sights	p144
⊗	Eating	p147
🍷	Drinking	p152
✪	Entertainment	p155
🛍	Shopping	p156

Hokien St

Nankin St

Chin Chew St

China St

Pekin St

South Bridge Rd

Cross St

Kenko Wellness Spa

Mohamed La

Club St

Ann Siang Hill

Ann Siang Rd

Arnoy St

Telok Ayer St

Telok Ayer

Cross St

Cecil St

Market St

Robinson Rd

Amoy St

Telok Ayer St

Boon Tat St

Cross St

Thian Hock Keng Mural

Thian Hock Keng Temple

Stanley St

Boon Tat St

Singapore Musical Box Museum

Ann Siang Hill Park

McCallum St

Cecil St

Robinson Rd

Maxwell Link

Shenton Way

Telok Ayer St

McCallum St

Telok Ayer Park

Shenton Way

Cecil St

Robinson Rd

Maxwell Link

Maxwell Rd

Shenton Way

Shenton Way

0   200 m
0   0.1 miles

Sights

Baba House

MUSEUM

1 ◉ MAP P142, A5

Baba House is one of Singapore's best-preserved Peranakan heritage homes. Built in the 1890s, this beautiful blue three-storey building was donated to the National University of Singapore (NUS) by a member of the family that used to live here. The NUS then set about renovating it so that it best matched how it would have looked in 1928 when, according to the family, Baba House was at its most resplendent. The only way in is on a guided/self-guided tour; bookings are essential. Children must be 12 years or older. (☏6227 5731; http://babahouse.nus.edu.sg; 157 Neil Rd; S$10; ⊙1hr tour 10am Tue-Fri, self-guided tour 1.30pm, 2.15pm, 3.15pm & 4pm Sat; Ⓜ Outram Park)

Buddha Tooth Relic Temple

BUDDHIST TEMPLE

2 ◉ MAP P142, D3

Consecrated in 2008, this hulking, five-storey Buddhist temple is home to what is reputedly a tooth of the Buddha, discovered in a collapsed stupa (Buddhist relic structure) in Mrauk U, Myanmar. While its authenticity is debated, the relic enjoys VIP status inside a 320kg solid-gold stupa in a dazzlingly ornate 4th-floor room. More religious relics await at the 3rd-floor Buddhism museum, while the peaceful rooftop garden features a huge prayer wheel inside a 10,000 Buddha Pavilion. (☏6220 0220; www.btrts.org.sg; 288 South Bridge Rd; admission free; ⊙7am-7pm, relic viewing 9am-6pm; Ⓜ Chinatown)

Thian Hock Keng Mural

PUBLIC ART

3 ◉ MAP P142, F3

Spanning 44m, this mural, painted by Singaporean artist Yip Yew Chong (accountant by weekday, artist by weekend), tells the story of Singapore's early Hokkien immigrants. You'll find it on the outside rear wall of the Thian Hock Keng Temple start from the right end and follow the immigrants' story, from leaving China to arriving in Singapore, and the sacrifices, hardships and joys they experienced along the way. Discover the mural's hidden secrets via the LocoMole app: instructions are to the mural's far left. (www.yipyc.com; Amoy St, rear wall of Thian Hock Keng Temple, 158 Telok Ayer St; Ⓜ Telok Ayer)

Thian Hock Keng Temple

TAOIST TEMPLE

4 ◉ MAP P142, F3

Surprisingly, Chinatown's oldest and most important Hokkien temple is often a haven of tranquillity. Built between 1839 and 1842, it's a beautiful place, and was once the favourite landing point of Chinese sailors, before land reclamation pushed the sea far down the road. Typically, the temple's design features are richly

Temple Tales

Before construction of the Thian Hock Keng Temple, the site was home to a much humbler joss house, where Chinese migrants would come to thank Mazu, the goddess of the sea, for their safe arrival. Their donations helped propel construction of the current temple, the low granite barrier of which once served to keep seawater out during high tide. Look up at the temple's ceiling in the right wing and you'll notice a statue of a man, seemingly lifting a beam. The statue is an ode to Indian migrants from nearby Chulia St, who helped construct the building. During restoration works in 1998, one of the roof beams revealed a surprising find – a scroll written by the Qing emperor Guangxu bestowing blessings on Singapore's Chinese community.

Once you're finished inside, make sure to head around to the rear wall on Amoy St. Here you'll discover the detailed Thian Hock Keng Mural by Yip Yew Chong, which depicts the story of Singapore's early Hokkien immigrants.

symbolic: the stone lions at the entrance ward off evil spirits, while the painted depiction of phoenixes and peonies in the central hall symbolise peace and good tidings respectively. (☏ 6423 4616; www.thianhockkeng.com.sg; 158 Telok Ayer St; admission free; ☻ 7.30am-5.30pm; Ⓜ Telok Ayer)

Singapore City Gallery
MUSEUM

5 ◉ MAP P142, D4

See into Singapore's future at this interactive city-planning exhibition, which provides compelling insight into the government's resolute policies of land reclamation, high-rise housing and meticulous urban planning. At the time of research, the gallery was closed for a revamp;

however, a number of temporary exhibits and the island-wide model remain available for viewing. The main gallery is due to reopen 2019. (☏ 6321 8321; www.ura.gov.sg/citygallery; URA Centre, 45 Maxwell Rd; admission free; ☻ 9am-5pm Mon-Sat; Ⓜ Chinatown, Tanjong Pagar)

Singapore Musical Box Museum
MUSEUM

6 ◉ MAP P142, F4

Walk through music history and be captivated by the exquisite melodies of these antique music boxes, some more than 200 years old. Peer into the inner workings of the very first, and rather basic, boxes all the way through to cupboard-sized, multi-instrument music makers. One was even

Public Housing Panorama

For killer city views at a bargain S$6, head to the 50th-floor rooftop of **Pinnacle@Duxton** (Map p142, A5; ☑8683 7760; www.pinnacle duxton.com.sg; Block 1G, 1 Cantonment Rd; ⊙9am-9pm; ⓂOutram Park), the world's largest public housing complex. Skybridges connecting the seven towers provide a 360-degree sweep of city, port and sea. Chilling out is encouraged, with patches of lawn, modular furniture and sun loungers. Find the 'blink or you'll miss it' ticket booth at level one, Block G, hand over your cash and register your Ez-Link transport card, before taking the lift up to the 50th floor, where you'll tap your card at the gate – stand inside the turnstile before tapping.

destined for the *Titanic* but missed the boat! There's something for everyone; the older generations will love the old-time tunes, and youngsters will marvel at what the first iPod looked like. (☑6221 0102; www.singaporemusicalboxmuseum. org; 168 Telok Ayer St; 40min tour per person S$12, child under 6yr free; ⊙10am-6pm Wed-Mon, tours run hourly from 10am-5pm; ⓂTelok Ayer)

Sri Mariamman Temple

HINDU TEMPLE

7 ◉ MAP P142, D2

Paradoxically in the middle of Chinatown, this is the oldest Hindu temple in Singapore, originally built in 1823, then rebuilt in 1843. You can't miss the fabulously animated, Technicolor 1930s *gopuram* (tower) above the entrance, the key to the temple's South Indian Dravidian style. Sacred-cow sculptures grace the boundary walls, while the *gopuram* is covered in kitsch

plasterwork images of Brahma the creator, Vishnu the preserver and Shiva the destroyer. (☑6223 4064; www.smt.org.sg; 244 South Bridge Rd; take photos/videos S$3/6; ⊙5.30am-noon & 6-9pm; ⓂChinatown)

People's Park Complex

MASSAGE

8 ◉ MAP P142, B1

Heady with the scent of Tiger balm, Singapore's oldest mall is well known for its cheap massage joints. Our favourite is **Mr Lim Foot Reflexology** (☑6327 4498; 20min foot reflexology S$10; ⊙10.30am-10pm), where you'll queue with regulars awaiting a robust rubdown. Feeling adventurous? Try one of the fish-pond foot spas, where schools of fish nibble the dead skin right off your feet. (www.peoplesparkcomplex.sg; 1 Park Cres; ⊙9am-10pm, shop hours vary; ⓂChinatown)

Kenko Wellness Spa
SPA

9 MAP P142, E2

Kenko is the McDonald's of Singapore's spas with branches throughout the city, but there's nothing drive-through about its foot reflexology and forceful Kenko massage (choose the Swedish massage for softer pressure). (☑ 6223 0303; www.kenko.com.sg; 199 South Bridge Rd; reflexology per 40min S$59, body massage per 60min S$120; ☺ 10am-10.30pm; M Chinatown)

Eating

Burnt Ends
BARBECUE $$$

10 ✖ MAP P142, B4

The best seats at this mod-Oz hot spot are at the counter, which offers a prime view of chef Dave Pynt and his 4-tonne, wood-fired ovens and custom grills. The affable Aussie cut his teeth under Spanish charcoal deity Victor Arguinzoniz (Asador Etxebarri), an education echoed in pulled pork shoulder in homemade brioche, and beef marmalade and pickles on chargrilled sourdough. (☑ 6224 3933; www.burntends.com.sg; 20 Teck Lim Rd; dishes S$8-45; ☺ 6-11pm Tue-Thu, 11.45am-2pm & 6-11pm Fri & Sat; M Chinatown, Outram Park)

A Noodle Story
NOODLES $$

11 ✖ MAP P142, F4

With a snaking line and proffered apology that 'we may sell out earlier than stipulated timing' on the facade, this one dish only stall is a magnet for Singapore

Pinnacle@Duxton

foodies. The object of desire is Singapore-style ramen created by two young chefs, Gwern Khoo and Ben Tham. It's Japanese ramen meets won-ton mee (noodles): pure bliss in a bowl topped with a crispy potato-wrapped prawn. (🖝 9027 6289; www.anoodlestorydot-com.wordpress.com; 01-39 Amoy Street Food Centre, cnr Amoy & Telok Ayer Sts; noodles S$8-15; ⏰ 11.15am-2.30pm & 5.30-7.30pm Mon-Fri, 10.30am-1.30pm Sat; Ⓜ Telok Ayer)

Maxwell Food Centre HAWKER $

12 ❌ MAP P142, D4

One of Chinatown's most accessible hawker centres, Maxwell is a solid spot to savour some of the city's street-food staples. While stalls slip in and out of favour with Singapore's fickle diners, endur-

ing favourites include **Tian Tian Hainanese Chicken Rice** (chicken rice from S$3.50; ⏰ 10am-8pm Tue-Sun) and **Rojak, Popiah & Cockle** (popiah S$1.50, rojak S$3-8; ⏰ 10am-10pm), as well as new favourite **Lad & Dad** (🖝 9247 7385; www.facebook.com/ladanddadsg; dishes S$4-12; ⏰ 11.30am-2.30pm & 5.30-9pm Mon-Fri) serving British fare. (cnr Maxwell & South Bridge Rds; dishes S$2.50-12; ⏰ 8am-2am, stall hours vary; 🖉; Ⓜ Chinatown)

Chinatown Complex HAWKER $

13 ❌ MAP P142, C3

Leave Smith St's revamped 'Chinatown Food Street' to the out-of-towners and join old-timers and foodies at this nearby labyrinth, now home to Michelin-starred **Hong Kong Soya Sauce Chicken Rice & Noodle** (Hawker Chan Soya Sauce Chicken Rice & Noodle; www.facebook.com/hawkerchan; dishes S$2-3; ⏰ 10.30am-3.30pm Thu-Tue). You decide if the two-hour wait is worth it. Other standouts include mixed claypot rice at **Lian He Ben Ji Claypot Rice** (🖝 6227 2470; dishes S$2.50-5, claypot rice S$5-20; ⏰ 4.30-10.30pm Fri-Wed) and the rich, nutty satay at **Shi Xiang Satay** (10 sticks S$6; ⏰ 4-9pm Fri-Wed). (335 Smith St; dishes from S$1.50; ⏰ stall hours vary; Ⓜ Chinatown)

Butcher Boy FUSION $$$

14 ❌ MAP P142, B4

Meat lovers will relish the Asian-inspired creations by chef-owner Andrew Walsh, formerly of tapas

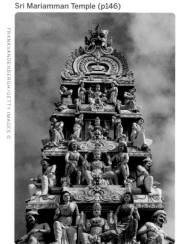

Sri Mariamman Temple (p146)

FRANKVANDENBERGH/GETTY IMAGES ©

Hawker Centre 101

Fragrant chicken rice, nutty satay, sweet and sour *rojak* (salad), spicy barbecue sambal stingray: Singapore's hawker food is the stuff of legend, and celebrity chefs, including the late Anthony Bourdain and *New York Times* writer Johnny Apple, have raved about the dazzling array of cheap, lip-smacking dishes available. There's really no better way to get into Singapore's psyche than through its cuisine, so roll up your sleeves, follow these instructions, and get ready to sweat it out over steaming plates of tried, tested and perfected local favourites.

○ Bag a seat first, especially if it's busy. Sit a member of your group at a table, or 'chope' (save) your seat by laying a packet of tissues there. Don't worry if there are no completely free tables; it's normal to share with strangers.

○ If there's a table number, note it as the stall owner uses it as a reference for food delivery.

○ If the stall has a self-service sign, you'll have to carry the food to the table yourself. Otherwise, the vendor brings your order to you.

○ Ignore wandering touts who try to sit you down and plonk menus in front of you.

○ It's customary to return your tray when finished, although there are a few roaming cleaners who'll take your empty dishes.

---

haven **Esquina** (☏6222 1616; www.esquina.com.sg), in this dimly lit shophouse grill and bar. Perfectly charred, the tender black Angus rib eye is not to be missed, and the masala roasted cauliflower has vegetarians swooning. The good vibes keep on rolling with wickedly strong cocktails.

Happy hour runs 5pm to 7pm daily and the bar seating is great for solo drinkers and diners. (☏6221 6833; www.butcherboy.com.sg; 31 Keong Siak Rd; mains S$24-42; ⊘noon-3pm Wed, Thu & Fri, 6-10.30pm

Sun-Thu, to 11pm Fri & Sat, bar 5pm-late; Ⓜ Chinatown, Outram Park)

Neon Pigeon JAPANESE $$$

15 ✕ MAP P142, B5

Join the crowd at this graffiti-pimped, cocktail-swilling izakaya for produce-driven, finger-licking Japanese sharing plates. Peck your beak at winners like fluffy soft-shell-crab bao with corn, avocado and black pepper teriyaki; moreish edamame Tokyo hummus with curry chips; and smoky baby back ribs with sake barbecue sauce. Six small dishes between two should suffice. The cocktail list is definitely worth sampling. (📞6222 3623; www.neonpigeonsg.com; 1A Keong Saik Rd; small dishes S$9-19, large dishes S$16-48; ⏰6pm-midnight Mon-Sat; 🛜; Ⓜ️Outram Park, Chinatown)

Ya Kun Kaya Toast   CAFE $

16 🍴 MAP P142, F2

Though it's now part of a chain, this airy, retro coffeeshop is an institution, and the best way to start the day the Singaporean way. The speciality is buttery *kaya* toast, dipped in runny eggs (add white pepper and a swirl of soy sauce) and washed down with strong *kopi*. Enjoy a giggle at the Singaporean humour posters. (📞6438 3638; www.yakun.com; 01-01 Far East Sq, 18 China St; kaya toast set S$4.80, kopi S$1.80; ⏰7.30am-7pm Mon-Fri, to 4.30pm Sat, 8.30am-3pm Sun; Ⓜ️Telok Ayer)

Coconut Club   MALAYSIAN $$

17 🍴 MAP P142, D3

Not just any old nasi lemak joint, here they're nuts about coconuts and only a certain Malaysian West African (MAWA) hybrid will do. Chicken is super crispy, encrusted in a flavour-punching lemongrass, ginger and galangal coating. The sambal (sauce of fried chilli, onions and prawn paste), however, is on the mild side. Save room for the refreshing *cendol* dessert. (📞6635 2999; www.thecoconutclub.sg; 6 Ann Siang

Hill; mains S$12.80; ⏰11am-3pm & 6-9.30pm Mon-Sat, 11am-3pm Sun; Ⓜ️Chinatown, Telok Ayer)

Lau Pa Sat   HAWKER $

18 🍴 MAP P142, H4

Lau Pa Sat means 'Old Market' in Hokkien, which is appropriate as the handsome iron structure shipped out from Glasgow in 1894 remains intact. It's a favourite spot for CBD workers, who flock here for hawker favourites like fishball noodles and chicken rice. In the evening, the facing Boon Tat St transforms into **Satay Street** (satay sticks around S$0.70; ⏰7pm-1am Mon-Fri, 3pm-1am Sat & Sun), the famous eating spot. (www.laupasat.biz; 18 Raffles Quay; dishes from S$4; ⏰24hr, stall hours vary; Ⓜ️Telok Ayer, Raffles Place)

Red Star   CHINESE $$

19 🍴 MAP P142, C1

Armed with trolley-clutching aunties who swoop like fighter jets, classic Red Star is perfect for a Hong Kong–style yum cha. Keep your ears pricked for the pork bao and *liu sha* bao, the latter a smooth bun filled with runny salted egg-yolk custard. The restaurant is tucked away on the 7th floor of a HDB block; look for red signs. (📞6532 5266; www.redstarrestaurant.com.sg; Level 7, 54 Chin Swee Rd; yum cha from S$3.50-8; ⏰yum cha 8am-3pm Mon-Sat, from 7am Sun, dinner 6-10pm Mon-Sat; Ⓜ️Chinatown)

Ci Yan Organic Vegetarian Health Food

VEGETARIAN $

20 MAP P142, D3

Excellent food, a very friendly manager and an informal atmosphere make this a fine choice for a no-fuss vegetarian meal in the heart of Chinatown. It tends to only have five or six dishes (when we ate here choices ranged from the delicious brown-rice set meal to minestrone soup, vegetarian Penang laksa and almond tofu), written up on a blackboard daily. (6225 9026; www.facebook.com/ciyanveg; 8-10 Smith St; mains S$4-9; noon-10pm; ; MChinatown)

Ginza Tendon Itsuki

JAPANESE $$

21 MAP P142, C6

Life's few certainties include taxes, death and a queue outside this dedicated *tendon* (tempura served on rice) eatery. Patience is rewarded with cries of *irrashai-mase!* (welcome) and generous bowls of Japanese comfort grub. Both the tempura and rice are cooked to perfection, drizzled in sweet and sticky soy sauce, and served with *chawanmushi* (Japanese egg custard), miso soup and pickled vegetables. A cash-only bargain. (6221 6678; www.tendon-itsuki.sg; 101 Tanjong Pagar Rd; mains S$13-14; 11.30am-2.30pm & 5.30-10pm; ; MTanjong Pagar)

Ya Kun Kaya Toast

DAVIDIONP/SHUTTERSTOCK ©

Tong Heng

BAKERY $

22 MAP P142, D3

Hit the spot at this veteran pastry shop, specialising in pastries, tarts and cakes from the southern Chinese province of Guangdong. While locals rightfully flock here for the melt-in-your-mouth diamond shaped egg tarts, leave room for the slightly charred perfection of the char siew su (barbecue pork puff). Addictive personalities beware. (📞6223 3649; www.tongheng.com. sg; 285 South Bridge Rd; snacks from S$1.70; ⏰9am-9pm; Ⓜ Chinatown)

Drinking

Operation Dagger

COCKTAIL BAR

23 MAP P142, E3

From the cloud-like light sculpture to the boundary-pushing cocktails, extraordinary is the keyword here. To encourage experimentation, drinks are described by flavour, not spirit, the latter shelved in uniform apothecary-like bottles. Sample the sesame-infused Gomashio or the textural surprise of the Hot & Cold. Head up the hill where Club St and Ann Siang Hill meet; a symbol shows the way. (📞6438 4057; www.operationdagger.com; 7 Ann Siang Hill; ⏰6pm-late Tue-Sat; Ⓜ Chinatown, Telok Ayer)

Employees Only

COCKTAIL BAR

24 MAP P142, F2

This outpost of the famous New York cocktail bar of the same name has brought a slice of big-city buzz to Singapore, along with a dazzling array of innovative drinks. Some of the sting from the eye-watering prices is soothed by the free-pour mixing method; lightweights may be knocked from their perch. A pink neon 'psychic' sign marks the entrance. (http://employeesonlysg. com; 112 Amoy St; ⏰5pm-1am Mon-Fri, to 2am Sat, 6pm-1am Sun; Ⓜ Telok Ayer)

HDB Caffeine Hit

The ground-floor space of Singapore's public housing blocks (HDBs) are usually scattered with gossipy uncles and aunties and shrieking kids. At Everton Park, however, you're just as likely to find third-wave coffee geeks. The HDB complex is home to **Nylon Coffee Roasters** (Map p142, A6; 📞6220 2330; www.nyloncoffee.sg; 01-40, 4 Everton Park; ⏰8.30am-5.30pm Mon & Wed-Fri, 9am-6pm Sat & Sun; Ⓜ Outram Park, Tanjong Pagar), a standing-room-only cafe-roastery helmed by a personable, gung-ho crew of coffee fanatics, chatting away with customers about their latest coffee-sourcing trip abroad (they deal directly with the farmers). Everton Park is 500m south of Outram Park MRT. Enter from Cantonment Rd, directly opposite the seven-tower Pinnacle@Duxton (p146).

Operation Dagger

Native

BAR

25 MAP P142, F4

This hidden bar, in hot-spot-heavy Amoy St, is the brainchild of bartender extraordinaire Vijay Mudaliar (formerly of Operation Dagger (p152)), and his concoctions have everyone talking. With spirits sourced from around the region – such as Thai rum and Sri Lankan arak, paired with locally foraged ingredients – expect the unexpected. (8869 6520; www.tribenative.com; 52A Amoy St; 6pm-midnight Mon-Sat; Telok Ayer)

Tippling Club

COCKTAIL BAR

26 MAP P142, C4

Tippling Club propels mixology to dizzying heights, with a technique and creativity that could turn a teetotaller into a born-again soak. Sample the Dreams & Desires menu before ordering by chewing your way through alcohol-infused gummy bears, which give a hint of what's to come. Our pick is the champagne-based Beauty, served with a cherry sorbet lipstick. (6475 2217; www.tipplingclub.com; 38 Tanjong Pagar Rd; noon-midnight Mon-Fri, from 6pm Sat; Tanjong Pagar)

Tea Chapter

TEAHOUSE

27 MAP P142, C4

Queen Elizabeth and Prince Philip dropped by this tranquil teahouse in 1989, and for S$10 you can sit at the table they sipped at. A minimum charge of S$8 per person will got you a heavenly pot of loose-leaf tea, prepared with traditional precision. The selection is excellent and the adjoining shop sells tea and a selection of beautiful tea sets.

Want to take your tea tasting to a new level? Book a tea appreciation package (from S$70 for two persons), either the 'fragrance and aroma' or 'shades of tea', and become a tea master. (6226 1175; www.teachapter.com; 9-11 Neil Rd; teahouse 11am-9pm Sun-Thu, to 10.30pm Fri & Sat, shop 10.30am-9pm Sun-Thu, to 10.30pm Fri & Sat; Chinatown)

Spiffy Dapper

COCKTAIL BAR

28 MAP P142, E4

Keep your eyes peeled for the Dapper Coffee sign and then quick, before anyone sees, scuttle

Beer Hawkers

Clink craft-beer glasses with locals at the Chinatown Complex (p148), where a few fancy beer hawkers such as Smith Street Taps (p154) and have opened their shutters right next to some of the best eats in town – the satays from nearby Shi Xiang Satay (p148) complement the suds perfectly. Don't be put off if the centre looks closed when you enter; check the map at the top of the escalator to find the stalls and join the party.

up the stairs and through the engraved doors. Choose from the list of classic cocktails or let the bar tenders do their thing – gin lovers, you're in for a treat as the collection here is legendary. (☑ 8742 8908; www.spiffydapper.com; 73 Amoy St; ☻ 5pm-late Mon-Fri, from 6pm Sat & Sun; M Telok Ayer)

Smith Street Taps   CRAFT BEER

Head to this hawker-centre stall in the Chinatown Complex (see 14 ✖ Map p142, C3) for a top selection of ever-changing craft and premium draught beers from around the world. A few food stalls stay open around this back section of the hawkers market, creating a local hidden-bar buzz. Tuck into a plate of smoky skewers from Shi Xiang Satay (p148) with your brew. Last call 15 minutes before closing.

Sister stall the **Good Beer Company** (02-58 Chinatown Complex; ☻ 6.30-10.30pm Mon-Sat) sells bottled suds. (☑ 9430 2750; www.facebook.com/smithstreettaps; 02-62 Chinatown Complex, 335 Smith St; ☻ 6.30-10.30pm Tue-Thu, 5-11pm Fri, 2-10.30pm Sat; M Chinatown)

Taboo   CLUB, LGBTIQ+

29   MAP P142, B4

Conquer the dance floor at what remains the favourite gay club in town. Expect the requisite line-up of shirtless gyrators, doting straight women and regular racy-themed nights. The dance floor goes ballistic from midnight and the beats bump till the wee hours of the morning. (☑ 6225 6256; www.taboo.sg; 65 Neil Rd; ☻ 8pm-2am Wed & Thu, 10pm-3am Fri, to 4am Sat; M Outram Park, Chinatown)

Potato Head Singapore   COCKTAIL BAR

30   MAP P142, B4

Offshoot of the legendary Bali bar, this standout, multi-level playground incorporates three spaces, all reached via a chequered stairwell embellished with creepy storybook murals and giant glowing dolls. Skip the Three Buns burger joint and head straight for the dark, plush glamour of cocktail lounge Studio 1939 or the laid-back frivolity of the rooftop tiki bar. (☑ 6327 1939; www.ptthead.com; 36 Keong Saik Rd; ☻ Studio 1939 & rooftop bar 5pm-late; 🛜; M Outram Park)

Entertainment

Chinese Theatre Circle OPERA

31 ⭐ MAP P142, D3

Teahouse evenings organised by this nonprofit opera company are a wonderful, informal introduction to Chinese opera. Every Friday and Saturday at 8pm there is a brief talk on Chinese opera, followed by a 45-minute excerpt from an opera classic, performed by actors in full costume. You can also opt for a pre-show Chinese meal at 7pm. Book ahead. (📞6323 4862; www.ctcopera.com; 5 Smith St; show & snacks S$25, show & dinner S$40; ⏰7-9pm Fri & Sat; Ⓜ Chinatown)

Singapore Chinese Orchestra CLASSICAL MUSIC

32 ⭐ MAP P142, G6

Using traditional instruments such as the *liuqin*, *ruan* and *sanxian*, the SCO treats listeners to classical Chinese concerts throughout the year. Concerts are held at the SCO Concert Hall as well as at various venues around the city, with occasional collaborations showcasing jazz musicians. Tickets can be purchased via SISTIC (p49) or at the on-site box office. Check the website for upcoming performances. (SCO; 📞6557 4034; www.sco.com.sg; Singapore Conference Hall, 7 Shenton Way, ⏰box office 10am-6.45pm Mon-Fri, 6-9pm SCO concert nights; Ⓜ Tanjong Pagar, Downtown)

Potato Head Singapore

Paper, Death & Sago Lane

The curious paper objects on sale around Chinatown – from miniature cars to computers – are offerings burned at funeral wakes to ensure the material wealth of the dead. Veteran **Nam's Supplies** (Map p142, D3; ☑6324 5872; www.facebook.com/namssupplies; 22 Smith St; ◷8am-7pm; Ⓜ Chinatown) has been peddling such offerings since 1948, when nearby Sago Lane heaved with so-called 'death houses', where the dying spent their final days.

Shopping

Tong Mern Sern Antiques
ANTIQUES

33 🔒 MAP P142, B5

An Aladdin's cave of dusty furniture, books, records, wood carvings, porcelain, and other bits and bobs, Tong Mern Sern is a curious hunting ground for Singapore nostalgia. A banner hung above the front door proclaims: 'We buy junk and sell antiques. Some fools buy. Some fools sell'. Better have your wits about you. (☑6223 1037; www.tmsantiques.com; 51 Craig Rd; ◷9.30am-5.30pm Mon-Sat, from 1.30pm Sun; Ⓜ Outram Park)

Anthony the Spice Maker
SPICES

If you want to re-create the aromas and tastes of Singapore at home, head to this tiny stall in the Chinatown Complex (see 14 ✕ Map p142, C3) where little brown airtight packets, which don't allow even the slightest whiff of the heady spices to escape, are uniformly lined up. Anthony is only too happy to help you choose, but we can personally recommend the meat *rendang* blend. (☑9117 7573; www.anthonythespicemaker.com; B1-169 Chinatown Complex, 335 Smith St; ◷8.15am-3.30pm Tue-Sun; Ⓜ Chinatown)

East Inspirations
ANTIQUES

34 🔒 MAP P142, D2

East Inspirations is jam-packed with antique figurines, trinkets and some furniture. Look out for the beautifully embroidered Chinese Manchu wedding shoes. There's a second outlet at 233 South Bridge Rd. (☑6224 2993; www.east-inspirations.com; 33 Pagoda St; ◷10.30am-6.30pm; Ⓜ Chinatown)

Eu Yan Sang
HEALTH & WELLNESS

35 🔒 MAP P142, D3

Get your *qi* back in order at Singapore's most famous and user-friendly Chinese medicine store. Pick up some Monkey Bezoar powder to relieve excess phlegm, or Liu Jun Zi pills to dispel dampness. You'll find herbal teas, soups and oils, and you can even consult a practitioner of Chinese medicine at the clinic next door (bring your

Anthony the Spice Maker

passport). (📞6223 6333; www.euyansang.com.sg; 269 South Bridge Rd; ⏲shop 9am-6.30pm Mon-Sat, clinic 8.30am-6pm Mon-Tue & Thu-Fri, from 9am Wed, 8.30am-7.30pm Sat; 🚇Chinatown)

innit   FASHION & ACCESSORIES

36 🔒 MAP P142, E3

Singaporean fashionistas swoon over the flowing fabrics and perfect pleating of Thai fashion house innit. Pieces are easily mixed and matched, and the high quality means you'll get plenty of wear from each item. (📞9781 7496; www.innitbangkok.com; 13 Ann Siang Hill; ⏲11am-8pm Wed-Sat; 🚇Chinatown, Telok Ayer)

Hear Records   MUSIC

37 🔒 MAP P142, C3

Rack upon rack of wooden boxes filled with music gold awaits those who like to flick at this vinyl-lovers paradise. Tucked at the end of a block near the Buddha Tooth Relic Temple, this bright-orange-painted store, with fun black-and-white 'sleeveface' picture wall, stocks new and used vinyl in pretty much every genre. (📞6221 3221; www.facebook.com/hearrecordschinatown; 01-98, Block 5, Banda St; ⏲11am-7.30pm Mon-Sat, noon-6pm Sun; 🚇Chinatown)

Walking Tour

A Lazy Morning in Tiong Bahru

Spend a late weekend morning in Tiong Bahru, three stops from Raffles Place on the East–West (green) MRT line. More than just hip boutiques, bars and cafes, this low-rise neighbourhood was Singapore's first public-housing estate, and its walk-up, art-deco apartments now make for unexpected architectural treats.

Walk Facts

Start Tiong Bahru Market
(M Tiong Bahru)

Finish We Need A Hero
(M Tiong Bahru)

Length 1.5km; one to two hours

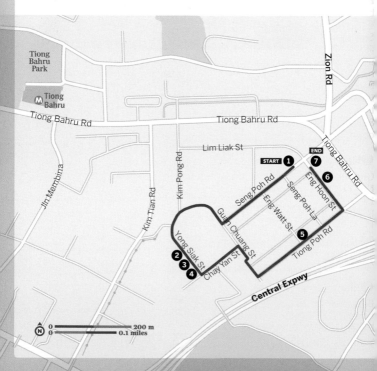

❶ Tiong Bahru Market

Whet your appetite exploring the wet market at the **Tiong Bahru Market & Food Centre** (83 Seng Poh Rd; dishes from S$3; ⊘6am-late, stall hours vary), then head upstairs to the hawker centre for *shui kueh* (steamed rice cake with diced preserved radish) at **Jian Bo Shui Kueh** (www.jianboshuikueh.com; 02-05 Tiong Bahru Market & Food Centre, 5 shui kueh S$2.50; ⊘5.30am-10pm).

❷ Book Hunting

BooksActually (☏6222 9195; www.booksactually.com; 9 Yong Siak St; ⊘10am-8pm Tue-Sat, to 6pm Mon & Sun) is one of Singapore's coolest independent bookshops, with often unexpected choices of fiction and non-fiction. For beautiful children's books, check out **Woods in the Books** (☏6222 9980; www.woodsinthebooks.sg; ⊘10am-7pm Tue-Fri, to 8pm Sat, to 6pm Sun), three doors down.

❸ Nana & Bird

Originally a pop-up concept store, **Nana & Bird** (www.nanaandbird.com; 1M Yong Siak St; ⊘noon-7pm Mon-Fri, from 11am Sat & Sun) is a sound spot for fresh independent fashion and accessories for women, with labels including Singapore designers Aijek and Rye.

❹ Plain Vanilla Bakery

If your idea of heaven involves frosted icing, head to **Plain Vanilla Bakery** (☏8363 7614; www.plainvanillabakery.com; 1D Yong Siak St;

cupcakes from S$4.20; ⊘8am-7pm Mon-Sat, 9am-6pm Sun). The passion project of ex-lawyer-turned-baker Vanessa Kenchington, this bakery-cafe peddles ridiculously scrumptious cupcakes in flavours such as Earl Grey lavender.

❺ Ah Chiang's

Join old-timers and Gen-Y nostalgics for a little Cantonese soul food at **Ah Chiang's** (☏6557 0084; www.facebook.com/ahchiangporridgesg; 01-38, 65 Tiong Poh Rd; porridge S$5-6; ⊘6am-11pm). The star turn at this retro corner *kopitiam* (coffeeshop) is fragrant, charcoal-fired congee.

❻ Tiong Bahru Bakery

The quintessential Frenchman, baker Gontran Cherrier has all and sundry itching for a little French lovin' at **Tiong Bahru Bakery** (☏6220 3430; www.tiongbahrubakery.com; 01-70, 56 Eng Hoon St; pastries S$2.20-4.60, sandwiches S$5.30-12; ⊘8am-8pm). Faultless pastries include flaky *kouign amanns* (Breton-style pastry); perfect with luscious coffee from Common Man Coffee Roasters.

❼ We Need a Hero

Especially for blokes, **We Need A Hero** (☏6222 5590; www.weneedahero.sg; 01-86, 57 Eng Hoon St; barber cut from S$60, shave from S$35; ⊘11am-9pm Mon-Fri, from 10am Sat, 10am-8pm Sun) is the perfect place to plonk yourself down and let the Hero team unleash their grooming superpowers – you'll be slick in no time.

Walking Tour 🚶

Geylang

Contradiction thrives in Geylang, a neighbourhood as famous for its shrines, temples and mosques as for its brothels and back-alley gambling dens. Catch the East–West (green) MRT line four stops from Raffles Place and spend the afternoon wandering quaint lorongs (alleys) and religious buildings, before heading back to neon-lit Geylang Rd for a lively evening of people-watching and lip-smacking local grub.

Walk Facts

Start Geylang Lor 9 Fresh Frog Porridge (Ⓜ Kallang/Aljunied)

Finish Rochor Beancurd (Ⓜ Paya Lebar)

Length 3km; two to four hours

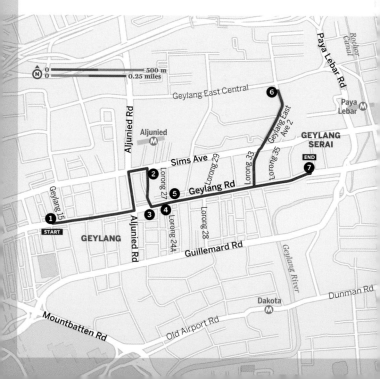

❶ Geylang Lor 9 Fresh Frog Porridge

Geylang is famous for its frog porridge and the best place to try it is **Geylang Lor 9 Fresh Frog Porridge** (235 Geylang Rd; frog porridge from S$8.50; ⏰3pm-3.30am). Its Cantonese-style version is beautifully smooth and gooey, and only live frogs are used, so the meat is always fresh.

❷ Amitabha Buddhist Centre

Take a class on dharma and meditation at the **Amitabha Buddhist Centre** (📞6745 8547; www.fpmtabc. org; 44 Lorong 25A; ⏰10.30am-6pm Tue-Sat, from 10am Sun); its upstairs meditation hall is open to the public and filled with devotional objects. Check the website for class schedules.

❸ No Signboard Seafood

Get messy over white-pepper crab at **No Signboard Seafood** (📞6842 3415; www.nosignboardsea food.com; 414 Geylang Rd; dishes S$15-60, crab per kg from S$80; ⏰11am-1am). Madam Ong Kim Hoi started out with an unnamed hawker stall (hence 'No Signboard'), but the popularity of her seafood made her a rich woman, with four restaurants.

❹ Lorong 24A

One alley worth strolling down is **Lorong 24A**, lined with reno-vated shophouses from which the sounds of chanting emerge.

Many have been taken over by the numerous small Buddhist associations in the area. Close by, tree-lined Lorong 27 is jammed with colourful shrines and temples.

❺ Geylang Thian Huat Siang Joss Paper

Old-school **Geylang Thian Huat Siang Joss Paper** (503 Geylang Rd; ⏰8am-9.30pm) sells paper offerings used at funeral wakes. You'll find everything from giant cash registers to lifelike shoes and piles of cash, all thrown into the fire to ensure a comfortable afterlife.

❻ Sri Sivan Temple

Built on Orchard Rd in the 1850s, the whimsically ornate **Sri Sivan Temple** (📞6743 4566; www.sst.org. sg; 24 Geylang East Ave 2; admission free; ⏰6am-noon & 6-9pm) was uprooted and moved to Serangoon Rd in the 1980s before moving to its current location in 1993. The Hindu temple is unique for its fusion of North and South Indian architectural influences.

❼ Rochor Beancurd

End on a sweet note at tiny **Rochor Beancurd** (📞6748 3989; www.rochorbeancurdhouse.wix. com/home; 745 Geylang Rd; dough sticks S$1.20, bean curd from S$1.60; ⏰24hr; 🖋). People head here from all over the city for a bowl of silky bean curd (opt for it warm). Order a side of dough sticks and dip to your heart's content. Oh, and did we mention the egg tarts?

Explore

Joo Chiat (Katong)

This picturesque neighbourhood of restored multicoloured shophouses has, in recent years, become known as the spiritual heartland of Singapore's Peranakan culture. Spend a few hours wandering the ornate shophouse-lined streets ducking in and out of heritage temples, dusty antiques workshops, Islamic fashion boutiques, low-fuss eateries and trendy cafes. Complete your day with a trip to breezy East Coast Park.

The Short List

○ **Peranakan Terrace Houses (p167)** Eyeing-up the exuberant architectural candy of Joo Chiat and Koon Seng Rds.

○ **328 Katong Laksa (p168)** Licking to the bottom of the bowl at this cult-status laksa shop.

○ **Katong Antique House (p165)** Delving into rich Peranakan culture.

○ **East Coast Park (p167)** Riding a bicycle or roller-blading along East Coast Park before plonking yourself down to rest, watch the ships in the strait and soak up the atmosphere.

Getting There & Around

Ⓜ Paya Lebar takes you to the north end of Joo Chiat Rd.

🚌 Buses 33 and 16 go to the centre of Joo Chiat, passing through Geylang; bus 14 goes from Orchard Rd to East Coast Rd. Bus 12 goes to East Coast Rd from Victoria St; bus 36 gets there from Bras Basah Rd.

Neighbourhood Map on p166

Koon Seng Road (p165) JOHN SEATON CALLAHAN/GETTY IMAGES ©

Walking Tour 🥾

Joo Chiat (Katong)

Also known as Katong, Joo Chiat is the heart of Singapore's Peranakan community. It's an evocative mix of multicoloured shophouses, tucked-away temples, and quaint workshops and studios – plus some of the city's best eating options. Try to head in during business hours, when locals hop in and out of heirloom shops in search of fabrics, produce and the next tasty snack.

Walk Facts

Start Geylang Serai Market (Ⓜ Paya Lebar)

Finish Katong Antique House (🚌 10, 12, 14, 32)

Length 2.5km; three to four hours

❶ Geylang Serai Market

Geylang Serai Market (1 Geylang Serai; ◷8am-10pm) packs in a lively wet market, hawker food centre and stalls selling everything from Malay CDs to skull-caps. Feeling peckish? Hunt down some *pisang goreng* (banana fritters) and wash them down with *bandung* (milk with rose cordial syrup).

❷ Joo Chiat Road

Eclectic Joo Chiat Rd is lined with dusty antiques workshops, Islamic fashion boutiques and low-fuss grocery shops. Detour into Joo Chiat Tce to admire the Peranakan terraces at Nos 89 to 129, adorned with *pintu pagar* (swinging doors) and colourful ceramic tiles.

❸ Long Phung

Down-to-earth Vietnamese eatery **Long Phung** (☏9105 8519; 159 Joo Chiat Rd; dishes S$7-23; ◷noon-10pm) serves up some of Singapore's best Vietnamese food. The fragrant *pho* (noodle soup) and tangy mango salad are simply gorgeous.

❹ Kuan Im Tng Temple

Located on a quiet side street, Buddhist temple **Kuan Im Tng** (☏6348 0967; www.kuanimtng.org.sg; 62 Tembeling Rd, cnr Tembeling Rd & Joo Chiat Lane; admission free; ◷5am-6pm) is dedicated to Kuan Yin, goddess of mercy. Temple fans will appreciate the ornate roof ridges adorned with dancing dragons.

❺ Koon Seng Road Terraces

Koon Seng Rd is famous for its two rows of pre-war, pastel-coloured Peranakan terrace houses (p167), lavished with stucco dragons, birds, crabs and brilliant glazed tiles imported from Europe.

❻ Sri Senpaga Vinayagar Temple

One of Singapore's most beautiful Hindu temples, **Sri Senpaga Vinayagar Temple** (☏6345 8176; www.senpaga.org.sg; 19 Ceylon Rd; admission free; ◷6am-12.30pm & 5.30-11pm) features a *kamalapaatham*, a specially sculptured granite foot-stone found in certain ancient Hindu temples. The roof of the inner sanctum is covered in gold.

❼ Kim Choo Kueh Chang

Joo Chiat is stuffed with bakeries, but few equal old-school **Kim Choo Kueh Chang** (☏6741 2125; www.kimchoo.com; 109-111 East Coast Rd; ◷9am-9pm). Pick up traditional pineapple tarts and other bite-sized Peranakan snacks, then pit stop at the adjoining boutique for Peranakan ceramics and clothing.

❽ Katong Antique House

Tiny shop-cum-museum **Katong Antique House** (☏6345 8544; 208 East Coast Rd; 45min tour S$15; ◷by appointment only, though it's sometimes open to the public) is the domain of Peter Wee, a noted expert on Peranakan culture, and packed with his collection of books, antiques and cultural artefacts.

A

B
Eunos

Sims Ave

Jln Eunos

C

D

0.25 miles

500 m

For reviews see

👁 Sights p167
✕ Eating p168
🍷 Drinking p170
★ Entertainment p171
🔒 Shopping p171

1

Eunos Rd 2

Changi Rd

2

Joo Chiat Rd

Onan Rd

Tembeling Rd

Crane Rd

Jousting
Painters
Mural Joo Chiat Tce

3 👁

11 ✕

Joo Chiat Pl

✕ 12

Joo Chiat La

Still Rd

JOO CHIAT
(KATONG)

Telok Kurau Rd

4 👁

Betel Box:
The Real
Singapore
Tours

9 ✕

Koon Seng Rd

Lorong L Teok Kurau

3

1 👁 Peranakan
Terrace
Houses

Duku Rd

Still Rd

Dunman Rd

13 👁

Joo Chiat Rd

Tembeling Rd

Cheow Keng Rd

East Coast Rd

10 ✕

St Patrick's Rd

Carpmael Rd

Onan Rd

Ceylon Rd

Marshall Rd

Fowlie Rd

Kuo Chuan Ave Jago Cl

✕ 8

Chapel Rd

Sea Ave

4

Haig Rd

6 7 15 16 🔒
✕ ✕

East Coast Rd

17 🔒

Joo Chiat Rd

★ 14

Still Rd South

5

Mountbatten Rd

Amber Gardens

Amber Rd

East Coast Rd

Brooke Rd

Parade Rd

Marine Parade Rd

Roland
Restaurant

5
👁
Marin
Cov

Amber Rd

East Coast Pkwy (ECP)

East Coast
Park

East Coast Park Service Rd

👁
2

Strait of
Singapore

6

A

B

C

D

Sights

Peranakan Terrace Houses

AREA

MAP P166, B3

Just off Joo Chiat Rd, Koon Seng Rd and Joo Chiat Pl feature Singapore's most extraordinary Peranakan terrace houses, joyously decorated with stucco dragons, birds, crabs and brilliantly glazed tiles. *Pintu pagar* (swinging doors) at the front of the houses are a typical feature, allowing cross breezes while retaining privacy. Those on Koon Seng Rd are located between Joo Chiat and Tembeling Rds, while those on Joo Chiat Pl run between Everitt and Mangis Rds. (Koon Seng Rd & Joo Chiat Pl; 10, 14, 16, 32)

East Coast Park

PARK

2 MAP P166, C6

This 15km stretch of seafront park is where Singaporeans come to swim, windsurf, wakeboard, kayak, picnic, bicycle, rollerblade, skateboard, and – of course – eat. You'll find swaying coconut palms, patches of bushland, a lagoon, sea-sports clubs and some excellent eating options.Renting a bike, enjoying the sea breezes, watching the veritable city of container ships out in the strait and capping it all off with a beachfront meal is one of the most pleasant ways to spend a Singapore afternoon. (1800 471 7300; www.nparks.gov.sg; P; 36, 43, 48, 196, 197, 401)

Jousting Painters Mural

PUBLIC ART

3 MAP P166, A2

This giant mural by Lithuanian-born street artist Ernest Zacharevic (www.ernestzacharevic.com) is fantastically playful, like all his works. It features two very real-looking boys prepared for battle on brightly painted horses. (cnr Everitt Rd & Joo Chiat Tce; M Paya Lebar)

Betel Box: The Real Singapore Tours

TOURS

4 MAP P166, A2

Insider tours led by Tony Tan and the team at Betel Box Hostel. Choose from culture and heritage walks, city kick scootering or food odysseys through the historic Joo Chiat, Kampong Glam or Chinatown neighbourhoods. If you're looking for a walk on the wild side, join the Friday night tour through red-light district in Geylang. (6247 7340; www.betelboxtours.com; 200 Joo Chiat Rd; S\$60-100; tours M Paya Lebar)

Marine Cove

PARK

5 MAP P166, D5

With a breezy seaside setting, this 3,500-sq-metre playground is the perfect place to let the kids run wild. Highlights include an 8m tall lighthouse gym, rock-climbing walls and digital game stations. A row of family-friendly restaurants complete this kiddie enclave. Weekday afternoons are the best times to go (weekends are manic), and don't forget your hat as there's little shade. (📞1800 471 7300; www.nparks.gov.sg; 1000 East Coast Park; admission free; ⏰24hr; 🅿🚻; 🚍36, 43, 48, 196, 197, 401)

Eating

328 Katong Laksa MALAYSIAN $

6 🍴 MAP P166, B4

For a bargain foodie high, hit this cult-status corner shop. The star is the namesake laksa: thin rice noodles in a light curry broth made with coconut milk and coriander, and topped with shrimps and cockles. Order a side of *otah* (spiced mackerel cake grilled in a banana leaf) and wash it down with a cooling glass of lime juice.

(📞9732 8163; www.328katonglaksa.com; 51 East Coast Rd; laksa S$5.50-7.50; ⏰10am-10pm; 🚍10, 12, 14, 32)

Birds of Paradise GELATO $

7 🍴 MAP P166, B4

This high-end boutique ice-cream shop is stocked with artisanal gelatos, taking flavour cues from nature: think white chrysanthemum and strawberry basil. Even the cone (S$1 extra) gets the botanical touch, infused with a subtle thyme fragrance. In homage to Singapore's heritage, there are also local flavours – try the heady masala spice, if available. (📞9678 6092; www.facebook.com/bopgelato; 01-05, 63 East Coast Rd; ⏰noon-10pm Tue-Sun; 🚍10, 14, 16, 32)

Katong laksa (spicy coconut broth with noodles)

The Invention of Chilli Crab

In 1956, Mr and Mrs Lim opened a seafood restaurant called the Palm Beach. It was here that Mrs Lim first concocted the now-famous tomato, chilli and egg sauce that makes the quintessential Singapore chilli crab. At least that's the story according to her son, who decades, on is the proprietor of his own giant restaurant, **Roland Restaurant** (Map p166, C5; ☑ 6440 8205; www.rolandrestaurant.com.sg; 06-750 Block 89, Marine Parade Central, Deck J, multistorey carpark; dishes S$12-60, crab per kg from S$73; ⏱ 11.30am-2.15pm & 6-10.15pm; ☐ 36, 48, 196, 197), where the chilli crab lures former prime minister Goh Chok Tong on National Day. The crabs are fleshy and sweet and the gravy milder than many of its competitors: good news if you're not a big spice fan.

Chin Mee Chin Confectionery

BAKERY $

8 ✖ MAP P166, C4

A nostalgia trip for many older Singaporeans, old-style baker-ies such as Chin Mee Chin are a dying breed, with their geomet-ric floors, wooden chairs and industrious aunties pouring *kopi* (coffee). One of the few Singa-porean breakfast joints that still makes its own *kaya* (coconut jam), it's also a good spot to pick up some pastries to go. (☑ 6345 0419; 204 East Coast Rd; kaya toast & coffee from S$2; ⏱ 8.30am-3.30pm Tue-Sun; ☐ 10, 12, 14, 32)

Loving Hut

VEGAN $$

9 ✖ MAP P166, A3

Bright, airy and oozing healthy vibes, this strictly plant-based cafe serves up traditional local fare. Try the sesame chicken clay-pot rice or manbo fillet with chilli nyonya moo siam; all are 100% vegan. (☑ 6348 6318; www.loving hut.com.sg; 01-01, 229 Joo Chiat Rd; dishes S$8-20; ⏱ 11.30am-2.30pm & 6-9pm Mon, Wed-Fri, 11.30am-9pm Sat & Sun; ☑; ☐ 10, 14, 16, 32)

Penny University

CAFE $

10 ✖ MAP P166, D3

Coffee snobs will appreciate this laid-back new-schooler, one of the few speciality coffeeshops on the East Coast. Grab a booth or sit at the communal table, sip an espresso and scan the menu for fresh, modern grub such as vanilla-infused yoghurt with granola or Turkish eggs (poached, on whipped yoghurt, topped with spicy Moroccan harissa sauce and oregano). (☑ 6345 9055; www.face book.com/pennyuniversity; 402 East Coast Rd; dishes S$6-16; ⏱ 8.30am-6pm, to 10.30pm Fri & Sat, to 7pm Sun; ☎; ☐ 10, 12, 14, 32)

Nonya Desserts

Peranakan (Nonya) desserts are typified by *kueh* (colourful rice cakes often flavoured with coconut and palm sugar) and sweet, sticky delicacies such as miniature pineapple tarts that are sold everywhere in small plastic tubs with red lids. The magnificent *kueh lapis,* a laborious layer cake, is a must-try. Head to old-school Kim Choo Kueh Chang (p165) to sample some of the island's best.

Smokey's BBQ   AMERICAN $$

11 🗙 MAP P166, A2

You'll be longing for sweet home Alabama at this breezy, all-American barbecue legend. Californian owner Rob makes all the dry rubs using secret recipes and the meats are smoked using hickory and mesquite woodchips straight from the USA. Start with the spicy buffalo wings with blue-cheese dipping sauce, then stick to slow-roasted, smoked meats such as ridiculously tender, fall-off-the-bone ribs. (☑ 6345 6914; www.smokeysbbq.com.sg; 73 Joo Chiat Pl; mains S$19-65; ⊙3-11pm, from 11am Sat & Sun; ⏺; Ⓜ Paya Lebar)

Guan Hoe Soon   PERANAKAN $$

12 🗙 MAP P166, A2

Famously, this is Singapore's oldest Peranakan restaurant (established 1953) and the late former-prime minister Lee Kuan Yew's favourite ... but even boasts like that don't cut much ice with picky Singaporeans if the food doesn't match up. Fortunately, its fame hasn't inspired complacency and the Nonya food here is top-notch. The definitive Peranakan ayam buah keluak (chicken with black nut) is a standout. (☑ 6344 2761; www.guanhoesoon.com; 38 Joo Chiat Pl; mains S$11-16; ⊙11am-3pm & 6-9.30pm; Ⓜ Paya Lebar)

Drinking

Cider Pit   BAR

13 🍺 MAP P166, B3

Wedged in a nondescript concrete structure, Cider Pit is easy to miss. Don't. The watering hole offers an extensive range of ciders on tap, and speciality beers such as Australia's Little Creatures. It's a refreshingly casual, unfussy kind of place, ideal for easygoing drinking sessions among expats in shorts, tees and flip-flops. (☑ 6440 0504; www.eastofavalon wines.com; 328 Joo Chiat Rd; ⊙3pm-1am, from 1pm Sat & Sun; ⏺; Ⓜ Paya Lebar)

Entertainment

Bldg, 278 Marine Parade Rd; 🚌12, 16, 36, 196)

Necessary Stage

THEATRE

14 ⭐ MAP P166, D4

Since the theatre's inception in 1987, artistic director Alvin Tan has collaborated with resident playwright Haresh Sharma to produce over 60 original works. Innovative, indigenous and often controversial, the Necessary Stage is one of Singapore's best-known theatre groups. Productions are performed at the Necessary Stage Black Box and other venues; check the website for current shows and purchase tickets through SISTIC (p49). (📞6440 8115; www.necessary. org; B1-02 Marine Parade Community

Shopping

Rumah Bebe

CLOTHING, HANDICRAFTS

15 🔒 MAP P166, B4

Bebe Seet is the owner of this 1928 shophouse and purveyor of all things Peranakan. She sells traditional kebayas (Nonya-style blouses with decorative lace) with contemporary twists and beautifully beaded shoes. If you've got time and the inclination, you can take one of the beading classes run by Bebe, including a two-session beginners course (S$450). (📞6247 8781, www.rumahbebe.com; 113 East

Rumah Bebe

Peranakan Culture

Peranakan heritage has been enjoying renewed interest, mainly triggered by *The Little Nonya,* a high-rating 2008 drama series focused on a Peranakan family, and the opening of Singapore's outstanding Peranakan Museum (p46). But who are the Peranakans?

Origins

In Singapore, Peranakan (locally born) people are the descendants of immigrants who married local, mostly Malay women. The largest Peranakan group in Singapore is the Straits Chinese. The men, called Babas, and the women, Nonya, primarily speak a patois that mixes Bahasa Malaysia, Hokkien dialect and English. The ancestors of the Straits Chinese were mainly traders from mainland China, their presence on the Malay peninsula stretching back to the Ming dynasty. The ancestors of Chitty Melaka and Jawi Peranakan were Indian traders, whose unions with local Malay women created their own unique traditions. All three groups are defined by an intriguing, hybrid culture created by centuries of cultural exchange and adaptation.

Weddings

No Peranakan tradition matches the scale of the traditional wedding. Originally spanning 12 days, its fusion of Fujian Chinese and Malay traditions included the consulting of a *sinseh pokwa* (astrologer) in the choosing of an auspicious wedding day, elaborate gifts delivered to the bride's parents in *bakul siah* (lacquered bamboo containers) and a young boy rolling across the bed three times in the hope for a male first-born. With the groom in Qing-dynasty scholar garb and the bride in a similarly embroidered gown and hat piece, the first day would include a tea ceremony. On the second day, the couple took their first meal together, feeding each other 12 dishes to symbolise the 12-day process, while the third day would see them offering tea to their parents and in-laws. On the *dua belah hari* (12th-day ceremony), the marriage was sealed and proof of the consummation confirmed with a discreet sighting of the stain on the bride's virginity handkerchief by the bride's parents and groom's mother.

Coast Rd; ⊙9.30am-6.30pm Tue-Sun; 🚌10, 14, 16, 32)

Cat Socrates   GIFTS & SOUVENIRS

16 🔒 MAP P166, B4

Complete with feline 'assistant shopkeeper', this eclectic boutique is filled with wares from independent local and foreign designers. Creatives flock here for the mix of whimsical stationery, lo-fi cameras, on-trend homewares, stylish jewellery and indie books. Souvenir hunters will love the Singapore–inspired curios, especially the Peranakan-themed notebooks

and tiles. (☎6348 0863; https://cat-socrates.myshopify.com; 448 Joo Chiat Rd; ⊙12.30-9.30pm Tue-Sun; 🚌10, 14, 16, 32)

112 Katong   MALL

17 🔒 MAP P166, B4

This contemporary mall is where East Coasters love to shop. You will find plenty of fashion and lifestyle stores, Kids will love the water playground on the 4th floor. (☎6636 2112; www.112katong.com.sg; 112 East Coast Rd; ⊙10am-10pm; 🚌10, 14, 16, 32)

Worth a Trip 🥾

Pulau Ubin

Singapore's 'Far East' has a slower, nostalgic style of local life. Vests, boardshorts and flip-flops are the look in chilled-out Changi Village, a place where low-rise buildings are the norm and out-of-towners are a less common sight. A short bumboat (motorised sampan) ride away, the rustic island of Pulau Ubin is the Singapore that development has left behind ... for now.

Getting There

Ⓜ Catch the East–West Line to Tanah Merah MRT Station.

🚌 Take bus 2 to Changi Village.

⛴ For Pulau Ubin catch a bumboat from Changi Point Ferry Terminal.

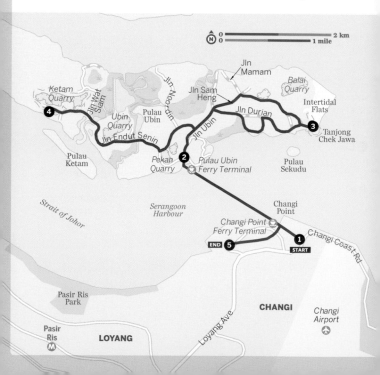

❶ Changi Village

Hugging Singapore's far north-east coast, Changi Village is well worth a wander to experience a curiously relaxed side of Sing apore. The vibe is almost village-like, and a browse around the area will turn up cheap clothes, batik, Indian textiles and electronics. Bumboats to Pulau Ubin depart from Changi Point Ferry Terminal (p180), beside the bus terminal.

❷ Pulau Ubin Village

Your landing spot on Pulau Ubin is Pulau Ubin Village. Although not technically a tourist sight, its ramshackle nature channels a long-lost Singapore. If you're feeling peckish, turn left for a handful of places to eat, mostly housed in *kampong* (village) huts. The village is also the place to rent bikes; day rentals cost around S$6 to S$25.

❸ Chek Jawa Wetlands

If you only have time for one part of Pulau Ubin, make it **Chek Jawa Wetlands** (☑1800 471 7300; www.nparks.gov.sg; admission free; ⊙8.30am-6pm). Located at the island's eastern end, its 1km coastal boardwalk juts out into the sea before looping back through protected mangrove swamp to the 20m-high Jejawi Tower, offering a stunning panorama.

❹ German Girl Shrine

The German Girl Shrine, near Ketam Quarry, is one of the island's quirkier sights. Legend has it that the young German daughter of a coffee-plantation manager was running away from British troops who had come to arrest her parents during WWI and fell fatally into a quarry. Somewhere along the way, this daughter of a Roman Catholic family became a Taoist deity.

❺ Coastal Settlement

Back in Changi, end the day with drinks at **Coastal Settlement** (☑6475 0200; www.thecoastal settlement.com; 200 Netheravon Rd; ⊙10.30am-11pm Tue-Thu, to midnight Fri, from 8.30am Sat & Sun; 🛜), an eclectic bar-lounge-restaurant pimped with retro objects and set in a black-and-white colonial bun-galow on lush, verdant grounds.

Survival Guide

Singapore skyline SAKDAWUT TANGTONGSAP/SHUTTERSTOCK ©

Before You Go

Book Your Stay

Staying in Singapore is expensive, especially in the CBD and around shoppers paradise Orchard Rd. However more modest and budget-friendly digs are available in the surrounding areas of Little India and Chinatown. Prices all over the island skyrocket during September's F1 night race so you should book early if visiting at that time. Accommodation options range from simple, shared back-packer dorms to some of the most historical and luxurious sleep spots in Asia.

Useful Websites

Lonely Planet (lonely planet.com/singapore/hotels) Recommendations and bookings.

StayinSingapore (www.stayinsingapore.com) Hotel-booking website managed by the Singapore Hotel Association.

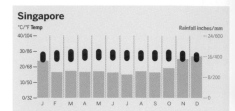

Singapore
°C/°F Temp — Rainfall inches/mm

When to Go

o **Jan & Feb** Buzzing night markets and Chinese New Year celebrations.

o **Jun & Jul** School holidays fall in June and July, the hottest time of year, so try to avoid travelling in these months if possible.

o **Dec** Moonsoon rains cool Singapore down a fraction.

LateRooms (www.laterooms.com) Great deals on rooms; book now and pay when you stay.

Best Budget

Adler Hostel (www.adlerhostel.com) This self-proclaimed 'poshtel' just near the Chinatown MRT comes with Chinese antiques.

COO (www.staycoo.com) A new-school hostel with neon lighting and a hip location in Tiong Bahru.

Dream Lodge (www.dreamlodge.sg) Spick-and-span capsule hostel in up-and-coming Jalan Besar.

BEAT. Capsules (www.beathostel.co) Sleek capsules smack bang on the Singapore River.

Kam Leng Hotel (www.kamleng.com) Retro hotel in the Jalan Besar district.

Best Midrange

Wanderlust (www.wanderlusthotel.com) Idiosyncratic rooms packed with imagination and designer twists in intriguing Little India.

Lloyd's Inn (www.lloydsinn.com) Minimalist boutique hotel a short stroll from Orchard Rd.

Holiday Inn Express Orchard Road (www. hiexpress.com) A fresh, good-value option just a block from Orchard Rd.

Hotel Indigo (www. hotelindigo.com) Peranakan-inspired hotel bursting with nostalgic memorabilia, steps from heritage-heavy Joo Chiat Rd.

Great Madras (www. thegreatmadras.com) Pastel art-deco gem right in the thick of Little India.

Best Top End

Fullerton Bay Hotel (www.fullertonhotels. com) Elegant, light-filled luxury perched right on Marina Bay.

Parkroyal on Pickering (www.parkroyalhotels. com) A striking architectural statement, with hanging gardens and a stunning infinity pool.

Capella Singapore (www.capellahotels. com) Cascading pools, lush gardens and chic interiors on Sentosa.

Six Senses Duxton (www.sixsenses.com) A tranquil haven, where no two rooms are the same, ensconced in a row of heritage shophouses.

Warehouse (www. thewarehousehotel. com) Industrial-chic interiors and a stunning infinity pool right by the Singapore River.

Arriving in Singapore

By Plane

Changi Airport (☎6595 6868; www.changiairport. com; Airport Blvd; 🛜; ⓂChangi Airport), 20km northeast of Singapore's central business district (CBD), has four main terminals with a fifth in the works. Regularly voted the world's best airport, it is a major international gateway, with frequent flights to all corners of the globe. You'll find free internet, courtesy phones for local calls, foreign-exchange booths, medical centres, left luggage, hotels, day spas, showers, a gym, a swimming pool and no shortage of shops.

The much-anticipated Jewel Changi Airport is a 10-storey complex with exciting attractions, including a canopy park, forest and rain vortex as well as retail, accommodation and dining offerings. At the time of research, it was slated to open in early 2019.

Transport options from Changi Airport include the following:

○ MRT trains run into town from the airport from 5.30am to 11.18pm; public buses run from 6am to midnight. The train and bus trips cost from S\$1.69.

○ The airport shuttle bus (adult/child S\$9/6) runs into the city 24 hours a day.

○ A taxi into the city will cost anywhere from S\$20 to S\$40, and up to 50% more between midnight and 6am, plus airport surcharges.

○ A four-seater limousine taxi from the airport to the city is S\$55, plus S\$15 surcharge per additional stop.

By Bus

Numerous private companies run comfortable bus services to Singapore from many destinations in Malaysia, including Melaka and Kuala Lumpur, as well as from cities such as Hat Yai in Thailand. Many of these services terminate at **Golden Mile Complex Bus Terminal** (5001 Beach Rd; M Bugis, Nicoll Hwy), near Kampong Glam. You can book at www.busonlineticket.com.

From Johor Bahru, commuter buses with Causeway Link Express (www.causewaylink.com.my) run regularly to various locations in Singapore (one way S$3.50/RM3.40, every 15 to 30 minutes, roughly 6am to 11.30pm), including Newton Circus, Jurong East Bus Terminal and Kranji MRT station.

By Train

Malaysian company Keretapi Tanah Melayu Berhad (www.ktmb.com.my) runs trains from Kuala Lumpur to JB Sentral station in Johor Bahru from where you get a shuttle train to **Woodlands Train Checkpoint** (11 Woodlands Crossing; 🚌 170, Causeway Link Express from Queen St terminal). Tickets for the shuttle (S$5) can be bought at the counter. Trains leave from here to Kuala Lumpur, with connections on to Thailand. You can book tickets at the Woodlands or JB Sentral stations or online at www.easybook.com.

By Ferry

Ferry services from Malaysia and Indonesia arrive at various ferry terminals in Singapore.

Changi Point Ferry Terminal (☑ 6545 2305; 51 Lorong Bekukong; ⏰ 24hr; 🚌 2)

HarbourFront Cruise & Ferry Terminal (☑ 6513 2200; www.singaporecruise.com; 1 Maritime Sq; 🚇; M HarbourFront)

Tanah Merah Ferry Terminal (☑ 6513 2200; www.singaporecruise.com.sg; 50 Tanah Merah Ferry Rd; 🚌 35)

Getting Around

Mass Rapid Transit (MRT)

The efficient Mass Rapid Transit (MRT) subway system is the easiest, quickest and most comfortable way to get around Singapore. The system operates from 5.30am to midnight, with trains at peak times running every two to three minutes, and every five to seven minutes off-peak.

The system consists of five colour-coded lines: North–South (red), North–East (purple), East–West (green), Circle Line (orange) and Downtown (blue). A sixth line, the Thomson–East Coast Line (brown), will open in five stages, with the first scheduled to open in 2019.

Single-trip tickets cost from S$1.40 to S$2.50, but if you're using the MRT a lot it can become a hassle buying tickets for every journey. A lot more convenient is the EZ-Link card (www.ezlink.com.sg). Alternatively, a **Singapore Tourist Pass** (www.thesingaporetouristpass.com.sg) offers unlimited train and bus travel (S$10 plus a S$10 refundable deposit) for one day.

Bus

Singapore's extensive bus service is clean, efficient and regular, reaching every corner of the island. The two main operators are **SBS Transit** (☏1800 225 5663; www.sbstransit.com.sg) and **SMRT** (☏1800 336 8900; www.smrt.com.sg). Both offer similar services.

Bus fares range from S$1 to S$2.10 (less with an EZ-Link card). When you board the bus, drop the exact money into the fare box (no change is given), or tap your EZ-Link card or Singapore Tourist Pass on the reader as you board, then again when you get off.

Train operator SMRT also runs late-night bus services between the city and various suburbs from 11.30pm to 4.35am on Fridays, Saturdays and the eve of public holidays. The flat rate per journey is S$4.50.

Taxi

You can flag down a taxi any time, but in the city centre taxis are technically not allowed to stop anywhere except at designated taxi stands.

Finding a taxi in the city at certain times is harder than it should be. These include during peak hours, at night, or when it's raining. Many cab drivers change shifts between 4pm and 5pm, making it notoriously difficult to score a taxi then.

The fare system is also complicated, but thankfully it's all metered, so there's no haggling over fares. The basic flagfall is S$3 to S$3.40 then S$0.22 for every 400m.

There's a whole raft of surcharges to note, among them 50% of the metered fare from midnight to 6am and 25% of the metered fare between 6am and 9.30am Monday to Friday, and 6pm to midnight daily. Airport journeys incur a surcharge of S$5 from 5pm to midnight Friday to Sunday and S$3 at all other times. There's also a S$3 city-area surcharge from 5pm to midnight and S$2.30 to S$8 for telephone bookings.

Tipping is not generally expected, but it's courteous to round up or tell the driver to keep the change.

Payment by credit card incurs a 10% surcharge. You can also pay using your EZ-Link transport card. For a comprehensive list of fares and surcharges, visit www.taxi singapore.com.
Comfort Taxi & City Cab (☏6552 1111; www.cdgtaxi.com.sg)

Premier Taxis (☏6363 6888; www.premiertaxi.com.sg)

SMRT Taxis (☏6555 8888; www.smrt.com.sg)

Essential Information

Accessible Travel

A wide-ranging and long-term government campaign has seen ramps, lifts and other facilities progressively installed around the island. Footpaths in the city are nearly all immaculate, MRT station all have lifts and more than half of public buses are wheelchair-friendly. Wheelchair-accessible taxis can sometimes be flagged down, but contact **SGMAXI.cab** (www.

sgmaxi.cab) to book wheelchair-accessible maxicabs for airport transfers or transport around the island.

The **Disabled People's Association Singapore** (www.dpa.org.sg) can provide information on accessibility in Singapore.

Download Lonely Planet's free Accessible Travel guides (http://shop.lonelyplanet.com/accessible-travel).

Business Hours

Banks 9.30am to 4.30pm Monday to Friday (some till 6pm or later); 9.30am to noon or later Saturday.

Restaurants Generally noon to 2.30pm and 6pm to 11pm. Casual restaurants and food courts open all day.

Shops 10am or 11am to 6pm; larger shops and department stores til 9.30pm or 10pm. Some smaller shops in Chinatown and Arab St close on Sundays.

Discount Cards

If you arrived on a SilkAir or Singapore Airlines flight, you can present your boarding pass to get discounts at shops, restaurants and attractions. See www.singaporeair.com/boardingpass for information.

Electricity

Type G
230V/50Hz

Emergencies

Country Code	📞65
Ambulance & Fire	📞995
Police	📞999

LGBTIQ+ Travellers

Sex between males is illegal in Singapore and carries a minimum sentence of 10 years. Singaporeans are fairly conservative about public affection.

Despite that, Singapore has a string of popular LGBTIQ+ bars. Websites **Travel Gay Asia** (www.travelgayasia.com), **PLUguide** (www.pluguide.com) or **Utopia** (www.utopia-asia.com) have coverage of venues and events.

Money

ATMs and money-changers are widely available. Credit cards are accepted in most shops and restaurants.

Credit Cards

Credit cards are widely accepted, apart from at local hawkers and food courts.

Public Holidays

The only holiday that has a major effect on the city is Chinese New Year, when virtually all shops shut down for two days. Public holidays are as follows:

New Year's Day 1 January

Chinese New Year Two days in January/February

Good Friday March/April

Labour Day 1 May

Vesak Day May

Hari Raya Puasa June

National Day 9 August

Hari Raya Haji August

Dewali October

Christmas Day 25 December

Responsible Travel

Support Local

For local tourism operators, check www.seeksophie.com – you'll find everything from gin tasting, to kayaking through mangroves.

Get a mani-pedi at The Nail Social (www.thenailsocial.co), a socially conscious salon that provides training and employment to local marginalised women who experience a higher barrier to employment.

Ex-offenders are given a second chance at The Caffeine Experience, a coffeeshop started by an ex-drug dealer and prison officer.

Taxes & Refunds

Visitors can get a refund of the 7% GST on purchases, under the following conditions:

- Present your passport and spend a minimum of S$100 at one retailer on the same day, for no more than three purchases.
- Get an eTRS (Electronic Tourist Refund Scheme) ticket issued by the shop or use a debit or credit card as a token to track purchases; no need to pay with the card.
- Scan your eTRS ticket or token debit/credit card at the kiosks at the airport or cruise terminal. If physical inspection of the goods is required present the goods, original receipts and your boarding pass at the Customs Inspection Counter.

Tourist Information

Singapore Visitors Centre @ Orchard (Map p84, F5; ☎1800 736 2000; www.yoursingapore.com; 216 Orchard Rd; ⏲8.30am-9.30pm; 📶; Ⓜ Somerset) This main branch has knowledgable staff who can help you organise tours, buy tickets and book hotels.

Visas

Citizens of most countries are granted 90-day entry on arrival. Citizens of India, the People's Republic of China, the Commonwealth of Independent States and most Middle Eastern countries must obtain a visa before arriving. Visa extensions can be applied for at the **Immigration & Checkpoints Authority** website (☎6391 6100; www.ica.gov.sg; Level 4, ICA Bldg, 10 Kallang Rd; ⏲8am-4pm Mon-Fri; Ⓜ Lavender).

Customs Regulations

You are not allowed to bring tobacco into Singapore unless you pay duty. You will be slapped with a hefty fine if you fail to declare and pay. You are permitted 1L each of wine, beer and spirits duty-free. Alternatively, you are allowed 2L of wine and 1L of beer, or 2L of beer and 1L of wine. You need to have been out of Singapore for more than 48 hours and to anywhere but Malaysia. It's illegal to bring chewing gum, firecrackers, obscene or seditious material, gun-shaped cigarette lighters, endangered species or their by-products, and pirated recordings or publications with you.

Language

The official languages of Singapore are Malay, Mandarin, Tamil and English. Malay is the national language, adopted when Singapore was part of Malaysia, but its use is mostly restricted to the Malay community.

The government's long-standing campaign to promote Mandarin, the main nondialectal Chinese language, has been very successful and increasing numbers of Singaporean Chinese speak it at home. In this chapter we've provided Pinyin (the official system of writing Mandarin in the Roman alphabet) alongside the Mandarin script.

Tamil is the main Indian language in Singapore; others include Malayalam and Hindi. If you read our pronunciation guides for the Tamil phrases in this chapter as if they were English, you'll be understood.

English is widespread and has been the official first language of instruction in schools since 1987. Travellers will have no trouble getting by with only English in Singapore.

To enhance your trip with a phrasebook, visit lonelyplanet.com.

Malay

Hello.	*Helo.*
Goodbye. (when leaving/staying)	*Selamat tinggal./ Selamat jalan.*
How are you?	*Apa khabar?*
Fine, thanks.	*Khabar baik.*
Please. (when asking/offering)	*Tolong./ Silakan.*
Thank you.	*Terima kasih.*
Excuse me.	*Maaf.*
Sorry.	*Minta maaf.*
Yes./No.	*Ya./Tidak.*
What's your name?	*Siapa nama kamu?*
My name is ...	*Nama saya ...*
Do you speak English?	*Bolehkah anda berbicara Bahasa Inggeris?*
I don't understand.	*Saya tidak faham.*
How much is it?	*Berapa harganya?*
Can I see the menu?	*Minta senarai makanan?*
Please bring the bill.	*Tolong bawa bil.*
Where are the toilets?	*Tandas di mana?*
Help!	*Tolong!*

Mandarin

Hello./Goodbye. 你好。/再见。 好。你呢？	*Nǐhǎo./Zàijiàn.* *Hǎo. Nǐ ne?*
How are you? 你好吗？	*Nǐhǎo ma?*
Fine. And you? 好。你呢？	*Hǎo. Nǐ ne?*
Please ... 请……	*Qǐng ...*
Thank you. 谢谢你。	*Xièxie nǐ.*

Excuse me. (to get attention)
劳驾。 *Láojià.*

Excuse me. (to get past)
借光。 *Jièguāng.*

Sorry.
对不起。 *Duìbùqǐ.*

Yes./No.
是。/不是。 *Shì./Bùshì.*

What's your name?
你叫什么
名字? *Nǐ jiào shénme
míngzi?*

My name is ...
我叫…… *Wǒ jiào ...*

Do you speak English?
你会说
英文吗? *Nǐ huìshuō
Yīngwén ma?*

I don't understand.
我不明白。 *Wǒ bù míngbái.*

How much is it?
多少钱? *Duōshǎo qián?*

Can I see the menu?
能不能给我看
一下菜单? *Néng bù néng gěiwǒ
kàngyīxià càidān?*

Please bring the bill.
请给我账单。 *Qǐng gěiwǒ
zhàngdān.*

Where are the toilets?
厕所在哪儿? *Cèsuǒ zài nǎr?*

Help!
救命! *Jiùmìng!*

Tamil

Hello.
வணக்கம். *va·nak·kam*

Goodbye.
போய வருகிறேன். *po·i va·ru·ki·reyn*

How are you?
நீங்கள் நலமா? *neeng·kal na·la·maa*

Fine, thanks. And you?
நலம், நன்றி.
நீங்கள்? *na·lam nan·dri
neeng·kal*

Please.
தயவு செய்து. *ta·ya·vu chey·tu*

Thank you.
நம்றி. *nan·dri*

Excuse me.
தயவு செய்து. *ta·ya·vu sei·du*

Sorry.
மன்னிக்கவும். *man·nik·ka·vum*

Yes./No.
ஆமாம்./இல்லை. *aa·maam/il·lai*

What's your name?
உங்கள் பெயர்
என்ன? *ung·kal pe·yar
en·na*

My name is ...
என் பெயர்... *en pe·yar ...*

Do you speak English?
நீங்கள் ஆங்கிலம்
பேசுவீர்களா? *neeng·kal
aang·ki·lam
pey·chu·veer·ka·la*

I don't understand.
எனக்கு
விளங்கவில்லை. *e·nak·ku
vi·lang·ka·vil·lai*

How much is it?
இது என்ன
விலை? *i·tu en·na
vi·lai*

I'd like the bill/menu, please.
எனக்கு தயவு
செய்து
விலைச்சீட்டு/
உணவுப்பட்டியல்
கொடுங்கள். *e·nak·ku ta·ya·vu
chey·tu
vi·laich·cheet·tu/
u·na·vup·pat·ti·yal
ko·tung·kal*

Where are the toilets?
கழிவறைகள்
எங்கே? *ka·zi·va·rai·kal
eng·key*

Help!
உதவு! *u·ta·vi*

Behind the Scenes

Send Us Your Feedback

We love to hear from travellers – your comments help make our books better. We read every word, and we guarantee that your feedback goes straight to the authors. Visit **lonelyplanet.com/contact** to submit your updates and suggestions.

Note: We may edit, reproduce and incorporate your comments in Lonely Planet products such as guidebooks, websites and digital products, so let us know if you don't want your comments reproduced or your name acknowledged. For a copy of our privacy policy visit lonelyplanet.com/privacy.

Ria's Thanks

Thank you to my Destination Editor Tanya Parker for all her help in guiding me through my Lonely Planet adventure, and to all those I met along my travels who kindly shared their knowledge, time and Singapore secrets with me. To Craig, Cisca and William, my travelling circus tribe.

Acknowledgements

Cover photograph: Shophouses, Chinatown, Ronnie Chua/ Shutterstock ©; back cover photograph: Haw Par Villa (p121), siraphat/ Shutterstock ©

Photographs pp 30-31 (clockwise from left): siraphat/Shutterstock ©, Komar/Shutterstock ©, tapanuth/Shutterstock ©, Peter Adams/Getty Images ©, leungchopan/Getty Images ©

This 7th edition of Lonely Planet's *Pocket Singapore* guidebook was researched and written by Ria de Jong. The previous two editions were written by Ria and Cristian Bonetto. This guidebook was produced by the following:

Destination Editor
Tanya Parker

Senior Product Editors
Daniel Bolger, Kate Chapman

Cartographers
Alison Lyall, Mark Griffiths, Julie Sheridan

Product Editors
Amy Lysen, Claire Rourke

Book Designers
Gwen Cotter, Fergal Condon

Assisting Editors
Judith Bamber, Sandie Kestell, Rosie Nicholson, Gabrielle Stefanos, Angela Tinson, Monica Woods

Cover Researcher
Ania Bartoszek

Thanks to:
Ronan Abayawickrema, Grace Dobell, Marcus Feaver, Christine Hanne, Martin Heng, Alison Killilea, Amy Lynch, Kate Morgan, Claire Naylor, Karyn Noble, Genna Patterson, Ambika Shree, Eleanor Simpson, James Smart, Peter Tudor

Index

See also separate subindexes for:

- 😊 Eating p189
- 😊 Drinking p190
- 😊 Entertainment p191
- 😊 Shopping p191

Our Writer

Ria de Jong

Ria started life in Asia, born in Sri Lanka to Dutch/ Australian parents. She has always relished the hustle and excitement of this continent of contrasts. After growing up in Townsville, Australia, Ria moved to Sydney as a features writer before packing her bags for a five-year stint in the Philippines. Having moved t' Singapore in 2015 with her husband and two small children, Ria is loving discovering every nook and cranny of this tiny city, country, nation. This is Ria's fourth Singapore update for Lonely Planet. Follow Ria on Twitter @ria_in_transit.

Published by Lonely Planet Global Limited
CRN 554153
7th edition – April 2022
ISBN 978 1 78868 375 3
© Lonely Planet 2022 Photographs © as indicated 2022
10 9 8 7 6 5 4 3 2 1
Printed in Singapore

Museum of Sydney MUSEUM

4 ⊙ MAP P62, D1

Built on the site of Sydney's first Government House, the MoS is a fragmented, storytelling museum, which uses installations to explore the city's history. The area's long Indigenous past is highlighted, plus there's interesting coverage of the early days of contact between the Gadigal (Cadigal) people and the colonists. Key figures in Sydney's planning and architecture are brought to life, while there's a good section on the First Fleet itself, with scale models. (MoS; ☎02-9251 5988; www.sydneylivingmuseums.com.au; cnr Phillip & Bridge Sts; adult/child $12/8; ◷10am-5pm; ☒Circular Quay)

St Mary's Cathedral CHURCH

5 ⊙ MAP P62, E4

Sydney has traditionally been quite a Catholic city, and this is the hub of the faith. Built to last, this 106m-long sandstone Gothic Revival–style cathedral was begun in 1868, consecrated in 1905 and substantially finished in 1928, though the massive, 75m-high spires weren't added until 2000. The **crypt** ($5 admission, 10am to 4pm weekdays) has bishops' tombs and an impressive cross-shaped terrazzo mosaic floor depicting the Creation, inspired by the Celtic-style illuminations of the *Book of Kells* (☎02-9220 0400, www.stmaryscathedral.org.au; St Marys Rd; ◷6.30am-6.30pm; ☒St James)

Sydney Tower Eye

Anzac Memorial

MEMORIAL

6 ◎ MAP P62, D6

Fronted by the Pool of Reflection, this dignified art-deco memorial (1934) commemorates the soldiers of the Australia and New Zealand Army Corps (Anzacs) who served in WWI. The interior dome is studded with 120,000 stars: one for each New South Welsh soldier who served. These twinkle above Rayner Hoff's poignant sculpture *Sacrifice*. A modern addition is the Hall of Service, which features names and soil samples of all the NSW places of origin of WWI soldiers. (✆02-9267 7668; www. anzacmemorial.nsw.gov.au; Hyde Park; admission free; ◷9am-5pm; ℞Museum)

St James' Church

CHURCH

7 ◎ MAP P62, D3

Built from convict-made bricks, Sydney's oldest church (1819) is widely considered to be architect Francis Greenway's masterpiece. It was originally designed as a courthouse, but the brief changed and the cells became the crypt. Check out the dark-wood choir loft, the sparkling copper dome, the crypt and the 1950s stained-glass 'Creation Window'. It's worth reading the marble plaques along the walls for some insights into early colonial life and exploration. A more recent plaque commemorates Gough and Margaret Whitlam. (✆02-8227 1300; www.sjks.org.au; 173 King St; ◷10am-4pm Mon-Fri, to 1pm Sat, 7.30am-2pm Sun; ℞St James)

Sydney Town Hall

HISTORIC BUILDING

8 ◎ MAP P62, C5

Mansard roofs, sandstone turrets, wrought-iron trimmings and over-the-top balustrades: the French Second Empire wedding-cake exterior of the Town Hall (built 1868–89) is something to behold. Unless there's something on, you can poke your head into an ornate hall inside; for further access you'll need to take the two-hour **guided tour** ($5, Tuesdays 10.30am). The wood-lined concert hall has a **giant organ** with nearly 9000 pipes, once the largest in the world. It's used regularly for recitals, some of which are free. (www.sydneytownhall. com.au; 483 George St; ◷8am-6pm Mon-Fri; ℞Town Hall)

The Mint

HISTORIC BUILDING

9 ◎ MAP P62, D3

The stately Mint building (1816) was originally the southern wing of the infamous Rum Hospital (p61), built by two Sydney merchants in return for a monopoly on the rum trade (Sydney's currency in those days). It became a branch of the Royal Mint in 1854, the first outside England. It's now head office for the Historic Houses Trust. Beyond the upstairs restaurant and a boutique downstairs, there's not a whole lot to see or do, but it's a worthwhile diversion nonetheless. (✆02-8239 2288; www.sydneylivingmuseums.com. au; 10 Macquarie St; admission free; ◷9am-5pm Mon-Fri; ℞St James)

Great Synagogue

SYNAGOGUE

10 🔘 MAP P62, D4

The heritage-listed Great Synagogue (1878) is the spiritual home of Sydney's oldest Jewish congregation, established in 1831. It's considered the Mother Synagogue of Australia and is architecturally the most important in the southern hemisphere, combining Romanesque, Gothic, Moorish and Byzantine elements. Tours include the **AM Rosenblum Museum** artefacts and a video presentation on Jewish beliefs, traditions and history in Australia. (📞02-9267 2477; www.greatsynagogue.org.au; 187a Elizabeth St; tours adult/child $10/5; ⏱tours noon Thu & 1st & 3rd Tue; 🚇St James)

Eating

Gumshara

RAMEN $

11 🔀 MAP P62, B6

Prepare to queue for some of Sydney's best broth at this cordial ramen house in a popular Chinatown budget-price food court. They boil down over 100kg of pork bones for a week to make the gloriously thick and sticky liquid. There are lots of options, including some that pack quite a punch. Ask for extra back fat for real indulgence. (📞0410 253 180; Shop 211, 25-29 Dixon St; ramen $12-19; ⏱11.30am-9pm Tue-Sat, to 8.30pm Sun & Mon; 🚇Paddy's Markets, 🚇Central)

Restaurant Hubert

FRENCH $$

12 🔀 MAP P62, D1

The memorable descent into the sexy old-time ambience plunges you straight from suity Sydney to some 1930s cocktail movie. Delicious French fare comes in old-fashioned portions – think terrine, black pudding or duck, plus a few more avant-garde creations. Candlelit tables and a long whisky-backed counter provide seating. No bookings for small groups, so wait it out in the bar area.

This is one of the few top-quality venues in Sydney to serve food this late. The bar in itself makes a great destination for a few cocktails – check out the vast collection of miniature bottles on your way down. (📞02-9232 0881; www.restauranthubert.com; 15 Bligh St; mains $15-48; ⏱noon-3pm & 5pm-1am Mon-Fri, 5pm-1am Sat; 🚇Martin Place)

Pablo & Rusty's

CAFE $$

13 🔀 MAP P62, C4

Busy and loud, with close-packed tables, this excellent cafe is high-energy. The inviting wood-and-brick decor and seriously good coffee (several single-origins available daily) is complemented by a range of appealing breakfast and lunch specials ranging from large sourdough sandwiches to wholesome Mediterranean- and Asian-influenced combos such as tuna poke with brown rice or lychee and ginger tapioca. (📞02-9283 9543; www.pabloandrustys.com.au; 161 Castlereagh St; light meals $9-25;

🕐 6.30am-5pm Mon-Fri, 8am-3pm Sat; 🛜 ✏️; 🚇 Town Hall)

Mr Wong CHINESE $$

14 MAP P62, C1

Classy but comfortable in an attractive, low-lit space on a CBD laneway, this has exposed-brick colonial warehouse chic and a huge team of staff and hanging ducks in the open kitchen. Lunchtime dim sum offerings bristle with flavour and the salad offerings are mouth-freshening sensations. Mains such as crispy pork hock are sinfully sticky, while Peking duck rolls are legendary.

An impressive wine list and attentive, sassy service seals the deal. (✏️ 02-9240 3000; www.merivale.com.au/mrwong; 3 Bridge Lane; mains $22-40; 🕐 lunch noon-3pm Mon-Fri, 10.30am-3pm Sat & Sun, dinner 5.30-11pm Mon-Wed, to midnight Thu-Sat, to 10pm Sun; 🛜 ✏️; 🚇 Wynyard)

Grounds of the City CAFE $$

15 MAP P62, C4

Peddling everything from takeaway snacks and scientifically roasted coffee to fuller meals and cocktails in a striking curiosity-shop interior, this scion of its Alexandria (p95) parent represents a significant hipster conquest of the somewhat staid CBD fortress. There's an amazing range of eating and drinking, from fresh-baked breakfast rolls to flower-strewn gin concoctions and delights wheeled around on the dessert trolley. (✏️ 02-9699 2235; www.thegroundscity.com.au; 500 George St; lunch mains $20-35; 🕐 7am-5pm Mon, to 9.30pm Tue-Thu, to 10pm Fri, 8am-10pm Sat, 8am-9.30pm Sun; 🛜; 🚇 Town Hall)

Chat Thai THAI $$

16 MAP P62, C7

Cooler than your average Thai joint, this Thaitown linchpin is so popular that a list is posted outside for you to affix your name to should you want a table. Expat Thais flock here for the dishes that don't make it onto your average suburban Thai restaurant menu – particularly the more unusual sweets. (✏️ 02-9211 1808; www.chatthai.com.au; 20 Campbell St; mains $13-25; 🕐 10am-2am; ✏️; 🚊 Capitol Square, 🚉 Central)

Yum Cha 🍽️

Despite the larger restaurants seating hundreds of dumpling devotees, there always seem to be queues in Chinatown on weekend mornings for yum cha. Literally meaning 'drink tea', it's really an opportunity to gorge on small plates of dim sum, wheeled between the tables on trolleys. Popular places for traditional fare include Marigold (www.marigold.com.au, 683 George St) and Golden Century (p71). Outside the district, Bodhi (p69) is great for vegans, while Mr Wong (p68) puts a contemporary twist on the dishes.

Yum cha

Sydney Madang KOREAN $

17 MAP P62, C6

Down a teensy Little Korea lane is this backdoor gem – an authentic BBQ joint that's low on interior charisma but high on quality and quantity. Noisy, cramped and chaotic, yes, but the chilli seafood soup will have you coming back. Try the delicious cold noodles, too. Prepare to queue at weekends. (02-9264 7010; 371a Pitt St; mains $14-28; 11.30am-2am; Museum)

Bodhi VEGAN, ASIAN $$

18 MAP P62, E4

Bodhi scores highly for its cool design and leafy position near St Mary's Cathedral. With its pretty outdoor area, it's a relaxing Asian haven from CBD stress. Vegan yum cha is served until 4pm, switching to 'Oriental tapas' and more substantial plates until close. The barbecue buns rule. (02-9360 2523; www.bodhirestaurant.com.au; Cook + Phillip Park, 2-4 College St; dishes lunch $9-10, dinner mains $23-30; 11am-4pm Mon, to 10pm Tue-Sun; ; St James)

Azuma JAPANESE $$$

19 MAP P62, D2

Tucked away upstairs in Chifley Plaza, this is one of Sydney's finest Japanese restaurants. Sushi and sashimi are of stellar quality and too pretty to eat – almost. Other options include sukiyaki and hot-pot DIY dishes and excellent tasting menus. It's a great place to get acquainted with high-class modern Japanese fare.

Food Courts 🍽

Though they aren't necessarily visible from the street, Sydney's CBD is absolutely riddled with food courts, which can be great places for a budget meal, especially at lunchtime. Look for them in shopping centres and major office towers. Some worthwhile ones are in Westfield Sydney, in Australia Square, at the north end underground in the QVB, between George and Pitt Sts north of Liverpool St, in World Square and in the Sussex Centre.

Sushi places in particular tend to start discounting in the mid-afternoon; Friday afternoons see a big sell-off at CBD food courts.

It also has some moreish sake by the carafe. (☑02-9222 9960; www. azuma.com.au; Level 1, Chifley Plaza, Hunter St; mains $29-39, tasting menus $70-110; ☺noon-2.30pm & 6-10pm Mon-Fri, 6-10pm Sat; 🚇Martin Place)

Rockpool Bar & Grill STEAK $$$

21 🔖 MAP P62, D2

You'll feel like a 1930s Manhattan stockbroker when you dine at this sleek operation in the fabulous art-deco City Mutual Building. The bar is famous for its dry-aged, full-blood Wagyu burger (make sure you order a side of the hand-cut fat chips), but carnivores will be equally enamoured with the succulent steaks, stews and fish dishes served in the grill. (☑02-8078 1900; www.rockpoolbarandgrill.com. au; 66 Hunter St; mains $35-65, bar mains $19-35; ☺noon-3pm & 6-11pm Mon-Fri, 5.30-11pm Sat, 6-10pm Sun; 🚇Martin Place)

Tetsuya's FRENCH, JAPANESE $$$

21 🔖 MAP P62, B5

Concealed in a villa behind a historic cottage amid the high-rises, this extraordinary restaurant is for those seeking a culinary journey rather than a simple stuffed belly. Settle in for 10-plus courses of French- and Japanese-inflected food from the genius of legendary Sydney chef Tetsuya Wakuda. It's all great, but the seafood is sublime. Great wine list. Book well ahead. (☑02-9267 2900; www. tetsuyas.com; 529 Kent St; degustation menu $230, matching wines $125; ☺5.30-10pm Tue-Fri, noon-3pm & 5.30-10pm Sat; 🚇Town Hall)

Bentley Restaurant & Bar MODERN AUSTRALIAN $$$

22 🔖 MAP P62, C2

Its chic corporate veneer blending plush with industrial, Bentley has been turning heads in Sydney for the sheer quality of its imaginative dishes. Many of these have a distinctly Australian taste, with native fruits and seeds lending their unusual flavours. The bar is also a good spot to hang out, with pricey but delicious share plates of similar fare. (☏02-8214 0505; www.thebentley.com.au; cnr Pitt & Hunter Sts; mains $46-70, tasting menus $120-150; �noon-3pm & 6pm-midnight Mon-Fri, 6pm-midnight Sat; 🛜🍸; 🚉Wynyard)

Golden Century CHINESE, SEAFOOD $$$

23 MAP P62, B6

The fish tank at this frenetic Cantonese place, a Chinatown classic, forms a window-wall to the street, filled with fish, crabs, lobsters and abalone. Splash out on the whole lobster cooked in ginger and shallots or try the delicious beef brisket with turnips It's open very late but is also wildly popular for weekend yum cha. (☏02-9212 3901; www. goldencentury.com.au; 393-399 Sussex St; mains $25-43; �noon-4am; 🍸; 🚉Town Hall)

Drinking

Uncle Ming's COCKTAIL BAR

24 MAP P62, B2

We love the dark romantic opium-den atmosphere of this small bar secreted away in a basement by a shirt shop. It's an atmospheric spot for anything from a quick beer before jumping on a train at Wynyard to a leisurely exploration of the cocktail menu. It also does an excellent line in dumplings and, usually, has very welcoming bar staff. (www.unclemings.com.au; 55 York St; �noon-midnight Mon-Fri, 4pm-midnight Sat; 🚉Wynyard)

Frankie's Pizza BAR

25 🚇 MAP P62, D2

Descend the stairs and you'll think you're in a 1970s pizzeria, complete with plastic grapevines, snapshots covering the walls and tasty pizza slices ($6). But open the nondescript door in the corner and an indie wonderland reveals itself. Bands play here at least four nights a week (join them on Tuesdays for live karaoke) and there's another bar hidden below. (www.frankies pizzabytheslice.com; 50 Hunter St; �4pm-3am Sat-Thu, noon-3am Fri; 🛜; 🚉Martin Place)

Baxter Inn BAR

26 🚇 MAP P62, B3

Yes, it really is down that dark lane and through that unmarked door (there are two easily-spotted bars on this courtyard, but this is through a door to your right). Whisky's the main poison and the friendly bar staff really know their stuff. There's an elegant speakeasy atmosphere and a mighty impressive choir of bottles behind the bar. (www.thebaxterinn.com; 152-156 Clarence St; �4pm-1am Mon-Sat; 🚉Town Hall)

Ivy BAR, CLUB

27 🚇 MAP P62, C2

Hidden down a lane off George St, Ivy is the HQ of the all-pervading Merivale Group. It's a fashionable complex of bars, restaurants... even a swimming pool. It's also

Sydney's most hyped venue; expect lengthy queues of suburban kids teetering on high heels, waiting to shed $40 on a Saturday for Sydney's hottest club nights, run by Ministry of Sound. (⏺02-9254 8100; www.merivale.com/ivy; Level 1, 330 George St; ⏲noon-midnight Mon-Fri, 8.30pm-3.30am Sat, plus pool party 1pm-midnight Sun Oct-Mar; 🛜; 🚉Wynyard)

Slip Inn & Chinese Laundry
PUB, CLUB

28 📍 MAP P62, B3

Slip in to this cheerfully colourful atmospheric warren on the edge of Darling Harbour and bump hips with the kids. There are bars, pool tables, a beer garden and Mexican food, courtesy of El Loco. On Friday and Saturday nights the bass cranks up at the long-running attached Chinese Laundry nightclub, accessed via Slip St below. (⏺02-9254 8088; www.merivale.

Small Bars

Though the CBD can be a bit lacking in atmosphere at night, once the office workers have gone home, there's more going on than first meets the eye. An array of 'small bars' are tucked away in hard-to-guess locations around the area. You can fashion a rewarding cocktail crawl of them…if you can find the way in.

com.au/chineselaundry; 111 Sussex St; club $28-33; ⏲11am-1am Mon-Thu, to 3am Fri, 2pm-3am Sat, Chinese Laundry 9pm-3.30am Fri & Sat; 🛜; 🚉Wynyard)

Barber Shop
COCKTAIL BAR

29 📍 MAP P62, B3

No, it's not a themed bar but a real barber. Walk on past the blokes getting a short-back-and-sides and you'll find a seductive spot peddling gin, cocktails and quality beers. The courtyard space out the back is great for a mingle on a hot summer night. You can also enter from Clarence St, down the laneway between 152 and 156. (⏺02-9299 9699; www.thisisthe barbershop.com; 89 York St; ⏲4pm-midnight Mon-Wed & Sat, 3pm-midnight Thu & Fri; 🛜; 🚉Town Hall)

Palmer & Co
BAR

30 📍 MAP P62, C1

A self-consciously hip member of Sydney's speakeasy brigade, this 'legitimate importer of bracing tonics and fortifying liquid' attracts a cashed-up, fashionable clientele. Inside, it's an atmospheric, brick-vaulted space with excellent cocktails. Prepare to queue later, as it's one of the few late-opening bars of this type. Get there before office-out at 5pm if you want a table. (⏺02-9254 8088; www.merivale.com.au/palmer andco; Abercrombie Lane; ⏲5pm-3am Sun-Wed, 3pm-3am Thu & Fri, 4pm-3am Sat; 🛜; 🚉Wynyard)

Grandma's
COCKTAIL BAR

31 MAP P62, B4

Billing itself as a 'retrosexual haven of cosmopolitan kitsch and faded granny glamour', Grandma's hits the mark. A stag's head greets you on the stairs and ushers you into a tiny subterranean world of parrot wallpaper and tiki cocktails. Very quirky, very relaxed and casual for a CBD venue. Toasted sandwiches provide sustenance. Look for it behind the Fender shop. (02-9264 3004; www.grandmasbarsydney.com.au; Basement, 275 Clarence St; 3pm-midnight Mon-Fri, 5pm-1am Sat; Town Hall)

Establishment
BAR

32 MAP P62, C1

Establishment's cashed-up crush proves that the art of swilling cocktails after a hard city day is not lost. Sit at the majestic marble bar or in the swish courtyard, or be absorbed by a leather lounge as stockbrokers scribble their digits on coasters for flirty new acquaintances. The bar was a scene-setter when it opened and is still iconic. (02-9240 3100; www.merivale.com /establishmentbar; 252 George St; 11am-late Mon-Fri, noon-late Sat, noon-10pm Sun; ; Wynyard)

O Bar
COCKTAIL BAR

33 MAP P62, C1

The cocktails at this 47th-floor revolving bar aren't cheap, but they're still substantially cheaper than admission to Sydney Tower (p64) – and it's considerably more glamorous. The views are truly wonderful; get up there shortly after opening time, and kick back to enjoy the sunset and transition into night. There's also smart food on offer. (02-9247 9777; www.obardining.com.au; Level 47, Australia Square, 264 George St; 5pm-midnight Sat-Thu, noon-midnight Fri; ; Wynyard)

Entertainment

City Recital Hall
CLASSICAL MUSIC

34 MAP P62, C2

Based on the classic configuration of the 19th-century European concert hall, this custom-built 1200-seat venue boasts near-perfect acoustics. Catch top-flight companies here, such as **Musica Viva** (1800 688 482; https://musicaviva.com.au), the **Australian Brandenburg Orchestra** (ABO; 02-9328 7581; www.brandenburg.com.au; tickets $70-170) and the **Australian Chamber Orchestra** (ACO; 02-8274 3888; www.aco.com.au). (02-8256 2222; www.cityrecitalhall.com; 2 Angel Pl; box office 9am-5pm Mon-Fri; Wynyard)

Metro Theatre
LIVE MUSIC

35 MAP P62, C6

The Metro is easily Sydney's best mid-sized venue for catching local and alternative international acts in intimate, well-ventilated, easy-seeing comfort. Other offerings include comedy, cabaret and dance parties. (02-9550 3666; www.metrotheatre.com.au; 624 George St; Town Hall)

State Theatre

THEATRE

36 ⭐ MAP P62, C4

The 2000-seat State Theatre is a lavish, gilt-ridden, chandelier-dangling palace. It hosts the **Sydney Film Festival** (www.sff.org.au; ⏱Jun), concerts, comedy, opera, musicals and the odd celebrity chef. (📞box office 13 61 00; www.statetheatre.com.au; 49 Market St; 🚉Town Hall)

Shopping

Abbey's

BOOKS

37 🔒 MAP P62, C4

Easily central Sydney's best bookshop, Abbey's has many strengths. It's good on social sciences and has excellent resources for language learning, including a great selection of foreign films on DVD. There's also a big sci-fi and fantasy section. Staff are great and generally very experienced. (📞02-9264 3111; www.abbeys.com.au; 131 York St; ⏱8.30am-6pm Mon-Wed & Fri, to 8pm Thu, 9am-5pm Sat, 10am-5pm Sun; 🚉Town Hall)

Strand Arcade

SHOPPING CENTRE

38 🔒 MAP P62, C3

Constructed in 1891, the beautiful Strand rivals the QVB in the ornateness stakes. The three floors of designer fashions, Australiana and old-world coffee shops will make your shortcut through here considerably longer. Some of the top Australian designers and other iconic brands have stores here – chocolatiers included! Aesop, Haighs, Leona Edmiston, Dinosaur Designs and more are all present. (📞02-9265 6800; www.strandarcade.com.au; 412 George St; ⏱9am-5.30pm Mon-Wed & Fri, to 9pm Thu, to 4pm Sat, 11am-4pm Sun; 🚉Town Hall)

Queen Victoria Building

SHOPPING CENTRE

The QVB (see 1 ◎ Map p62, C4) takes up a whole block and boasts nearly 200 shops on five levels. It's a neo-Gothic masterpiece – without doubt Sydney's most beautiful shopping centre. (QVB; 📞02-9265 6800; www.qvb.com.au; 455 George St; ⏱9am-6pm Mon-Wed, Fri & Sat, to 9pm Thu, 11am-5pm Sun; 🚉Town Hall)

Strand Arcade

STRUCTURESXX/SHUTTERSTOCK ©

Red Eye Records

MUSIC

39 🔒 MAP P62, C4

Partners of music freaks beware: don't let them descend the stairs into this shop unless you are prepared for a lengthy delay. The shelves are stocked with an irresistible collection of new, classic, rare and collectable LPs, CDs, rock T-shirts, books, posters and music DVDs. (☑02-9267 7440; www.redeye.com.au; 143 York St; ⏲9am-6pm Mon-Wed, Fri & Sat, to 9pm Thu, 10am-5pm Sun; 🚇Town Hall)

Paspaley

JEWELLERY

40 🔒 MAP P62, C2

This shell-shaped shop sells lustrous pearls farmed along uninhabited coastline, from Darwin in the Northern Territory to Dampier in Western Australia. Classic and modern designs start at $450 for a ring, rising to more than $1 million for a hefty strand of perfect pink pearls. (☑02-9232 7633; www.paspaley.com; 2 Martin Pl; ⏲10am-6pm Mon-Wed & Fri, to 7.30pm Thu, to 5pm Sat, 11am-5pm Sun; 🚇Martin Place)

Strand Hatters

FASHION & ACCESSORIES

Got a cold or wet head, or a serious case of the *Crocodile Dundees*? Strand Hatters (see **38** 🔒 Map p62, C3)

will cover your crown with a classically Australian Akubra bush hat (made from rabbit felt). Staff will block and steam hats to customer requirements (crocodile-teeth hatbands cost extra). (☑02-9231 6884; www.strandhatters.com.au; Strand Arcade, 412 George St; ⏲9am-5.30pm Mon-Wed & Fri, to 8pm Thu, to 4pm Sat, 11am-4pm Sun.; 🚇Queen Victoria Building, 🚇Town Hall)

Paddy's Markets

MARKET

41 🔒 MAP P62, B7

Cavernous, thousand-stall Paddy's is the Sydney equivalent of Istanbul's Grand Bazaar, but swap the hookahs and carpets for mobile phone covers, Eminem T-shirts and cheap sneakers. Pick up a VD singlet or wander the aisles in capitalist awe. (www.paddysmarkets.com.au; 9-13 Hay St; ⏲10am-6pm Wed-Sun; 🚇Paddy's Markets, 🚇Central)

Karlangu

ARTS & CRAFTS

42 🔒 MAP P62, B2

Some excellent Aboriginal art is for sale at this gallery near Wynyard, and staff are knowledgable and helpful. They can also arrange packing and postage. (☑02-9279 2700; www.karlangu.com; 47 York St; ⏲9.30am-6pm Mon-Fri, 10am-6pm Sat & Sun; 🚇Wynyard)

Explore
Darling Harbour & Pyrmont

Unashamedly tourist-focused, Darling Harbour will do its best to tempt you to its shoreline bars and restaurants with fireworks displays and a sprinkling of glitz. On its western flank, Pyrmont, though it appears to be sinking under the weight of its casino and motorway flyovers, still has a historic feel in parts, and strolling its harbourside wharves is a real pleasure.

Every other inch of this former dockland is given over to visitor amusements, bars and restaurants. It makes sense to start at Wynyard station and head for Barangaroo South (p81) through the tunnel. From here, following the curve of the bay right around to the other side will take you past most of the key sights, as well as numerous waterfront restaurants and bars. Next, dive into Pyrmont for historic converted warehouses and a more local Sydney scene. If you like, there's some sensational harbourside strolling here, far removed from the tourist beat.

Getting There & Around

🚆 The eastern edge of Darling Harbour is within walking distance of Town Hall train station. For King Street Wharf and Barangaroo South, Wynyard station is closer.

🚊 There are light-rail stops all through Pyrmont.

⚓ Ferry wharves at Barangaroo and Pyrmont Bay.

Darling Harbour & Pyrmont Map on p78

Wharves at Darling Harbour JOONHWAN LEE/SHUTTERSTOCK ©

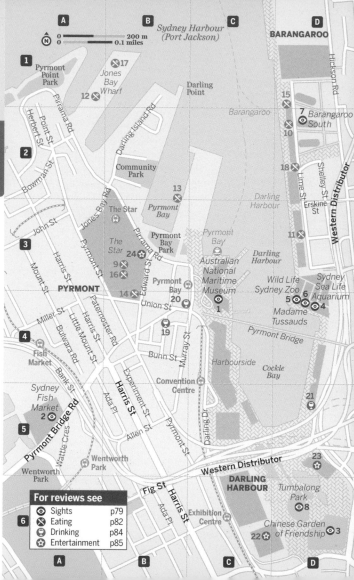

Darling Harbour & Pyrmont

Sydney Harbour
(Port Jackson)

BARANGAROO

0   200 m
0   0.1 miles

1
Pyrmont
Point
Park

Jones
Bay Wharf

17

12

Darling
Point

15

Barangaroo

7 Barangaroo
South

10

Pirrama Rd

Point St

Herbert St

Darling Island Rd

Hickson Rd

2
Bowman St

Community
Park

18

Lime St

Shelley St

Erskine St

Western Distributor

The Star

13

Pyrmont
Bay

Darling
Harbour

John St

Jones Bay Rd

3
Mount St

Harris St

Pyrmont St

The
Star

Pirrama Rd

24

9
16

Pyrmont
Bay Park

Pyrmont
Bay

Pyrmont
Bay

Australian
National
Maritime
Museum

Darling
Harbour

11

Sydney
Sea Life
Aquarium

PYRMONT

Miller St

Paternoster Rd

Edward St

Wild Life
Sydney Zoo

5 6

4

4
Harris St

Bulwara Rd

Little Mount St

14

Pyrmont
Bay

Union St

Murray St

20

1

Madame
Tussauds

Pyrmont Bridge

Fish
Market

Bank St

19

Bunn St

Harbourside

Cockle
Bay

Sydney
Fish
Market

5
Pyrmont Bridge Rd

Wattle Cres

Ada Pl

Harris St

Experiment St

Allen St

Pyrmont St

Convention
Centre

Darling Dr

21

Wentworth
Park

Wentworth
Park

Western Distributor

DARLING
HARBOUR

23

Fig St

Harris St

Ada Pl

Exhibition
Centre

Tumbalong
Park

8

Chinese Garden
of Friendship

3

22

For reviews see

⊙	Sights	p79
✗	Eating	p82
⊖	Drinking	p84
✩	Entertainment	p85

6

Sights

Australian National Maritime Museum
MUSEUM

1 ◉ MAP P78, C4

Beneath a soaring roof, the Maritime Museum sails through Australia's inextricable relationship with the sea. Exhibitions range from Indigenous canoes to surf culture, immigration to the navy. The worthwhile 'big ticket' (adult/child $32/20) includes entry to some of the vessels moored outside, including the atmospheric submarine HMAS *Onslow* and the destroyer HMAS *Vampire*. The high-production-value short film *Action Stations* sets the mood with a re-creation of a mission event from each vessel. Excellent free **guided tours** explain each vessel's features.

You can also visit a lighthouse and an 1874 square rigger, the *James Craig*, which periodically offers **sailing trips** (📞02-9298 3888; www.shf.org.au; Wharf 7, Pyrmont; adult/child from $120/60; 🚢Pyrmont Bay, 🚊The Star). Normally a replica of Cook's *Endeavour* also drops anchor here. There's plenty to do for kids, especially at weekends. Other parts of the museum include a free exhibition on wooden boats in the next building north, and, opposite Pyrmont Bay ferry stop, the **Welcome Wall**, a commemoration of migration to Australia that seems particularly relevant in the current political climate. (📞02-9298 3777; www.anmm.gov.au; 2 Murray St, Pyrmont; permanent collection free, temporary exhibitions adult/child $20/free; ⏰9.30am-5pm, to 6pm Jan; ♿; 🚌389, 🚊Pyrmont Bay)

Sydney Fish Market
MARKET

2 ◉ MAP P78, A5

This piscatorial precinct on Blackwattle Bay shifts over 15 million kilograms of seafood annually, and has retail outlets, restaurants, a sushi bar, an oyster bar, and a highly regarded **cooking school** (📞02-9004 1111; www.sydneyfishmarket.com.au/seafood-school; Sydney Fish Market, Pyrmont Bridge Rd, Pyrmont; 2-/4-hr courses $90/165). Chefs, locals and overfed seagulls haggle over mud crabs, Balmain bugs, lobsters and slabs of salmon at the daily fish auction, which kicks off at 5.30am weekdays. Check it out on a behind-the-scenes tour (adult/child $35/10). (📞02-9004 1108; www.sydneyfishmarket.com.au; Bank St, Pyrmont; ⏰7am-4pm Mon-Thu, to 5pm Fri-Sun; 🚊Fish Market)

Chinese Garden of Friendship
GARDENS

3 ◉ MAP P78, D6

Built according to Taoist principles, the Chinese Garden of Friendship is usually an oasis of tranquillity – although one increasingly dwarfed by assertive modern buildings. Designed by architects from Guangzhou (Sydney's sister city) for Australia's bicentenary in 1988, the garden interweaves pavilions, waterfalls, lakes, paths and lush plant life. There's also a **tea house**. (☏02-9240 8888; www.chinesegarden. com.au; Harbour St, Central Sydney; adult/child $6/3; ⏱9.30am-5pm Apr-Sep, to 5.30pm Oct-Mar; ☒Town Hall)

Sydney Sea Life Aquarium

AQUARIUM

4 ◉ MAP P78, D4

As well as regular wall-mounted tanks and ground-level enclosures, this impressive complex has two large pools that you can walk through – safely enclosed in Perspex tunnels – as an intimidating array of sharks and rays pass overhead. Other highlights include clownfish (g'day, Nemo!), platypuses, moon jellyfish (in a disco-lit tube), sea dragons and the swoon-worthy finale: the two-million-litre Great Barrier Reef tank.

The aquarium's two dugongs were rescued after washing up orphaned on Queensland beaches. Attempts to return them to the wild failed, so the Dugong Island enclosure was built to house them. As sad as it is to see such large marine mammals in captivity, it offers a fascinating and rare opportunity to get close to them. Needless to say, kids

Sydney's Chinese Community

Chinese immigrants started to come to Australia around 1840, when convict transportation ceased and labouring jobs became freely available. Initially they were considered a solution to labour shortages, but as gold-rush fever took hold, racial intolerance grew. The tireless Chinese were seen as threats, and state entry restrictions were enforced from the early 19th century into much of the 20th century.

In 1861 the NSW government enacted the White Australia policy, aimed at reducing the influx of Chinese. This included a ban on naturalisation, work-permit restrictions and acts such as the 1861 *Chinese Immigration Regulation & Restriction Act* (an immigrant tax). As a result of this policy (and the fact that many Chinese people returned to China after the gold rush), the Chinese population remained low. The White Australia policy wasn't completely dismantled until 1973.

Sydney's Chinese community eventually gravitated to Dixon St near Darling Harbour, an area once known for opium and gambling but now better known for tasty and great-value food.

A major immigration wave from pre-handover Hong Kong boosted the Cantonese population in the 1980s and 1990s; more recently there has been a strong increase in arrivals from the mainland, as well as a very significant temporary population of students.

Today people of Chinese extraction make up some 10% of Sydney's population, with around half of these born in Australia.

love this place; arrive early to beat the crowds. It's cheaper to book online, and there are various combo deals with other attractions run by the same company, including the zoo and Madame Tussauds. (☑02-8251 7800; www.sydneyaquarium.com.au; Aquarium Pier, Central Sydney; adult/child $42/30; ☻9.30am-6pm; ☒Town Hall)

Wild Life Sydney Zoo
ZOO

5 ◉ MAP P78, D4

Complementing its sister and neighbour, Sea Life, this large complex houses an impressive collection of Australian native reptiles, butterflies, spiders, snakes and mammals (including kangaroos and koalas). The nocturnal section is particularly good, bringing out the extrovert in the quolls, potoroos, echidnas and possums. As interesting as Wild Life is, it's not a patch on Taronga Zoo (p51). Still, it's worth considering as part of a combo with Sea Life, or if you're short on time. Tickets are cheaper online. (☑02-9333 9245; www.wildlifesydney.com.au; Aquarium Pier, Central Sydney; adult/child $42/30; ☻9.30am-5pm; ☒Town Hall)

Madame Tussauds
MUSEUM

6 ◉ MAP P78, D4

In this celebrity-obsessed age, it's hardly surprising that Madame Tussauds' hyperrealistic waxwork dummies are just as popular now as when the eponymous madame lugged her macabre haul of French Revolution death masks to London in 1803. Where else do mere mortals get to strike a pose with Hugh Jackman and cosy up to Kylie? There are various combination entrance deals with the adjacent zoo and aquarium; book online for best rates. (www.madametussauds.com.au; Aquarium Pier, Central Sydney; adult/child $42/30; ☻9.30am-6pm; ☒Town Hall)

Barangaroo South
AREA

7 ◉ MAP P78, D2

The latest product of Sydney's port redevelopment is this extension of the CBD's office-land. There are three rather lofty skyscrapers and pedestrian alleys beneath, busy with corporate types rushing about, coffee in hand. On the harbourfront itself is a handsome promenade with lots of decent bars and eateries, merging into the similar King Street Wharf and Cockle Bay strips to the south. The food is generally better at Barangaroo than the other two. There's a major ferry stop here, too. (www.thestreetsofbarangaroo.com; Central Sydney; ☲Barangaroo, ☒Wynyard)

Tumbalong Park
PARK

8 ◉ MAP P78, D6

Flanked by the modern **Darling Walk** development, this grassy circle on Darling Harbour's southern rump is set up for family fun. Sunbakers and frisbee-throwers occupy the lawns, tourists dunk their feet in fountains on hot summer afternoons and there's an excellent children's playground with a 21m flying fox (zip line). (Harbour St, Central Sydney; 🛝; 🚊Town Hall)

Eating

Café Court

FOOD HALL $

9 🔀 MAP P78, B3

The Star has done a great job of filling its ground-floor food court with some of the best operators of their kind, with top-quality dumpling rollers, fish 'n' chip fryers, patisserie wizards and gelato makers. (www.star.com.au; The Star, 80 Pyrmont St, Pyrmont; ⏰11am-9pm Sun & Mon, to 11pm Tue-Sat; 📶; 🚊The Star)

Anason

TURKISH $$

10 🔀 MAP P78, D2

Outdoor eating is a pleasure of the Barangaroo strip, and this is one of the best places to do it. Modern takes on generous Turkish flavours are upbeat and delicious, with plenty of breads and dippable dishes alongside grilled seafood and hearty meat. It gets very busy in the noon-to-2pm lunch break. (📞02-9188 1581; www.anason.com.au; 5/23 Barangaroo Ave, Central Sydney; mains $24-36; ⏰11.30am-11pm; 🚢Barangaroo, 🚊Wynyard)

Malaya

MALAYSIAN $$

11 🔀 MAP P78, D3

There's something really life-affirming about quality Malaysian cooking, and what you get here is certainly that. Dishes bursting with flavour and spice make it a very authentic experience, while fabulous views over Darling Harbour (fireworks on Saturday nights) add romance. The atmosphere is a very Sydney blend of upmarket and casual. À la carte is better than the set menu. (📞02-9279 1170; www.themalaya.com.au; 39 Lime St, Central Sydney; mains $26-35; ⏰noon-3pm & 6-10pm Mon-Fri, noon-3pm & 5.30-10pm Sat, 5.30-10pm Sun; 📶📄; 🚢Barangaroo, 🚊Wynyard)

Cafe Morso

CAFE $$

12 🔀 MAP P78, A1

On pretty Jones Bay Wharf, this makes a fine venue for breakfast or lunch (though it gets busy, so you may want to book). There's a mixture of Channel 7 workers and yacht skippers. Sassy breakfasts – try the bacon gnocchi – morph into proper cooked lunches, or you can just grab a sandwich. (📞02-9692 0111; www.cafemorso.com.au; Jones Bay Wharf, Pyrmont; breakfast $13-20, lunch mains $18-28; ⏰7am-3.30pm Mon-Fri, 9am-2.30pm Sat, 8am-3.30pm Sun; 📶📄; 🚊The Star)

LuMi

ITALIAN $$$

13 🔀 MAP P78, B2

This wharf spot sits right alongside the bobbing boats, though views aren't quite knock-me-down. Hidden just steps from the Star, it offers casual competence and strikingly innovative Italian-Japanese fusion cuisine. The degustation is a tour de force;

memorable creations include extraordinary pasta dishes. The open kitchen is always entertaining, service is smart and both wine and sake lists are great. (☎02-9571 1999; www.lumidining.com; 56 Pirrama Rd, Pyrmont; 7/10 courses $120/150, 5-course lunch Fri $85; ⏱6.30-10.30pm Wed & Thu, noon-2.30pm & 6-10.30pm Fri-Sun; 🛜; 🚊Pyrmont Bay, 🚈The Star)

Sokyo
JAPANESE $$$

14 🍴 MAP P78, B4

Bringing an injection of Toyko glam to the edge of the casino complex, Sokyo serves well-crafted sushi and sashimi, delicate tempura, tasty robata grills and sophisticated mains. It also dishes up Sydney's best Japanese-style breakfast. Solo travellers

should grab a counter seat by the sushi kitchen to watch all the action unfurl. (☎02-9657 9161; www.star.com.au/sokyo; The Star, 80 Pyrmont St, Pyrmont; breakfast $23-38, mains $32-65; ⏱7-10.30am & 5.30-10pm Sun-Thu, 7-10.30am, noon-2pm & 5.30-10.30pm Fri & Sat; 🛜🚭; 🚈The Star)

Cirrus
SEAFOOD $$$

15 🍴 MAP P78, D1

The curved glass windows of this excellent Barangaroo seafood restaurant offer a water view more ambient than spectacular, but the tinny (simple fishing boat) suspended from the ceiling hints at another focus. Sustainably sourced fish and extremely tasty molluscs and crustaceans form the backbone of the menu, which

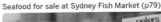
Seafood for sale at Sydney Fish Market (p79)

KOROVAY/SHUTTERSTOCK ©

features dishes with exquisite flavour pairings and presentation, designed to share.

The wine list is first-class, with lots of imports and carafe options. (☏02-9220 0111; www.cirrusdining.com.au; 10/23 Barangaroo Ave, Central Sydney; mains $38-56; ☺noon-3pm & 6-10.30pm; ☻Barangaroo, ☒Wynyard)

Momofuku Seiōbo
MODERN AUSTRALIAN $$$

16 ☒ MAP P78, B3

The first restaurant outside the US opened by New York's gastronomic darling David Chang, Momofuku Seiōbo is a key foodie favourite. Bringing together the techniques, concepts and ideas of Japanese *kaiseki* (multi-course eating) and classical Western degustation, it's not one for the short of time, or funds. (☏02-9657 9169; www.seiobo.momofuku.com; The Star, 80 Pyrmont Street, Pyrmont; degustation menu $185; ☺6-10pm Mon-Fri, noon-2pm & 6-10pm Sat; ☒The Star)

Flying Fish
SEAFOOD $$$

17 ☒ MAP P78, B1

On a lovely Pyrmont wharf, this is everything a seafood restaurant should be, with crisp white tablecloths, gleaming glasses and water views. Romance and city lights work their magic here, aided by excellent food and an indulgent cocktail list. Its toilets are the coolest in town – the clear glass frosts over when you close the stall door.

The little **cocktail bar** is a pleasant destination in itself, a fine place to lounge harbourside away from the bustle. (☏02-9518 6677; www.flyingfish.com.au; Jones Bay Wharf, Pyrmont; mains $40-50; ☺6-10.30pm Mon, noon-2.30pm & 6-10.30pm Tue-Sat, noon-2.30pm Sun; ☒The Star)

Bea
MODERN AUSTRALIAN $$$

18 ☒ MAP P78, D2

Looking like a double-decker salad burger with its concentric rings and verdant planter boxes, **Barangaroo House** is a striking addition to Sydney's waterfront. Halfway up, this upbeat bistro offers super outdoor seating and tighter indoor tables. Fusion ingredients are spiced up with bush tucker; the *umami* kick of tyrant ants on asparagus is a standout. Some great wines populate a fat list. (Barangaroo House; ☏02-8587 5400; www.barangaroohouse.com.au; 35 Barangaroo Ave, Central Sydney; mains $32-48; ☺noon-3pm & 5.30-11pm; ☏; ☻Barangaroo, ☒Wynyard)

Drinking

Smoke
COCKTAIL BAR

On the top floor of the Barangaroo House building, Smoke (see 18 ☒ Map p78, D2) has a most pleasant outlook over the busy ferry comings and goings at the ferry wharf below. It takes cocktails seriously – the seasonal G&T is a standout dose of refreshment. Get here early to bag one of the outdoor tables before the 5pm office crowd invades. (☏02-8587 5400; www.barangaroohouse.com.au; 35 Barangaroo Ave, Central Sydney; ☺3pm-midnight Mon-Wed, noon-midnight Thu-Sun; ☏; ☻Barangaroo, ☒Wynyard)

Peg Leg
BAR

19 🍺 MAP P78, B4

In what was once one of Sydney's older hotels, this small bar has a pirate theme and a feel of the Spanish Main. It's got plenty of interesting spirits, including quality rum. It takes food seriously and the little wood-clad dining area is a great place for seafood and steak grills. (www.facebook.com/pegleg pyrmont; 11 Pyrmont Bridge Rd, Pyrmont; ⏰3pm-midnight Mon-Thu, 11am-midnight Fri-Sun; 🚊Pyrmont Bay)

Pyrmont Bridge Hotel
PUB

20 🍺 MAP P78, B4

Standing like a guardian of tradition at the entrance to Pyrmont, this solid pub is a bastion of no-frills Sydney drinking culture. With an island bar and rooftop terrace, there are many handsome features; there's also lots of character and regular live music. Its biggest selling point is its 24-hour license – the CBD lockout zone ends several metres away. In practice, it usually closes for an hour or two around 5am.(☎02-9660 6996; www.pyrmontbridgehotel.com; 96 Union St, Pyrmont; ⏰24hr; 🛜; 🚊Pyrmont Bay)

Home
BAR, CLUB

21 🍺 MAP P78, D5

Welcome to the pleasuredome: a three-level, 2100-capacity timber-and-glass 'prow' that's home to a dance floor, countless bars, outdoor balconies, and sonics that make other clubs sound like transistor radios. The club often features big-name DJs; you can catch live music most nights at the attached **Tokio Hotel bar** downstairs (www.tokiohotellive.com.au). (☎02-9266 0600; www.homesydney.com; 1 Wheat Rd, Cockle Bay Wharf, Central Sydney; ⏰club 9pm-4am Thu-Sat, 10pm-4am Sun; 🛜; 🚊Town Hall)

Entertainment

ICC Sydney
LIVE MUSIC, THEATRE

22 ⭐ MAP P78, C6

The International Convention Centre at Darling Harbour has three theatres, including one that seats 8000, and principally holds big touring bands. It replaces the former Entertainment Centre. (☎02-8297 7600; www.iccsydney.com.au; Darling Dr; 🚊Exhibition Centre)

Monkey Baa Theatre Company
THEATRE

23 ⭐ MAP P78, D5

Bring your budding culture vultures here to watch Australian children's books come to life. This energetic company devises and stages its own adaptations. (☎02-8624 9340; www.monkeybaa.com.au; 1 Harbour St, Central Sydney; tickets around $25; 🚼; 🚊Town Hall)

Sydney Lyric Theatre
THEATRE

24 ⭐ MAP P78, B3

This high-quality 2000-seat theatre within the Star casino stages big-name musicals and the occasional concert. (☎02-9509 3600; www.sydneylyric.com.au; The Star, Pirrama Rd, Pyrmont; 🚊The Star)

Explore ◈
Inner West

The bohemian sweep of the Inner West is an array of suburbs crowded with great places to eat and drink. The quiet streets of Glebe and louder Newtown, grouped around the University of Sydney, are the most well-known of these tightly packed suburbs, but Enmore, Marrickville, Summer Hill, Petersham and more are all worth investigating. All the essential hangouts for students – bookshops, cafes and pubs – are present in abundance, but the Inner West is a lifestyle choice for a whole swathe of Sydney society.

The Inner West is a sociological stew of students, urban hippies, lifestyle-focused professional couples, artists and more. The most high-profile suburb, Newtown, where stoners and home renovators collide, shadows sinuous King St, lined with quirky boutiques, bookshops, yoga studios, cafes and Thai restaurants. It's climbing the social rungs, but is still free-thinking and bolshy.

Getting There & Around

🚆 Central and Redfern train stations are handy for Darlington and Chippendale, while Newtown and several other suburbs have their own station.

🚆 Glebe has two light-rail stops.

🚌 Buses from the city ply Glebe Point Rd (370, 431–433), Parramatta Rd (413, 436–440, 461, 480–483, M10) and City Rd/King St (352, 370, 422–428, M30).

Inner West Map on p90

Powerhouse Museum (p92) SARAH1810/SHUTTERSTOCK ©

Walking Tour 🚶

Studying the University of Sydney

Australia's oldest tertiary institution (1850) has well over 50,000 students and even boasts its own postcode. You don't need to have a PhD to grab a free campus map and wander around. The university completely dominates the surrounding suburbs of Camperdown, Darlington, Chippendale, and to a lesser extent, Glebe and Newtown.

Walk Facts

Start Verge Gallery
Finish Sappho Books
Length 1.8km, 45 minutes

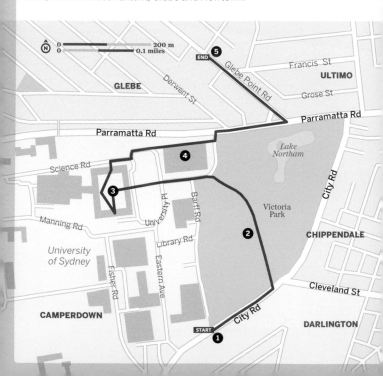

❶ Head to the Verge

On the Darlington side of City Road, this university-affiliated **gallery** (📞02-9563 6218; www.verge-gallery.net; City Rd, Darlington; admission free; ⏰10am-5pm Tue-Fri, 11am-4pm Sat; 🚌352, 370, 422, 423, 426, 428, M30; 🚉Redfern) has two exhibition spaces and a mission to get people involved with the artworks via a program of talks and other activities.

❷ Venture into Victoria Park

The green gateway to the Inner West and the University of Sydney, **Victoria Park** (cnr Parramatta & City Rds; 🚌352, 370, 422, 423, 426, 428, M30) is a 9-hectare grassy wedge revolving around pond-like Lake Northam. The 50m pool here serves as Newtown and Glebe's beach.

❸ Cross the Quadrangle

Flanked by two grand halls that wouldn't be out of place in Harry Potter's beloved Hogwarts, the Quadrangle has a Gothic Revival design that tips its mortarboard towards the stately colleges of Oxford. It was designed by colonial architect Edmund Blacket and completed in 1862; he also built St Andrew's Cathedral in the city.

❹ Check out the Chau Chak Wing

Billionaire Chinese Australian property developer Chau Chak Wing made a substantial donation towards the cost of this new **museum** (📞02-9351 2222; http://sydney.edu.au; University Pl, University of Sydney; admission free; 🚌412, 413, 436, 438-40, 461, 480, 483, M10) which opened in 2020. It displays the university's art, natural history and ethnographic collections. It also incorporates the **Nicholson Collection**, a must see for ancient history geeks, with a beautifully displayed collection of Greek, Roman, Cypriot, Egyptian and Near Eastern antiquities and a marvellous Lego Pompeii

❺ Slink into Sappho Books

Combining the essentials of student life – books, coffee, alcohol and lesbian poetry – Sappho has a beautiful bohemian garden **cafe** (📞02-9552 4498; www.sapphobooks.com.au; 51 Glebe Point Rd, Glebe; light meals $6-19; ⏰8.30am-6pm Mon-Sat, 9am-6pm Sun; ✐; 🚌431, 433, 🚊Glebe), its walls scrawled with generations of graffiti. Wine and tapas kick in after 6pm.

Inner West

500 m
0.25 miles

PYRMONT

Harris St

Pier St

Exhibition Centre

2 Powerhouse Museum

45

ULTIMO

University of Technology Sydney (UTS)

Central

3 Park

White Rabbit

Abercrombie St

1

4

10

15

Broadway

Knox St

CHIPPENDALE

Myrtle St

City Rd

44

Bulwarra Rd

Bulwarra Rd

Jones St

William Henry St

Mary Ann St

S Ann St

Wattle St

Mountain St

Bay St

Quarry St

Victoria Park

Lake Northam

Science Rd

Manning Rd

Wentworth Park

Wentworth Park

Bridge Rd

Ferry Rd

Blackwattle Bay

Blackwattle Park

26

Bellevue St

Darghan St

Darling St

Gottenham St

Talfourd St

Glebe

GLEBE

Broughton St

Glebe St

Greek St

Francis St

41

23

9 47

50

Glebe Point Rd

Derwent St

Westmoreland St

Mt Vernon St

Catherine St

Parramatta Rd

Ross St

Forest Rd

FOREST LODGE

Stewart St

Cook St

Forsyth St

Avona Ave

27

30

Glebe Point Rd

Allen St

Mansfield St

Wigram Rd

Boyce St

Toxteth Rd

Arcadia Rd

Hereford St

St James Reserve

Bridge Rd

Ross St

Rosins St

St Johns Rd

22

Edward St

Avenue Rd

Jubilee Park

Bicentennial Park

Federal Park

Jubilee Park

Johnstons Creek

Lewis Hoad Reserve

Minogue Cres

Charles St

Ross St

Hogan Park

Barr St

Pyrmont Bridge Rd

49

Parramatta Rd

The Crescent

ANNANDALE

Trafalgar St

Nelson St

Nelson St

Booth St

Taylor St

Booth St

Nelson St

Johnston St

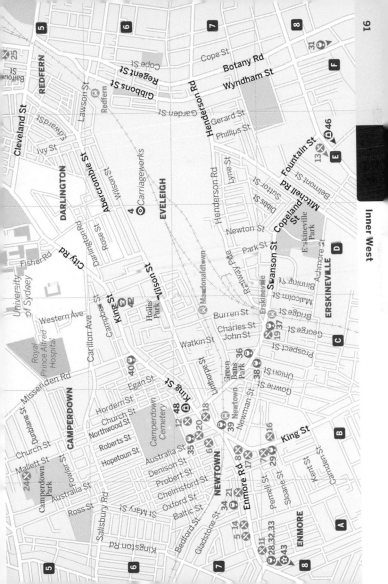

Inner West

REDFERN

DARLINGTON

Cleveland St

Ivy St

Edwards

Lawson St

Redfern

Gibbons St

Regent St

Cope St

Botany Rd

Wyndham St

Gerard St

Phillips St

Henderson Rd

Garden St

Cope St

31

46

13

F

E

Fountain St

Mitchell Rd

Belmont St

Fisher Rd

University of Sydney

Abercrombie St

Darlington Rd

Rose St

Wilson St

Carriageworks

4

EVELEIGH

Henderson Rd

Lyne St

Sutter St

Dibbs St

Copeland St

Swanson St

Newton St

Park St

Railway Pde

Erskineville

Erskineville Park

Ashmore St

Malcolm St

Binning St

Bridge St

George St

ERSKINEVILLE

D

Royal Prince Alfred Hospital

Missenden Rd

Western Ave

City Rd

Carlton Ave

King St

Campbell St

Wilson St

Hollis Park

Watkin St

Macdonaldtown

Burren St

Charles St

John St

Prospect St

19 37

C

CAMPERDOWN

Church St

Dunblane St

Mallett St

Australia St

Fowler St

Egan St

Hordern St

Church St

Northwood St

Roberts St

Hopetoun St

Camperdown Cemetery

King St

Linthorpe St

Green Bans Park

36

Newtown

Newman St

39

Gowrie St

Union St

38

40

48

24

Camperdown Park

12

20

18

35

6

NEWTOWN

Enmore Rd

8

17

16

King St

76

29

Kent St

Camden St

B

Denison St

Probert St

Chelmsford St

Oxford St

Baltic St

Bedford St

Gladstone St

34

21

Enmore Rd

Pernell St

Sloane St

A

Ross St

St Mary St

Kingston Rd

Salisbury Rd

5 14

28 32 33

11

43

ENMORE

8

Sights

White Rabbit
GALLERY

1 MAP P90, F4

If you're an art lover or a bit of a Mad Hatter, this particular rabbit hole will leave you grinning like a Cheshire Cat. There are so many works in this private collection of cutting-edge, contemporary Chinese art that only a fraction can be displayed at one time. Who knew that the People's Republic was turning out work that was so edgy, funny, sexy and idiosyncratic? It's probably Sydney's best contemporary art gallery. There's an on-site tearoom. (☏02-8399 2867; www.whiterabbitcollection.org; 30 Balfour St, Chippendale; admission free; ☺10am-5pm Wed-Sun, closed Feb & Aug; ☒Central)

Powerhouse Museum
MUSEUM

2 MAP P90, F2

A short walk from Darling Harbour, this cavernous science and design museum whirs away inside the former power station for Sydney's defunct, original tram network. The collection and temporary exhibitions cover everything from robots and life on Mars to steam trains to climate change to atoms to fashion, industrial design and avant-garde art installations. There are great options for kids of all ages but it's equally intriguing for adults. Grab a map of the museum once you're inside. Disabled access is good.

The Powerhouse is due to move to a new location in Parramatta that is set to be completed in 2024. (Museum of Applied Arts & Sciences/MAAS; ☏02-9217 0111; www.powerhousemuseum.com; 500 Harris St, Ultimo; adult/child $15/free; ☺10am-5pm; ♿; ☒Exhibition Centre)

Central Park
AREA

3 MAP P90, F4

Occupying the site of an old brewery, this major residential and shopping development is a striking sight. Most impressive is Jean Nouvel's award-winning, vertical-garden-covered tower, **One Central Park**. The canti-levered platform high above has been designed to reflect sunlight onto the greenery below. Its lower floors have plenty of food options, **cinemas** (☏02-9190 2290; www.palacecinemas.com.au; Level 3, Central Park, 28 Broadway; ☒Central), shops, a supermarket and gallery spaces, while adjacent Kensington St and Spice Alley (p95) offer further gastronomic pleasure. (☏02-8096 9900; www.centralparksydney.com; 28 Broadway, Chippendale; ☺10am-8pm; ☒Central)

Carriageworks
ARTS CENTRE

4 MAP P90, D6

Built between 1880 and 1889, this intriguing group of huge Victorian-era workshops was part of the Eveleigh Railyards. The rail workers chugged out in 1988, and in 2007 the artists moved in. It's now home to various avant-garde arts and performance projects, and there's usually something interesting to check out; have a look on the website to see what's on. There's a very pleasant cafe-bar here and an excellent Saturday morning farmers market (p105). (☏02-8571 9099; www.carriageworks.com.au; 245 Wilson St, Eveleigh; admission free; ☉10am-6pm; ☒Redfern)

Eating

Cow & the Moon   ICE CREAM $

5 ☒ MAP P90, A7

Forget the diet and slink into this cool corner cafe, where an array of sinful truffles and tasty tarts beckons seductively. Ignore them and head straight for the world's best gelato – the title this humble little place won in 2014 at the Gelato World Tour title in Rimini, Italy. There's decent coffee too. (☏02-9557 4255; 181 Enmore Rd, Enmore; small gelati $6.50; ☉8.30am-10.30pm Sun-Thu, to 11.30pm Fri & Sat; 🛜🥄🚻; ☒Newtown)

Black Star Pastry   BAKERY $

6 ☒ MAP P90, B7

Wise folks follow the black star to pay homage to excellent coffee, a large selection of sweet things and a few very good savoury things (gourmet pies and the like). There are only a couple of tables; it's more a snack-and-run or picnic-in-the-park kind of place. Prepare to queue. Other outposts have cropped up around town. (☏02-9557 8656; www.blackstarpastry.com.au; 277 Australia St,

Cow & the Moon

Newtown; snacks $4-10; ⏱7am-5pm Sun-Wed, 7am-5.30pm Thu-Sat; ; ®Newtown)

Lentil as Anything

VEGETARIAN $

7 MAP P90, B8

With tasty vegetarian and vegan fare on a voluntary contribution basis, this heartening project brings people together at communal tables. It's deservedly popular with everyone, from latte-sipping laptoppers to backpackers, students and some people who really need the feed. For those not in the know, the name is a pun on legendary Australian pop-rockers Mental as Anything. (☎02-8283 5580; www.lentilasanything.com; 391 King St, Newtown; donation; ⏱noon-3pm & 6-9pm Mon-Fri, 10am-3pm & 6-9pm Sat & Sun; 🖋; ®Newtown)

Golden Lotus

VEGAN, VIETNAMESE $

8 🍴 MAP P90, B7

Delicious bowls of pho, crunchy textures and fresh flavour bursts make this perhaps the best of Newtown's sizeable crop of vegan and vegetarian restaurants. As well as vegetable-based meals, there are lots of dishes involving soy-based chicken and fish substitutes. It's BYO alcohol. (☎02-8937 2838; www.goldenlotus-vegan.com; 343 King St, Newtown; mains $14-18; ⏱5.30-10.30pm Mon-Wed, noon-3pm & 5.30-10.30pm Thu-Sun; 🖋; ®Newtown)

Wedge

CAFE $

9 🍴 MAP P90, D3

Cut a corridor out of the side of a building, open it to the street and add artful industrial decor and you have the Wedge, which has delicious single-origin espressos and

---

Out in the Inner West

Newtown's King St and Enmore Rd are among the city's most diverse eating streets, with Thai restaurants sitting alongside Vietnamese, Greek, Lebanese and Mexican, but the scene is replicated on a smaller scale in nearly every inner west suburb. Many restaurants allow you to BYO wine. When it comes to coffee culture, all roads point this way, too.

And devotees of the comfortable, atmospheric local pub rejoice! The Inner West has plenty of pubs in varying degrees of gentrification, ranging from 'not at all' to 'within an inch of its life'. A thirsty student population sustains a barrage of bars and live-music venues, the hipster crowd means post-ironic cocktail tomfoolery is gloriously in vogue, and a sizeable LGBTIQ+ community also makes its presence felt. Night owls can take heart that the Inner West is outside the central city's restricted alcohol zone – meaning no lockouts. Family-friendly pubs with play areas are common.

cold brews as well as wholesome, artfully presented breakfasts, sandwiches and lunch specials. The quality and atmosphere are great, and sitting at the sill gazing over the street is a pleasure. (📞02-9660 3313; www.thewedgeglebe.com; cnr Cowper St & Glebe Point Rd, Glebe; light meals $8-18; ☺7am-4pm Mon-Sat, 8am-3pm Sun; 🛜📶; 🚃431, 433, 🚃Glebe)

Spice Alley
ASIAN $

10 ✖ MAP P90, F4

This little laneway off Kensington St by Central Park is a picturesque outdoor eating hub serving street-foody dishes from various Asian cuisines. Grab your noodles, dumplings or pork belly and fight for a stool. Quality is reasonable rather than spectacular, but prices are low and it's fun. It's cashless: pay by card or load up a prepay card from the drinks booth.

The drinks booth is soft-drink only, but you can BYO alcohol; there are two bottleshops nearby. (📞02-9281 0822; www.spice-alley.com.au; Kensington St, Chippendale; dishes $8-16; ☺11am-10pm Sun-Wed, to 10.30pm Thu-Sat; 📶; 🚃Central)

Faheem Fast Food
PAKISTANI $

11 ✖ MAP P90, A8

This Enmore Rd stalwart offers a totally no-frills dining atmosphere but very tasty and authentic curry and tandoori options served until late. Its Haleem lentil-and-beef curry is memorably tasty, while the

brain *nihari* is another standout, and not as challenging as it sounds. (📞02-9550 4850; 194 Enmore Rd, Enmore; dishes $12-14; ☺5pm-midnight Mon-Fri, noon-midnight Sat & Sun; 📶; 🚃423, 426, 428)

Mary's
BURGERS $

12 ✖ MAP P90, B7

Not put off by the grungy aesthetics, the ear-splitting heavy metal or the fact that the graffiti-daubed building was previously a sexual health clinic and a Masonic Temple? Then head up to the mezzanine of this dimly lit hipster bar for some of the best burgers and fried chicken in town. (www.getfat.com.au; 6 Mary St, Newtown; mains $13-18; ☺4pm-midnight Mon-Thu, noon-midnight Fri & Sat, noon-10pm Sun; 🛜📶; 🚃Newtown)

Grounds of Alexandria
CAFE $$

13 ✖ MAP P90, E8

A quite extraordinary Alexandria spot, the Grounds goes well beyond converted industrial chic. This former pie factory now sports futuristic coffee technology, tip-top baking and delicious food, but it's the enormous garden setting that has the biggest impact: chickens, a waste-chewing pig and greenery all around. It's a real sight to behold. You won't behold it alone though...prepare to queue.

Also here is the **Potting Shed** (mains $24-37; ☺11.30am-9pm Mon-Thu, to 10pm Fri, 11am-10pm Sat, to 9pm Sun; 🛜📶), another riot of plants open for evening drinks

Potting Shed at the Grounds of Alexandria (p95)

and food. (☑02-9699 2225; www.
thegrounds.com.au; 2 Huntley St,
Alexandria; dishes $15-26; ⊙7am-4pm
Mon-Fri, 7.30am-4pm Sat & Sun; ⎙ 🚼;
🚌348, 🚆Green Square)

Stanbuli
TURKISH $$

14 ⊗ MAP P90, A7

Hidden by the vintage pink-and-
purple facade of a '60s hair salon,
this sophisticated exploration
of traditional Istanbul dishes is
excellent. The handsomely tiled
downstairs bar area is a sociable
spot for a shot of raki and some
delicious share plates, or head
upstairs for more formal dining.
Flavours are intense, with an em-
phasis on Mediterranean seafood
and charcoal-grilled meats. (☑02-
8624 3132; www.stanbuli.com.au; 135
Enmore Rd, Enmore; mains $20-30;

⊙6pm-midnight Wed-Sat, to 10pm Sun;
🚆Newtown)

Koi Dessert Bar
DESSERTS $$

15 ⊗ MAP P90, F4

Having made the nation salivate
on *Master Chef Australia*, Reynold
Poernomo now produces his
fabulous desserts for public con-
sumption at this two-level spot by
Central Park. Downstairs is a cafe
with scrumptious sweet fare on
offer. Pre-book and head upstairs
(6pm to 9.30pm) for the ultimate
luxury; a four-course dessert degustation. It also does a savoury
degustation menu. (☑02-9212
1230; www.koidessertbar.com.au; 46
Kensington St, Chippendale; dessert
degustation $65; ⊙10am-10pm Tue-
Sun; 🚆Central)

Bloodwood
MODERN AUSTRALIAN $$

16 ✖ MAP P90, B8

Relax over a few drinks and a progression of small plates (we love those polenta chips!) in the front bar, or make your way to the rear to enjoy soundly conceived and expertly cooked dishes from across the globe. The decor is industrial-chic and the vibe is alternative – very Newtown. (☎02-9557 7699; www.bloodwoodnewtown.com; 416 King St, Newtown; share plates $17-32; ⊗5-11pm Mon-Fri, noon-3pm & 5-11pm Sat & Sun; ✐; ☒Newtown)

3 Olives
GREEK $$

17 ✖ MAP P90, B7

There's something very life-affirming about a good Greek restaurant, and this family-run *taberna* ticks all the boxes. The decor is restrained, with olive-coloured walls, but there's nothing restrained about the portions or aromas: mounds of perfectly textured BBQ octopus, big chunks of melt-in-the-mouth lamb *kleftiko*, warm flatbread, hearty meatballs and more-ish olives. It's an excellent celebration of traditional eating. (☎02-9557 7754; 365 King St, Newtown; mains $24-27, meze dishes $13-16; ⊗5.30pm-midnight Wed-Sun; ☒Newtown)

Thai Pothong
THAI $$

18 ✖ MAP P90, B7

The menu at this crowd-pleasing restaurant is full of long-time favourites and people still queue for them. The army of staff are efficient and friendly, and the food reliably excellent. Top choice is a window seat to watch the Newtowners pass by. If you pay cash, you get a discount, paid in a local currency only redeemable in the gift shop. (☎02-9550 6277; www.thaipothong.com.au; 294 King St, Newtown; mains $18-31; ⊗noon-3pm daily, plus 6-10.30pm Mon-Thu, 6-11pm Fri & Sat, 5.30-10pm Sun; P✐; ☒Newtown)

Maggie's
THAI $$

19 ✖ MAP P90, C8

Worth the short stroll downhill from the Newtown strip, or as the focus of a night out in pleasant Erskineville itself, this small neighbourhood Thai restaurant is a real gem. A short menu and blackboard specials offer intense, flavour-packed dishes from the open kitchen with great presentation and some unusual flavours. Intelligent service adds to the experience, as does outdoor seating. (☎02-9516 5270; www.maggiesthai.com.au; 75 Erskineville Rd, Erskineville; mains $18-26; ⊗5-9pm Sat-Wed, 11am-2.30pm & 5-9pm Thu & Fri; ✐; ☒Erskineville)

Continental
DELI $$

20 ✖ MAP P90, B7

It's a pleasure to sit at the counter at this artfully-designed deli and snack on charcuterie and fish preserves while quaffing a glass of vermouth or a deeply-flavoured amaro. Staff look after you exceptionally well here. The bistro upstairs opens for dinner and weekend lunches and features inventive, well-presented dishes partly based on the deli fare. (📱02-8624 3131; www.continental delicatessen.com.au; 210 Australia St, Newtown; charcuterie $10-20; ⏲noon-11pm Mon-Thu, to midnight Fri & Sat, to 10pm Sun; ℝNewtown)

The Stinking Bishops CHEESE $$

21 MAP P90, A7

A pungent array of artisanal cheeses is the raison d'être of this popular shop and eatery. Choose the varieties you want, pick a wine or craft beer to accompany, and off you go. There are also very tasty charcuterie boards. All its wares are sourced from small producers and available to take home too.

(📱02-9007 7754; www.thestinking-bishops.com; 63 Enmore Rd, Newtown; 2-/3-/4-cheese boards $21/29/37; ⏲5-9pm Tue-Thu, noon-3.30pm & 5.30-10pm Fri & Sat; 🖊; ℝNewtown)

Tramsheds Harold Park FOOD HALL $$

22 MAP P90, B2

Sydney's latest foodie hangout is this refurbished centenarian brick tram depot at the northern end of Glebe. It's a handsome rede-velopment with a supermarket, provedores and modern-thinking eateries, including one specialising in fresh pasta, another in organic meats, a sustainable fish restaurant, a contemporary Middle Eastern, a Spanishy tapas place from the Bodega team and Messina gelati.

The Stinking Bishops

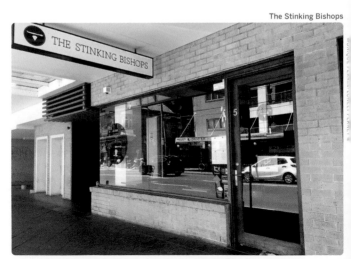

(📞02-8398 5695; www.tram
shedssydney.com.au; Maxwell Rd, Glebe;
⏰7am-10pm; ✳🛜; 🚉Jubilee Park)

Despaña
TAPAS $$

23 ✗ MAP P90, D3

Though service can be a little
scatty, there's some excellent
tapas-sharing to be done at this
welcoming Glebe restaurant. A
good selection of cured meats
is backed up by full-of-flavour,
loosely Spanish creations, with
delicious artichokes, mushrooms
and cauliflower dishes com-
plemented by succulent lamb
skewers, braised beef cheek and a
selection of cheeses. The wine list
covers both Spain and Argentina.
(📞02-9660 2299; www.despana.com.
au; 101 Glebe Point Rd, Glebe; tapas
$9-18; ⏰5-11pm Mon-Fri, noon-10pm
Sat & Sun; 🚲; 🚌431, 433, 🚉Glebe)

Acre
MODERN AUSTRALIAN $$

24 ✗ MAP P90, B5

Part of Camperdown Commons, a
conversion of a bowling club into
organic farm and family-friendly
cafe, eatery and play area, Acre is
a breezy, good-looking, open-plan
bungalow-style restaurant. Plenty
of space between tables, tasty
tap beers and excellent, care-
fully selected produce make this
a pleasurable experience. The
share plates of meat and fish are
great. A shipping container out
front serves coffee daily. (Camperdown Commons; 📞02-9194 3100;
www.acreeatery.com.au; 31a Mallett

Changing Glebe

Glebe is home to a long-
established Aboriginal community, students, academics,
hipsters and cool bookstores.
The First Fleet's chaplain was
granted church land here (a
'glebe'); which later degen-
erated into slums. In the
mid-1970s Gough Whitlam's
federal government rejuve-
nated the area for low-income
families, many of whom have
lived here for generations.
These days, though, you
won't be low-income if you've
just bought a pretty old terrace here.

St, Camperdown; mains $27-38,
⏰restaurant noon-10pm Wed-Sat, to
9pm Sun; 🛜👫)

Ester
MODERN AUSTRALIAN $$$

25 ✗ MAP P90, F5

Ester exemplifies Sydney's
contemporary dining scene: in-
formal but not sloppy; innovative
without being overly gimmicky;
hip, but never try-hard. Influences
straddle continents and dishes
are made to be shared. How do
the dishes achieve that much
flavour and texture? It's a seri-
ously impressive place. If humanly
possible, make room for dessert.
(📞02-8068 8279; www.ester-
restaurant.com.au; 46/52 Meagher
St, Chippendale; share plates $18-50;

⏱6-10pm Mon-Thu, 6-11pm Fri, noon-3pm & 6-11pm Sat, noon-6pm Sun; 🥢; 🚊Central)

Boathouse on Blackwattle Bay

SEAFOOD $$$

26 🍴 MAP P90, D1

The best restaurant in Glebe, and one of the best seafood restaurants in Sydney. Offerings range from oysters so fresh you'd think you shucked them yourself, to a snapper pie that'll go straight to the top of your favourite-dish list. The views over the bay and Anzac Bridge are stunning. Arrive by water taxi for maximum effect. (📞02-9518 9011; www.boathouse.net.au; 123 Ferry Rd, Glebe; mains $42-48; ⏱6-10pm Tue-Thu, noon-3pm & 6-11pm Fri-Sun; 🚊Glebe)

Glebe Point Diner

MODERN AUSTRALIAN $$$

27 🍴 MAP P90, C1

A sensational neighbourhood diner, where only the best local produce is used and everything – from the home-baked bread and hand-churned butter to the nougat finale – is made from scratch. The food is creative and comforting at the same time: a rare combination. The menu changes regularly and is backed up by blackboard specials. (📞02-9660 2646; www.glebepointdiner.com.au; 407 Glebe Point Rd, Glebe; mains $32; ⏱noon-3pm Wed-Sun, 6-10pm Mon-Thu, 5.30-11pm Fri & Sat; 🚌431, 🚊Jubilee Park)

Drinking

Lazybones Lounge

BAR

28 🚇 MAP P90, A8

Roomy and extravagantly decorated, Lazybones is an excellent bar-lounge with live music nightly and a decent line in cocktails and food. At weekends it gets likeably louche, with a happy crowd dancing until late. Even the bouncers are friendly.

There's a cover charge for the bands ($10 to $20); it's free later on. Enter on Illawarra Rd. (📞0450 008 563; www.lazybones lounge.com.au; 294 Marrickville Rd, Marrickville; ⏱7pm-midnight Mon-Wed, 5pm-3am Thu-Sat, 5-10pm Sun; 📶; 🚊Marrickville)

Earl's Juke Joint

BAR

29 🚇 MAP P90, B8

Inspired by America's Deep South, Earl's serves craft beers and killer cocktails to the Newtown hip-erati. It's hidden behind the down-at-heel facade of the butcher's shop it used to be, but once in, you're in swinging New Orleans, with a bar as long as the Mississippi. (www.facebook.com/earlsjukejoint; 407 King St, Newtown; ⏱4pm-midnight Mon-Sat, 4-10pm Sun; 🚊Newtown)

Timbah

WINE BAR

30 🚇 MAP P90, C2

Quite a way down Glebe Point Rd is an excellent independent bottleshop; turn right to find this convivial wine bar it runs downstairs. It's a lovely space decked out in wood; there's always something interesting available by the glass, and staff are open to cracking something on demand. Tapas-style food (not Sundays) is tasty, with Australian native flavours and home-grown herbs. (📞02-9571 7005; www.timbahwinebar.com.au; 375 Glebe Point Rd, entrance on Forsyth St, Glebe; 🕙4-10pm Tue-Thu, 4-11pm Fri & Sat, 4-8pm Sun; 🚌431, 🚊Glebe)

Archie Rose Distilling Co. BAR

 31 🚇 MAP P90, F8

This distillery has made quite an impact with its excellent gins and where better to try them than the place itself? The bar is appropriately industrial chic; the mezzanine is a great spot to sit and observe the action. Try different gins in a flight, or pick your perfect G&T combination or cocktail. It also has some decent wine and beer. (📞02-8458 2300; www.archierose.com.au; 85 Dunning Ave, Rosebery; 🕙noon-10pm Sun & Mon, to 11.30pm Tue-Sat; 📶; 🚌343, 🚊Green Square)

The Henson PUB

32 🚇 MAP P90, A8

Offering something for everyone, this excellent neighbourhood pub sums up the modern Inner West vibe. Sip craft ale in various indoor spaces, watch charcuterie being sliced in the deli/beer shop or order up a plateful of delicious food. The beer garden sees a lot of action, and there's a great children's play area here, making it

The butcher's-shop frontage of Earl's Juke Joint

very popular with families. (☏02-9569 5858; www.thehenson.com.au; 91 Illawarra Rd, Marrickville; ⏰11am-midnight Mon-Sat, to 10pm Sun; 👶; 🚌423, 426, 428, M30)

Gasoline Pony BAR

33 🚇 MAP P90, A8

With a friendly, 30-plus local crowd, this is an excellent bar with streetside seating, local live music and a relaxing backyard area if you don't fancy the sounds. The food is ok but you're here for the welcoming atmosphere and that Marrickville vibe. (☏02-9569 2668; www.gasolinepony.com; 115 Marrickville Rd, Marrickville; ⏰5-11.30pm Tue-Thu, 3-11.30pm Fri & Sat, 3-9.30pm Sun; 🚌418, 423, 425, 426, M30, 🚉Sydenham)

Young Henry's BREWERY

34 🚇 MAP P90, A7

Conviviality is assured in this craft brewery bar, where the beer is as fresh as you'll get. Basically, they've filled a bit of warehouse with high tables, a loud stereo system and a counter to serve their delicious beer, opened the roller door and filled it with happy locals. It doesn't do eats, but there's a different food truck outside each weekend. (☏02-9519 0048; www.younghenrys.com; 76 Wilford St, Newtown; ⏰noon-7pm; 🚉Newtown)

Courthouse Hotel PUB

35 🚇 MAP P90, B7

A block back from the King St fray, the 150-year-old Courthouse is one of Newtown's best pubs,

Erskineville Hotel ('The Erko')

the kind of place where everyone from goths to magistrates can have a beer and feel right at home. It packs out for Sydney Swans games. The beer garden is one of Sydney's best: spacious, sheltered and cheerful, with decent pub food available. (02-9519 8273; www.solotel.com.au; 202 Australia St, Newtown; 10am-midnight Mon-Sat, to 10pm Sun; Newtown)

Erskineville Hotel PUB

36 MAP P90, C7

The Erko's art-deco glory is something to behold, and it also happens to be one of the area's best pubs. The wood-lined beer garden, local characters, range of curious spaces to drink in, and good pub food served in generous portions makes it a real gem of the community. Unusually for Sydney pubs, it's even got some street-side tables. (02-9565 1608; www.theerko.com.au; 102 Erskineville Rd, Erskineville; 11am-midnight Mon-Sat, 11am-10pm Sun; ; Erskineville)

Hive Bar BAR

37 MAP P90, C8

In groovy Erskineville village, this breezy little corner bar lures the neighbourhood's hipsters with food, cocktails – try the Full Scottish Breakfast featuring marmalade and malt whisky – DJs spinning funk and soul, crazy murals and a quiet bolthole upstairs. Order a few plates to share over a glass of vino and pull up a foot-

Hive Bar

MONIQUE PERRIN/LONELY PLANET ©

path table. (02-9519 1375; www.thehivebar.com.au; 93 Erskineville Rd, Erskineville; noon-midnight Mon-Fri, 11am-midnight Sat, 11am-10pm Sun; ; Erskineville)

Imperial Hotel LGBTIQ+

38 MAP P90, C7

The art-deco Imperial is legendary as the starting point for *The Adventures of Priscilla, Queen of the Desert*. This old, late-opening LGBTIQ+ favourite has put on a new frock in recent years, reopening with a mainly vegetarian restaurant and a refurbished basement space for the drag shows. (02-9516 1766; www.imperialerskineville.com.au; 35 Erskineville Rd, Erskineville; noon-midnight Mon-Thu, noon-3am Fri & Sat, 11am-midnight Sun; Erskineville)

Bank Hotel

PUB

39 🚇 MAP P90, B7

The Bank didn't always sport the artful heritage-wood look that it has now, but it has consistently been a Newtown classic in its central railway-side position. Its large retractable-roofed beer garden at the back is a highlight, as is the craft beer bar above it, which always has interesting guest ales on tap. Food is based on Mexican-style barbecue options. (📞02-8568 1900; www.bankhotel.com.au; 324 King St, Newtown; ⏰11am-1am Mon-Wed, to 2am Thu, to 4am Fri & Sat, to midnight Sun; 📶; 🚆Newtown)

Marlborough Hotel

PUB

40 🚇 MAP P90, C6

One of many great old art-deco pubs in Newtown, the Marly has a front sports bar with live bands on weekends and a shady beer garden. Head upstairs for a great balcony, soul food and rockabilly bands at Miss Peaches, or downstairs for all sorts of kooky happenings at the Tokyo Sing Song nightclub on Friday and Saturday nights. (📞02-9519 1222; www.marlboroughhotel.com.au; 145 King St, Newtown; ⏰10am-4am Mon-Sat, 10am-midnight Sun; 🚆Macdonaldtown)

Friend in Hand

PUB

41 🚇 MAP P90, E3

At heart the Friend in Hand is still a working-class pub with a resident loud-mouth cockatoo and a cast of grizzly old-timers and local larrikins propping up the bar. But then there's all the other stuff: live music, life drawing, poetry readings, crab racing, comedy nights. Strewth Beryl, bet you weren't expecting that. (📞02-9660 2326; www.friendinhand.com; 58 Cowper St, Glebe; ⏰8am-midnight Mon-Fri, 10am-midnight Sat, 10am-10pm Sun; 📶; 🚆Wentworth Park)

Entertainment

Leadbelly

LIVE MUSIC

42 ⭐ MAP P90, C6

This dark and atmospheric bar does seriously good cocktails and some excellent jazz and blues-y live music at weekends. There are also pizzas and other food, so that's your whole night sorted. (📞02-9557 7992; www.theleadbelly.com.au; 42 King St, Newtown; ⏰6pm-midnight Tue-Thu, 6pm-1am Fri & Sat; 🚌352, 370, 422, 423, 426, 428, M30, 🚆Macdonaldtown)

Camelot Lounge

LIVE MUSIC

43 ⭐ MAP P90, A8

In increasingly hip Marrickville, this eclectic little venue hosts jazz, world music, blues, folk, comedy, cabaret and all manner of other weird stuff. There are two bars; it's worth booking online or getting here early as it often sells out. The atmosphere is one of sit-down-and-appreciate rather than stand and dance. It's very close to Sydenham station. Check the website for shows outside open nights. (📞02-9550 3777;

www.camelotlounge.com; 19 Marrickville Rd, Marrickville; ⏰6pm-late Thu-Sun; 🚃Sydenham)

Lansdowne Hotel   LIVE MUSIC

44 ⭐ MAP P90, E4

This famous Sydney venue is back in action after a period of closure. It's a likeably no-frills rock pub downstairs, with graffiti on the walls and food served until 2am. Upstairs, there are gigs most nights; prepare for around $20 cover charge at weekends, depending on the band(s). (📞02-8218 2333; www.thelansdownepub.com.au; 2 City Rd, Chippendale; ⏰noon-3am Mon-Sat, to midnight Sun; 🚌412, 413, 422, 423, 🚃Central)

Foundry 616   LIVE MUSIC

45 ⭐ MAP P90, F3

With live Australian and international contemporary jazz several times a week, this atmospheric and thoughtfully programmed venue has been a great shot in the arm for the Sydney live-music scene. Good-value meals are available if you want a table. (📞02-9211 9442; www.foundry616.com.au; 616 Harris St, Ultimo; 🚃Paddy's Markets, 🚃Central)

Shopping

Carriageworks Farmers Market   MARKET

Over 70 regular stallholders sell their goodies at Sydney's best farmers market (see 4 🚇 Map p90, D6), held in a heritage-listed

Camelot Lounge

railway workshop (p92). Food and coffee stands do a brisk business, and vegetables, fruit, meat and seafood from all over the state are sold in a convivial atmosphere. (http://carriage-works.com.au; Carriageworks, 245 Wilson St, Eveleigh; ⏱8am-1pm Sat; 🚉Redfern)

Mitchell Road Antique & Design Centre ANTIQUES, VINTAGE

46 🔒 MAP P90, E8

This extraordinary vintage and antique market is a warehouse full of retro chic, whether you are after original 1970s Lego, pre-loved rocking horses, a Georgian coronation tea set or Bakelite telephones. For some it will be a dive into a

past known only from movies, for others a trip down memory lane. (📞02-9698 0907; https://mitchell-road.wordpress.com; 17 Bourke Rd, Alexandria; ⏱10am-6pm; 🚉Green Square)

Little Bottleshop WINE

One of Sydney's best bottleshops for those interested in Australian wine, this unassuming place (see 30 🍷 Map p90, C2) features an excellent curated selection of small-vineyard wines from quality regions. Look out for their own 2037 (Glebe's postcode) bottlings. It runs a wine bar (p100) downstairs. (Glebe Liquor; 📞02-9660 1984; www.glebeliquor.com.au; 375 Glebe Point Rd, Glebe; ⏱10am-8pm Mon-Sat, to 7pm Sun; 🚌431, 🚉Glebe)

Antique cash register, Mitchell Road Antique & Design Centre

ARUP TATUZZOV/SHUTTERSTOCK ©

Gleebooks

BOOKS

47 🔒 MAP P90, D3

One of Sydney's best bookshops, Gleebooks' aisles are full of politics, arts and general fiction, and staff really know their stuff. Check its calendar for author talks and book launches. (📞02-9660 2333; www.gleebooks.com.au; 49 Glebe Point Rd, Glebe; ⏱9am-7pm Mon-Sat, 10am-6pm Sun; 🚌431, 433, 🚉Glebe)

Better Read Than Dead

BOOKS

48 🔒 MAP P90, B7

This is our favourite Newtown bookshop, and not just because of the pithy name and the great selection of Lonely Planet titles. Nobody seems to mind if you waste hours perusing the beautifully presented aisles, stacked with high-, middle- and deliciously low-brow reading materials. (📞02-9557 8700; www.betterread.com.au; 265 King St, Newtown; ⏱9.30am-9pm Sun-Wed, to 10pm Thu-Sat; 🚉Newtown)

Deus Ex Machina

FASHION & ACCESSORIES

49 🔒 MAP P90, B4

This kooky showroom is crammed with classic and custom-made motorcycles and surfboards. A hybrid workshop, cafe and offbeat boutique, it stocks men's and women's threads, including Deus-branded

Updated Alexandria

The warehouses of Alexandria, at one time Australia's largest industrial district, were once the unflattering first glimpse that many visitors got of Sydney as their cab drove them from airport to city. These days, though, there's all sorts going on in this up-and-coming area. Groundbreaking cafes, smart food culture, renovated pubs, creative industries and a range of outlet stores make it well worth discovering. Note that the distance between reconstructed areas makes cycling a good option here.

jeans, tees and shorts. (📞02-8594 2800; www.deuscustoms.com; 102-104 Parramatta Rd, Camperdown; ⏱9am-5pm Mon-Fri,10am-4pm Sat & Sun; 🚌436-440)

Glebe Markets

MARKET

50 🔒 MAP P90, D4

The best of the west: Sydney's hipster inner-city contingent beats a course to this crowded retro-chic market. There are some great handcrafts and design on sale, as well as an inclusive, community atmosphere. (www.glebemarkets.com.au; Glebe Public School, cnr Glebe Point Rd & Derby Pl; ⏱10am-4pm Sat; 🚌431, 433, 🚉Glebe)

Walking Tour 🥾

A Saturday in Paddington

Paddington is an elegant neighbourhood of restored terrace houses and steep leafy streets where fashionable folks (seemingly without the need to occupy an office) drift between boutiques, art galleries and bookshops. The suburb's pulsing artery is Oxford St, built over an ancient track used by the Gadigal (Cadigal) people. The liveliest time to visit is on Saturday, when the markets are effervescing.

Getting There

🚌 Buses 333 (Circular Quay to North Bondi) and 380 (Circular Quay to Watsons Bay via Bondi) head along Oxford St. Bus 389 (Maritime Museum to Bondi Junction) takes the back roads.

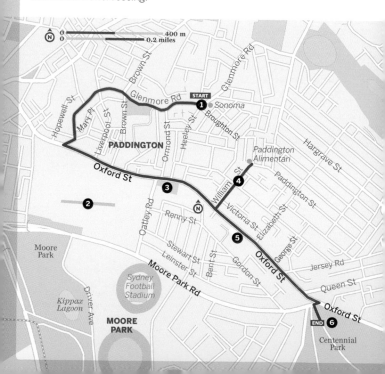

❶ Hang out in Five Ways

Oxford St may be the main drag, but the quirky cafes, galleries, shops and pub at the star-like junction of **Five Ways** (Glenmore Rd, Paddington; 🚌389) make it the hip heart of Paddington. Start with coffee in **Sonoma** (☑02-9331 3601; www.sonoma.com.au; 241 Glenmore Rd, Paddington; mains $6-18; ⏱7am-3pm Mon-Sat, 7am-2pm Sun; 🛜; 🚌389), a bakery-cafe specialising in sourdough bread and popular with the yummy-mummy set.

❷ Peer at Victoria Barracks

A manicured vision from the peak of the British Empire, these Georgian **barracks** (☑02-8335 5170, www.armymuseumnsw.com. au; Oxford St, Paddington; admission free; ⏱tours 10am Thu; 🚌333, 352, 380, 440, M40), built 1841–48, have been called the finest of their kind in the colonies. They're still part of an army base, so unless you return for the tour you'll have to peer through the gates.

❸ Stroll Through Paddington Reservoir Gardens

This impressive **park** (cnr Oxford St & Oatley Rd, Paddington; 🚌333, 352, 380, 440, M40) makes use of Paddington's long-abandoned 1866 water reservoir, incorporating the brick arches and surviving chamber into an interesting green space featuring a sunken garden, pond, boardwalk and lawns. They've even preserved some of the graffiti.

❹ Wander Down William St

William Street is an achingly pretty little slope whose cute terraced houses have been converted into upmarket clothing boutiques. It's a marvellous stroll; at the bottom, **Paddington Alimentari** (☑02-9358 2142; www.facebook.com/paddington. alimentari; 2 Hopetoun St, Paddington; light meals $5-13; ⏱7am-5pm Mon-Fri, 7.30am-4pm Sat; 🚌333, 352, 380, 440, M40) is a great cafe-deli that's an essential stop for local residents.

❺ Experience Paddington Markets

A cultural experience, these quirky, long-running **markets** (☑02-9331 2923; www.paddingtonmarkets.com.au; 395 Oxford St, Paddington; ⏱10am-4pm Sat; 🚌333, 380) turn Saturdays in Paddington into pandemonium. In the 1970s, when they started, Paddington Markets were distinctly counter-cultural. It's a tad more mainstream now, but still worth checking out for new and vintage clothing, crafts, jewellery, food and holistic treatments.

❻ Explore Centennial Park

Sydney's biggest **park** (☑02-9339 6699; www.centennialparklands.com. au; Oxford St, Centennial Park; ⏱gates sunrise-sunset; 🚈Moore Park, 🚈Bondi Junction) is a rambling 189-hectare expanse full of horse riders, joggers, cyclists and in-line skaters. Among the wide formal avenues, ponds and statues is the domed Federation Pavilion – the spot where Australia was officially proclaimed a nation.

Explore ◈
Surry Hills & Darlinghurst

Sydney's hippest neighbourhood is also home to its most interesting dining and bar scene. The plane trees and up-and-down of chic Surry Hills merge into the terraces of vibrant Darlinghurst. They are pleasant, leafy districts appealingly close to the centre.

Surry Hills bears little resemblance these days to the tightly knit, working-class community so evocatively documented in Ruth Park's classic Depression-era novels set here. The rows of Victorian terrace houses remain, but they're now upmarket residences home to inner-city types who keep the many excellent neighbourhood restaurants and bars in business.

Adjacent Darlinghurst is synonymous with Sydney's vibrant and visible LGBTIQ+ community. Oxford St has traditionally been Sydney's sequinned mile, and while it's seen better days it's still home to most of the city's dwindling gay venues and the Mardi Gras parade.

Getting There & Around

🚆 Exit at Museum train station for East Sydney and the blocks around Oxford St; Central for the rest of Surry Hills; and Kings Cross for the northern and eastern reaches of Darlinghurst.

🚌 Numerous buses traverse Cleveland, Crown, Albion, Oxford, Liverpool and Flinders Sts.

🚊 Sydney's L2 and L3 light-rail lines both conveniently stop in southern Surry Hills.

Surry Hills & Darlinghurst Map on p114

Terrace houses in Surry Hills CATRIN HAZE/SHUTTERSTOCK ©

Top Experience 📷

Learn About Aboriginal History at the Australian Museum

Under ongoing modernisation, this four-square sandstone museum, established just 40 years after the First Fleet dropped anchor, is doing a brilliant job. As well as natural history exhibits, it covers Indigenous Australia, dinosaurs, minerals and more.

◎ MAP P114, C1

📞 02-9320 6000

www.australianmuseum.
net.au

6 College St, Darlinghurst

adult/child $15/free

🕙 9.30am-5pm

🚇 Museum

Long Gallery

This elegant two-level space focuses on 100 key objects from the museum's extensive collection (from a platypus-skin rug to an Egyptian death-boat to the 'Bone Ranger', a spooky skeletal horserider) and, upstairs, 100 key Australians including household names and some who should be far better known.

Indigenous Galleries

Australia's Indigenous past and present gets good treatment in this standout section covering Aboriginal history and spirituality, from Dreaming stories to videos of the Freedom Rides of the 1960s. A collection of art and artefacts provides further insights.

Creatures

The excellent dinosaur gallery is a sure hit with kids and adults alike. Among several imposing beasts, it features enormous Jobaria as well as local bruisers like Muttaburrasaurus.

The stuffed-animal gallery of the natural history section manages to keep it relevant, while there are also interesting displays on extinct megafauna (giant wombats – simultaneously cuddly and terrifying) and current Australian creatures.

The Pacific

An intriguing collection of objects from a range of Pacific cultures is a real dose of colour and life after the stuffed animals. It's an assemblage of great quality that will at some point be incorporated into a new Oceania display.

★ **Top Tips**

○ Kidspace on level 2 is a mini-museum for the under-fives.

○ Even if you're not hungry, don't miss heading up to the cafe, which has brilliant views of St Mary's Cathedral and down to Woolloomooloo.

✗ **Take a Break**

The museum **cafe** is a fine spot for a snack and a drink with vistas.

Nearby Stanley Street still has a few remnants of its Little Italy heyday. **Bar Reggio** (☎ 02-9332 1129; www.barreggio. com.au; 135 Crown St, Darlinghurst; mains $14-30; ⏱ noon-11pm Mon-Sat; ✗; ℝ Museum), just round the corner, is one of the most typical.

Surry Hills & Darlinghurst

WOOLLOOMOOLOO

DARLINGHURST

PADDINGTON

HAYMARKET

Kings Cross

Craigend St

William St

Farrell Ave

Kirketon Rd

Victoria St

Nimrod St

Little Surrey St

West St

West St

Campbell Ave

Barcom Ave

Bourke St

Sydney Jewish Museum

St Vincents Hospital

Australian Design Centre

St Peters St

Forbes St

Liverpool St

Thomson St

Bourke St

Palmer St

Crown St

Kings La

Burton St

National Art School

Darlinghurst Rd

Green Park

Taylor Square

Surt St

Taylor St

Flinders St

Bourke St

Denham St

Little Oxford St

Foley St

Riley St

Yurong St

Oxford St

Liverpool St

Crown St

Poplar St

Goulburn St

Riley St

Campbell St

Hilder Reserve

Smith St

Mackey St

Ann St

Little Albion St

Crown St

Harmony Park

Hunt St

Mary St

Foster St

Reservoir St

Albion St

Wentworth Ave

Commonwealth St

Nithsdale St

Hay St

Belmore Park

Eddy Ave

Central

Stanley St

Francis St

Liverpool St

College St

Australian Museum

William St

Hyde Park

Pool of Reflection

Museum

Eastbound Cross City Tunnel

Bathurst St

Elizabeth St

Castlereagh St

Pitt St

Elizabeth St

Goulburn St

Elizabeth St

Surry Hills & Darlinghurst

For reviews see	
Top Experiences	p112
Sights	p116
Eating	p117
Drinking	p123
Entertainment	p127
Shopping	p127

400 m
0.2 miles

Oxford St

Moore Park Rd

Greens Rd

Napier St

Selwyn St

Iris St

Josephson St

Flinders St

Moore Park

Anzac Pde

South Dowling St

Floods La

South Dowling St

Hutchinson St

Nichols St

Bennett St

Prospect St

Fitzroy St

Fred Miller Park

Phelps St

Arthur St

Nobbs St

Parkham St

Mort S

Edge St

Bourke St

Albion St

Collins La

Rainford

Davies St

Raper St

Brett Whiteley Studio

Wiltshire St

Nickson St

Crown St

Foveaux St

Griffin St

Norton St

Tudor St

Arthur St

Riley St

Little Riley St

Surry Hills

Ward Park

Belvoir St

Goodlet St

Goodlet La

Riley St

Marlborough St

Cleveland St

Young St

Frog Hollow Reserve

Commonwealth St

Fitzroy St

SURRY HILLS

Adelaide St

Devonshire St

Butt St

Wilton St

James St

Cooper St

Foveaux St

Sophia St

Kippax St

Waterloo St

Hart St

Holt St

Cisdell St

Elizabeth St

Great Buckingham St

Chalmers La

Buckingham St

Mary St

Cooper St

Central Station

Chalmers St

Prince Alfred Park

Central

Sights

Brett Whiteley Studio   GALLERY

1 👁 MAP P114, C7

Acclaimed local artist Brett Whiteley (1939–1992) lived fast and without restraint. His hard-to-find studio (look for the signs on Devonshire St) has been preserved as a gallery for some of his best work. Pride of place goes to his astonishing *Alchemy,* a giant multi-panel extravaganza that could absorb you for hours with its broad themes, intricate details and humorous asides. The studio room upstairs also gives great insight into the character of this masterful draughtsman and off-the-wall genius.

At the door is a miniature of his famous sculpture *Almost Once,* which you can see in all its glory in the Domain. (📞02-9225 1881; www.artgallery.nsw.gov.au/brett-whiteley-studio; 2 Raper St, Surry Hills; admission free; 🕙10am-4pm Fri-Sun; 🚆Surry Hills, 🚆Central)

Sydney Jewish Museum   MUSEUM

2 👁 MAP P114, E3

This recently revamped museum revolves around a detailed and expertly curated exhibition on the Holocaust, with sobering personal testimonies and moving objects as well as a memorial section for the 1.5 million child victims. Other sections cover the history and practice of Judaism itself and Australian Jewish history, culture and tradition.

Another examines the role of Jews in Australia's military, while temporary exhibitions are always excellent. There's a kosher cafe upstairs.

Sydney has had an important Jewish history from the time of the First Fleet (which included 16 known Jews), to the immediate aftermath of WWII (when Australia became home to the greatest number of Holocaust survivors per capita, after Israel), to the present day. Visiting on a Sunday or weekday afternoon is recommended, as the museum often packs out with school groups. (📞02-9360 7999; www.sydneyjewishmuseum.com.au; 148 Darlinghurst Rd, Darlinghurst; adult/teen/child $15/9/free; 🕙10am-4pm Sun-Thu, to 2pm Fri; 🚆Kings Cross)

National Art School   HISTORIC SITE, GALLERY

3 👁 MAP P114, E3

Until 1912 these sandstone buildings were Darlinghurst Gaol: writer Henry Lawson was repeatedly incarcerated here for debt (he called the place 'Starvinghurst'). If today's art students think they've got it tough, they should spare a thought for the 732 prisoners crammed in here, or the 76 who were hanged. The central circular building was the chapel. A tiny former morgue near the Burton St exit has creepy skull-and-crossbone carvings. There's also a cafe and an excellent on-site gallery showcasing students' work. (www.nas.edu.au; Forbes St, Darlinghurst; admission free; 🕙gallery 11am-5pm Mon-Sat; 🚆Kings Cross)

Australian Design Centre

GALLERY

4 MAP P114, D1

The non-profit Australian Design Centre has a gallery, Object, that presents innovative exhibitions of new craft and design from Australia and overseas. Furniture, fashion, textiles and glass are all on show, and there's an appealing shop. (☑02-9361 4555; www.object.com.au; 101 William St, Darlinghurst; admission free; ☺11am-4pm Tue-Sat; ☒Museum)

Eating

Bourke Street Bakery

BAKERY $

5 MAP P114, D7

Queuing outside this teensy bakery is an essential Surry Hills experience. It sells a tempting selection of pastries, cakes, bread and sandwiches, along with sausage rolls that are near legendary in these parts. There are a few tables inside but on a fine day you're better off on the street. Offshoots around town offer a bit more space. (☑02-9699 1011; www.bourkestreetbakery.com.au; 633 Bourke St, Surry Hills; items $5-14; ☺7am-6pm Mon-Fri, to 5pm Sat & Sun; ☒; ☒301, ☒Surry Hills, ☒Central)

Le Monde

CAFE $

6 MAP P114, B5

Some of Sydney's best breakfasts are served between the demure dark wooden walls of this small street-side cafe. Top-notch coffee and a terrific selection of tea will gear you up to face the world, while dishes such as truffled

Entrance to the National Art School

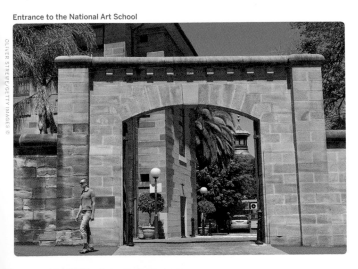

poached eggs or confit pork belly make it worth walking up the hill for. (📞02-9211 3568; www.lemonde cafe.com.au; 83 Foveaux St, Surry Hills; dishes $10-16; ⏰6.30am-4pm Mon-Fri, 7am-2pm Sat; 🛜; 🚇Central)

Reuben Hills
CAFE $

 MAP P114, B5

An industrial fitout and Latin American menu await here at Reuben Hills (aka hipster central), set in a terrace and its former garage. Fantastic single-origin coffee, roasted on the premises, and fried chicken, but the eggs, tacos and *baleadas* (Honduran tortillas) are no slouches, either. (📞02-9211 5556; www.reubenhills.com.au; 61 Albion St, Surry Hills; mains $9-22; ⏰7am-4pm Mon-Sat, 7.30am-4pm Sun; 🛜🍴; 🚇Central)

The Surry Scene

Once upon a time, this neighbourhood was known for its grungy live-music pubs and high-octane LGBTIQ+ scene. Many of the music venues have subsequently been converted into chic bar-restaurants and the gay bars have dwindled, but this area still contains some of Sydney's best nightspots – you just have to look harder to find them. The 'small bar' phenomenon has taken off here, with many of he city's best lurking down the most unlikely lanes.

Messina
ICE CREAM $

 MAP P114, F2

Join the queues of people who look like they never eat ice cream at the counter of the original store of Sydney's most popular gelato shop. Clearly even the beautiful people can't resist quirky flavours such as figs in marsala and pannacotta with fig jam and amaretti biscuit. It's all delicious, and there are several dairy-free options. There are several more outlets around town now.

Book well ahead for the sumptuous $130-a-head dessert degustations that they put on at one table next door. (📞02-9331 1588; www.gelatomessina.com; 241 Victoria St, Darlinghurst; 1/2/3 scoops $4.80/6.80/8.80; ⏰noon-11pm Sun-Thu, to 11.30pm Fri & Sat; 🍴; 🚇Kings Cross)

Formaggi Ocello
CAFE $

 MAP P114, D5

Love a cheesy grin? Then Formaggi Ocello is for you. This excellent Italian deli has a great range of cheeses, mostly Italian, Spanish and French, with some top Aussie selections, too. Check out the humongous cheese wheels in the ageing room. It's also a great place for a panino or tasting platter, accompanied by a glass of wine or two. (📞02-9357 7878; www.ocello. com.au; 425 Bourke St, Surry Hills; light meals $8-16; ⏰10am-6pm Mon-Fri, 9am-6pm Sat; 🍴; 🚇Central)

Sydney Jewish Museum (p116)

Spice I Am

THAI $

10 MAP P114, B3

Once the preserve of expat Thais, this place now has queues out the door. No wonder, as the food is superfragrant and superspicy. It's been so successful that it's opened the upmarket version in **Darlinghurst** (☏02-9332 2445; 296-300 Victoria St, Darlinghurst; mains $19-24; ⏱5-10pm; 🍴; ᴿKings Cross). The sign is unobtrusive so it's easy to walk past: don't. (☏02-9280 0928; www.spiceiam. com; 90 Wentworth Ave, Surry Hills; mains $15-20; ⏱11.30am-3.30pm & 5-10pm Tue-Sun; 🍴; ᴿCentral)

Nada's

LEBANESE $

11 MAP P114, A7

There are swisher Lebanese restaurants around, but for a no-frills delicious feed at a very fair price, it's hard to beat this old family-run favourite. The set meal at $29 a head is a bargain; just don't fill up too much on the bread and dips or you won't manage the sizeable chunks of Turkish delight at the end. BYO with no corkage. (☏02-9690 1289; www.nadasrestaurant.com; 270 Cleveland St, Surry Hills; mains $13-16; ⏱noon-2.30pm & 6-10pm Wed-Mon, 6-10pm Tue; 🍴; 🚌372, ᴿCentral)

Erciyes

TURKISH $

12 MAP P114, C8

Shamelessly kitsch Erciyes flaunts its fluoro lighting, mirror-faced wall, plastic tablecloths, disco ball and audience-participatory belly-dancing on Friday and Saturday nights. It's a well-loved spot that's been around for yonks: a good-value, good-time Turkish eatery. It has a few wine options, but it's also BYO. (📞02-9319 1309; www.erciyesrestaurant.com.au; 409 Cleveland St, Surry Hills; mains $15-26; ⏰11am-11.30pm; 🚗; 🚌372, 393, 395)

Porteño

ARGENTINE $$

13 🍴 MAP P114, B6

This upbeat and deservedly acclaimed Argentine restaurant is a great place to eat. The 'animal of the day' is slow-roasted for eight hours before the doors even open and is always delicious. Other highlights include the homemade chorizo and morcilla, but lighter touches are also in evidence, so it's not all meat-feast. There's a decent Argentine wine list too. (📞02-8399 1440; www.porteno.com.

au; 50 Holt St, Surry Hills; sharing plates $20-50; ⏰6pm-midnight Tue-Sat, plus noon-3pm Fri; 🚉Central)

The Bishop

BISTRO $$

14 🍴 MAP P114, C7

Reviving the disappearing Sydney tradition of shopfront-style restaurants in terraced houses, this two-level European-influenced spot offers quality bistro eating at very acceptable prices for stylish Surry Hills. Home-made charcuterie, decent wine choices and appealingly presented and executed seafood, meat and pasta dishes make this a reliably good choice. You'll feel a world away from the busy Sydney street corner photo featured upstairs. (📞02-8065 7223; www.thebishop. com.au; 527 Crown St, Surry Hills;

Meat pie from the Bourke Street Bakery (p117)

CATHERINE SUTHERLAND/LONELY PLANET ©

2/3 courses $49/59, degustation $77; ⊘noon-11pm Tue-Sat; ⊚Surry Hills)

Baccomatto Osteria ITALIAN $$

15 ⊗ MAP P114, C3

Sleek and modern, this smart Italian restaurant nevertheless conserves the warm and genuine welcome of your favourite trattoria. There's a real verve to the updated but faithful Italian cooking and some extraordinary flavours. The $20 pasta-and-wine lunches are a top deal. (⊘02-9215 5140; www.baccomattoosteria.com.au; 212 Riley St, Surry Hills; mains $29-35; ⊘6-10pm Mon-Thu, noon-3pm & 6-10pm Fri-Sun; ⊚; ⊚J01-2, 352)

Muum Maam THAI $$

16 ⊗ MAP P114, B6

Packing a punch for eyes and taste-buds, this is a buzzy spot beloved of those creative types who work hereabouts. It has a double identity that really works, with a food cart doling out lunch specials before the open kitchen turns to more serious, lavishly presented Thai creations in the evening. There's a big communal table but you can also go solo. (⊘02-9318 0881; www.muummaam. com.au; 50 Holt St, Surry Hills; lunch dishes $14-16, dinner mains $18-32; ⊘11.30am-3pm & 6-10.30pm Mon-Fri, 6-10.30pm Sat; ⊚; ⊚Central)

Single O CAFE $

17 ⊗ MAP P114, B4

Unshaven graphic designers roll cigarettes at little outdoor tables in the bricky hollows of Surry Hills, while inside impassionedcaffeine fiends prepare their beloved brews, along with a tasty selection of cafe fare. Something of a trendsetter a few years back, this place still does coffee as good as anywhere in Sydney. The hole-in-the-wall alongside does takeaways. (Single Origin Roasters; ⊘02-9211 0665; www.singleo. com.au; 60-64 Reservoir St, Surry Hills; mains $14-23; ⊘6.30am-4pm Mon-Fri, 7.30am-3pm Sat, 8am-3pm Sun; ⊚⊚; ⊚Central)

Bodega TAPAS $$

18 ⊗ MAP P114, B5

The coolest progeny of Sydney's tapas explosion, Bodega has a casual vibe, good-lookin' staff and a funky matador mural. Dishes vary widely in size and price and are very loosely rooted in Central American and Spanish cuisine. Wash 'em down with Spanish and South American wine, sherry, port or beer, and plenty of Latin gusto. (⊘02-9212 7766; www.bodegatapas. com; 216 Commonwealth St, Surry Hills; tapas $12-24, share plates $20-32; ⊘noon-2pm Fri, 6-10pm Tue-Sat; ⊚; ⊚Central)

Chaco JAPANESE $$

19 ⊗ MAP P114, D3

This little place has a simple, effortless Japanese cool and some seriously good food. The ramen are good, and there are very succulent gyoza and delicious meatball sticks to dip in egg. The yakitori skewers are available

Tuesday to Saturday nights and are a highlight, bursting with flavour. (📞02-9007 8352; www. chacobar.com.au; 238 Crown St, Darlinghurst; skewers $4-9; ⏱ramen 5.30-9pm Mon, 11.30am-2.30pm Wed-Sun, yakitori 5.30-10pm Tue-Sat; 🚉Museum)

Dead Ringer
TAPAS $$

20 ⊗ MAP P114, D4

This charcoal-fronted terrace is a haven of quality eating and drinking in a laid-back format. Barstool it or grab an outdoor table and graze on the short menu that changes slightly daily and runs from bar snacks through tapas to mains. Though well-presented, the food's all about flavour combinations rather than airy artistry. There's always something interesting by the glass to accompany. (📞02-9331 3560; http://deadringer.wtf; 413 Bourke St, Surry Hills; dishes $18-37; ⏱4-11pm Mon-Thu, 4pm-midnight Fri, 11am-midnight Sat, 11am-11pm Sun; 🛜🖊; 🚌333, 380, 440)

Devon
CAFE $

21 ⊗ MAP P114, A6

If it's boring old bacon and eggs you're after, look elsewhere. Devon energetically fuses the cuisines of multicultural Australia to deliver an extremely creative menu, with plenty of twists on old favourites and things like pork belly and miso salmon popping up on the menu. It doesn't look like much from the street, but has

a pleasant back courtyard area. (📞02-9211 8777; www.devoncafe. com.au; 76 Devonshire St, Surry Hills; dishes $14-24; ⏱7am-3.30pm Mon-Fri, 8am-3.30pm Sat & Sun; 🛜; 🚉Central)

Firedoor
GRILL $$$

22 ⊗ MAP P114, B4

All the dishes in this moodily attractive sunken space are produced over a blazing fire, chef Lennox Hastie matching different woods to the flavours of meat, seafood and vegetables to create extraordinary dishes with huge depth of flavour. (📞02-8204 0800; www.firedoor.com.au; 33 Mary St, Surry Hills; mains $25-67, degustation $90; ⏱5.30-11pm Tue, Wed & Sat, noon-3pm & 5.30-11pm Thu & Fri; 🚉Central)

Nomad
MEDITERRANEAN $$$

23 ⊗ MAP P114, B3

Though this large open space has a modern industrial look, the cuisine takes its inspiration from more traditional vectors. Excellent share options apply old-school techniques like pickling and marinating to a range of ingredients, creating Mediterranean masterpieces with soul. The all-Australian wine list is short but has some super smallvineyard gems on it.. (📞02-9280 3395; www. nomadwine.com.au; 16 Foster St, Surry Hills; share plates $25-48; ⏱noon-2.30pm & 5.30-10pm Mon-Sat; 🚉Central)

Love, Tilly Devine

Red Lantern on Riley

VIETNAMESE $$$

24 MAP P114, D1

This atmospheric eatery is run by TV presenters Luke Nguyen and Mark Jensen and sister/wife author Pauline Nguyen. It serves modern takes on classic Vietnamese dishes. (📞02-9698 4355; www.redlantern.com.au; 60 Riley St, Darlinghurst; mains $38-45; ⏰6-10pm Sun-Thu, noon-3pm & 6-11pm Fri, 6-11pm Sat; 🖼; 🚇Museum)

Drinking

Love, Tilly Devine

WINE BAR

25 🍸 MAP P114, D1

This dark and good-looking split-level laneway bar is pretty compact, but the wine list certainly isn't. It's an extraordinary document, with some exceptionally well-chosen wines and a mission to get people away from their tried-and-tested favourites and explore. Take a friend and crack open a leisurely bottle of something. Italian deli bites and fuller plates are on hand too. (📞02-9326 9297; www.lovetillydevine.com; 91 Crown Lane, Darlinghurst; ⏰5pm-midnight Mon-Sat, to 10pm Sun; 🚇Museum)

Wild Rover

BAR

26 🍸 MAP P114, B3

Look for the unsigned wide door and enter this supremely cool brick-lined speakeasy, where a big range of craft beer is served in chrome steins and jungle animals peer benevolently from the green walls. The upstairs bar opens for trivia and live bands. (☑02-9280 2235; www.thewildrover.com.au; 75 Campbell St, Surry Hills; ☺4pm-midnight Mon-Sat; ☒Central)

Shakespeare Hotel PUB

27 ☺ MAP P114, B6

This is a classic Sydney pub (1879) with art-nouveau tiled walls, skuzzy carpet, the horses on the TV and cheap bar meals. There are plenty of cosy hidey-holes upstairs and a cast of local characters.

It's a proper convivial all-welcome place that's the antithesis of the more gentrified Surry Hills drinking establishments. (☑02-9319 6883; www.shakespearehotel. com.au; 200 Devonshire St, Surry Hills; ☺10am-midnight Mon-Sat, 11am-10pm Sun; ☒Surry Hills, ☒Central)

Vasco COCKTAIL BAR

28 ☺ MAP P114, C8

Like the much, much hipper and better-looking Italian cousin of a Hard Rock Cafe, Vasco serves beer, wine and rock-themed cocktails in a room lined with band photos and with a Dave Grohl guitar on the wall.

Order a plate of salumi or homemade gnocchi to snack on as you sip your creation, while Jagger pouts on the screen. (☑0406 775 436; www.vascobar.com; 421 Cleveland St, Redfern; ☺5pm-midnight Mon-Sat; ☎; ☒372)

Shady Pines Saloon BAR

29 ☺ MAP P114, D3

With no sign or street number on the door and entry via a shady back lane (look for the white door before Bikram Yoga on Foley St), this subterranean honky-tonk bar caters to the urban boho. Sip whisky and rye with the good ole hipster boys amid Western memorabilia and taxidermy. (www. shadypinessaloon.com; 4/256 Crown St, Darlinghurst; ☺4pm-midnight; ☒333, 380, ☒Museum)

Eau-de-Vie COCKTAIL BAR

30 ☺ MAP P114, E2

Take the door marked 'restrooms' at the back of the main bar at the **Kirketon Hotel** (☑02-9332 2011; www.kirketon.com.au; 229 Darlinghurst Rd, Darlinghurst; r $149-389; ☀❄☎; ☒Kings Cross) and enter this sophisticated, black-walled speak-easy, where a team of dedicated shirt-and-tie-wearing mixologists concoct the sort of beverages that win best-cocktail gongs. (☑0422 263 226; www.eaudevie.com.au; 229 Darlinghurst Rd, Darlinghurst; ☺6pm-1am Mon-Sat, to midnight Sun; ☎; ☒Kings Cross)

Beresford Hotel PUB

31 ☺ MAP P114, D5

The well-polished tiles of the facade and interior are a real fea-ture at this elegantly refurbished historic pub. It's a popular pre-club venue for an upmarket mixed crowd at weekends but makes for

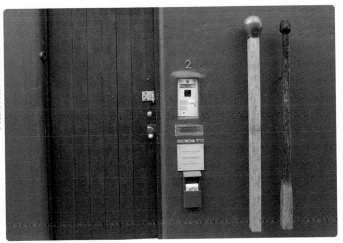

Brett Whiteley Studio (p116)

a quieter retreat midweek. The front bar is as handsome as they come; out the back is one of the area's best beer gardens, while upstairs is a schmick live-music and club space. (☎02-9114 7328; www.merivale.com.au/theberesfordhotel; 354 Bourke St, Surry Hills; ☺noon-midnight Mon-Thu, to 1am Fri-Sun; ☎; ☒374, 397, 399)

Local Taphouse   PUB

32 ☺ MAP P114, E5

Beer lovers can test their palates against the tasting notes as they work their way through dozens of craft beers at this angular old pub. There are around 20 on tap, rotating regularly, so there's always something new to try. There aren't any views but the little high-sided rooftop is a great spot to catch

the breeze. (☎02-9360 0088; www.taphousedarlo.com.au; 122 Flinders St, Darlinghurst; ☺noon-midnight Mon-Thu, to 1am Fri & Sat, to 11pm Sun; ☒396-399)

Winery   WINE BAR

33 ☺ MAP P114, C4

Beautifully situated back from the road in the leafy grounds of a historic water reservoir, this oasis serves dozens of wines by the glass to the swankier Surry Hills set. Sit for a while and you'll notice all kinds of kitsch touches lurking in the greenery: headless statues, upside-down parrots, iron koalas. It's a very fun, boisterous scene on weekend afternoons. (☎02-8322 2007; www.thewinerysurryhills.com.au; 285a Crown St, Surry Hills; ☺noon-midnight; ☎; ☒Central)

Palms on Oxford

LGBTIQ+, CLUB

34 MAP P114, D3

No one admits to coming here, but the lengthy queues prove they are lying. In this underground dance bar, the heyday of Stock Aitken Waterman never ended. It may be uncool, but if you don't scream when Kylie hits the turntables, you'll be the only one. Lots of fun and a friendly place. Entry is usually free; no open-toed shoes allowed. (📞02-9357 4166; 124 Oxford St, Darlinghurst; ⏰8pm-midnight Thu & Sun, to 3am Fri & Sat; 🚌333, 380)

Stonewall Hotel

LGBTIQ+, BAR

35 MAP P114, D3

Serving Sydney's LGBTIQ+ community for the past 23 years, Stonewall, in a good-looking building, has three levels of bars and dance floors. Cabaret, karaoke and quiz nights spice things up; there's something on every night of the week. Wednesday's Malebox nights are an inventive way to find a date. (📞02-9360 1963; www.stonewallhotel.com; 175 Oxford St, Darlinghurst; ⏰noon-4am; 🚌333,380)

Arq

LGBTIQ+, CLUB

36 MAP P114, D4

Situated just off Sydney's 'Golden Mile' of nightlife, this flash megaclub has everything; a cocktail bar, a recovery room, two dance floors with high-energy house, drag shows and a hyperactive smoke machine. (📞02-9380 8700; www.arqsydney.com.au; 16 Flinders St, Darlinghurst; ⏰9pm-3.30am Thu-Sun; 🚌333, 380)

Belvoir St Theatre

Entertainment

Golden Age Cinema & Bar

CINEMA

37 ⭐ MAP P114, B3

In what was once the Sydney HQ of Paramount pictures, a heart-warming small cinema has taken over the former screening room downstairs. It shows old favourites, art-house classics and a few recherché gems. There's a great small bar here too, with free gigs on Thursdays and Saturdays. All up, it's a fabulous place for a night out. (☏02-9211 1556; www.ourgolden age.com.au; 80 Commonwealth St, Surry Hills; adult/concession tickets $21/17; ☉4pm-midnight Tue-Fri 2.30pm-midnight Sat, 2.30-11pm Sun; ⊞Museum)

Belvoir St Theatre

THEATRE

38 ⭐ MAP P114, B7

In a quiet corner of Surry Hills, this intimate venue, with two small stages, is the home of an often-experimental and consistently excellent theatre company that specialises in quality Australian drama. It often commissions new works and is a vital cog in the Sydney theatre scene. (☏02-9699 3444; www.belvoir.com.au; 25 Belvoir St, Surry Hills; ⊞372, ⊞Surry Hills, ⊞Central)

Venue 505

LIVE MUSIC

39 ⭐ MAP P114, A8

Focusing on jazz, roots, reggae, funk, gypsy and Latin music, this small, relaxed venue is artist-run and thoughtfully programmed. The space features comfortable couches and murals by a local painter. It does pasta, pizza and share plates so you can munch along to the music. (☏0419 294 755, www.venue505.com; 280 Cleveland St, Surry Hills; ☉6pm-midnight Mon-Sat; ⊞372, ⊞Central)

Oxford Art Factory

LIVE MUSIC

40 ⭐ MAP P114, C2

Indie kids party against an arty backdrop at this two-room multipurpose venue modelled on Andy Warhol's NYC creative base. There's a gallery, a bar and a performance space that often hosts international acts and DJs. Check the website for what's on. (☏02-9332 3711; www.oxfordartfac tory.com; 38-46 Oxford St, Darling-hurst; ⊞Museum)

Shopping

Artery

ART

41 🔒 MAP P114, E2

Step into a world of mesmerising dots and swirls at this small gallery devoted to Aboriginal art. Artery's motto is 'ethical, contemporary, affordable', and while large canvases by established artists cost in the thousands, small, unstretched canvases start at around $35. There's also a good range of giftware as well as an offbeat sideline in preserved insects. (☏02-9380 8234; www.artery. com.au; 221 Darlinghurst Rd, Darling-hurst; ☉10am-5pm; ⊞Kings Cross)

Ariel
BOOKS

42 🔒 MAP P114, D3

This well-loved bookstore has moved down the road from Paddington. It's an eclectic, savvy place that's particularly good on art and design and is also a fine spot to pick up an offbeat gift for someone. (📞02-9332 4581; www.arielbooks.com.au; 98 Oxford St, Darlinghurst; ⊙9.30am-7pm Mon-Wed, 9.30am-8pm Thu & Fri, 10am-8pm Sat, 11am-6pm Sun; 🚌333, 380)

Route 66
CLOTHING, VINTAGE

43 🔒 MAP P114, C3

The name says it all. This store has been around for decades, furnishing Sydney with new and pre-owned jeans, cowboy boots

and other essential Americana. (📞02-9331 6686; www.route66.com.au; 255 Crown St, Darlinghurst; ⊙10.30am-6pm Mon-Wed, Fri & Sat, 10.30am-7.30pm Thu, noon-5pm Sun; 🚌330, 380, 🚆Museum)

Baby Likes to Pony
CLOTHING

44 🔒 MAP P114, E4

Stunning avant-garde lingerie, corsetry and accessories are on offer in this friendly store just off Oxford St where Darlinghurst blends into Paddington. (📞0488 766 966; www.babylikestopony.com; 319 South Dowling St, Darlinghurst; ⊙noon-6.30pm Mon-Wed, Fri & Sat, to 8pm Thu; 🚌333, 352, 380)

Title
BOOKS, MUSIC

45 🔒 MAP P114, C7

Focusing on distinct pop-cultural streams, seemingly determined at random (but probably at the owner's whim – very *High Fidelity*), this offbeat little store is well-stocked with glossy hardbacks (everything from rock photography to cookbooks), cult DVDs and an eclectic range of music on vinyl and CD. It's a browser's paradise. (📞02-9699 7333; www.titlemusicfilmbooks.com; 499 Crown St, Surry Hills; ⊙10am-6pm Mon-Sat, 11am-5pm Sun; 🚆Surry Hills, 🚆Central)

Sax Fetish
ADULT

46 🔒 MAP P114, D3

No, it's not a bar for jazz obsessives, but rather a sexy, dark-hearted shop selling high-

Route 66

FAIRFAX MEDIA VIA GETTY IMAGES ©

quality leather and rubber gear. All genders are catered for, and the 'accessories' range goes a little further than your standard belts and handbags (cufflinks and ties take on a whole new meaning here). (☑02-9331 6105; www.saxfetish.com; 110a Oxford St, Darlinghurst; ☺noon-6pm Sun & Mon, 11am-7pm Tue, Wed & Fri, 11am-8pm Thu, 11am-6pm Sat; ☐333, 380)

Robin Gibson Gallery

ART

47 🔒 MAP P114, E2

Housed in a beautiful three-storey terrace behind a lush stand of palm trees, this long-established gallery represents a coterie of Australian artists, and also stages the occasional exhibition by international superstars. (☑02-9331 6692; www.robingibson.net; 278 Liverpool St, Darlinghurst; ☺11am-6pm Tue-Sat; ☐Kings Cross)

Bookshop Darlinghurst

BOOKS

48 🔒 MAP P114, D4

This outstanding bookshop specialises in gay and lesbian tomes, with everything from queer crime and lesbian fiction to glossy pictorials and porn. A diverting browse, to say the least. (☑02-9331 1103; www.thebookshop.com.au; 207 Oxford

Robin Gibson Gallery

ANDREW HOLT/ALAMY STOCK PHOTO ©

St, Darlinghurst; ☺10am-7pm Mon-Sat, noon-6pm Sun; ☐333, 380)

Zoo Emporium

VINTAGE

49 🔒 MAP P114, D4

One of several vintage shops near the intersection of Crown and Campbell Streets, this has two floors of gloriously loud '70s and '80s apparel. The ground floor is mostly discounted items, including a bargain bin. (☑02-9380 5990; 180 Campbell St, Darlinghurst; ☺11am-6pm Mon-Wed, Fri & Sat, 11am-8pm Thu, noon-5pm Sun; ☐333, 380)

Explore ◈
Kings Cross & Potts Point

Traditionally Sydney's seedy red-light zone, the Cross has changed markedly in recent years. Lockout laws have killed the late-night bar life, and major building programs have accelerated gentrification in this so-close-to-the-city district. Adjoining the Cross, gracious, tree-lined Potts Point and Elizabeth Bay seem worlds away. Below by the water the old sailors' district of Woolloomooloo is a great spot for glitzy wharf restaurants and a handful of pubs of some character.

Kings Cross and its adjacent locales are ideal for exploring on foot; allocate half a day for the area to take in its quiet neighbourhood feel, but be sure to plan a revisit in the evening for the restaurant scene.

It makes sense to start around the Cross itself, at the top of William Street, and let gravity draw your wanders downwards.

Getting There & Around

🚊 Everywhere is within walking distance of Kings Cross train station.

🚌 Bus 311 hooks through Kings Cross, Potts Point, Elizabeth Bay and Woolloomooloo on its way from Railway Sq to the bottom of town. Buses 324 and 325 pass through Kings Cross (Bayswater Rd) en route between Walsh Bay, the City and Watsons Bay.

Kings Cross & Potts Point Map on p134

View over Woolloomooloo (p132) and Potts Point
OLGA KASHUBIN/SHUTTERSTOCK ©

Walking Tour 🥾

Wandering Around Woolloomooloo

Squeezed between the Domain and Kings Cross, Woolloomooloo (show us another word with eight Os!) is a suburb in transition. Once solidly working class, it still has some rough edges, but down by the water they're hard to spot. The navy base is still here, but drunken sailors are in short supply.

Walk Facts

Start Embarkation Park
Finish Old Fitzroy
Length 2.1km, 45 minutes

❶ Embarkation Park

This hidden **park** (Victoria St, Potts Point; ⓡ Kings Cross) on the roof of a navy car park is a prime spot for surveying Woolloomooloo beneath your feet. There are usually a couple Royal Australian Navy ships moored at the Garden Island base below.

❷ Descend McElhone Stairs

These stone **stairs** (Victoria St, Potts Point; ⓡ Kings Cross) were built in 1870 to connect spiffy Potts Point with the Woolloo-mooloo slums below. The steep steps run past an apartment block: residents sip tea on their balconies and stare bemusedly at the fitness freaks punishing themselves on the 113-stair uphill climb.

❸ Snack at Harry's Cafe de Wheels

Sure, it's a humble pie cart, but **Harry's** (Cowper Wharf Roadway, Woolloomooloo) is a tourist attraction nonetheless. Open since 1938 (except when founder Harry 'Tiger' Edwards was on active service), Harry's has served the good stuff to everyone from Pamela Anderson to Colonel Sanders.

❹ Woolloomooloo Wharf

A former wool and cargo dock, this beautiful Edwardian wharf (p135) faced oblivion for decades before a 2½-year demolition-workers' green ban on the site in the late 1980s saved it. It received a huge spruc-ing up in the late 1990s and has emerged as one of Sydney's most exclusive eating, drinking, sleeping and marina addresses.

❺ Space Out in Artspace

Artspace (p135) is spacey: its eternal quest is to fill the void with vigorous, engaging contemporary art. Things here are decidedly avant-garde – expect lots of con-ceptual pieces, audio visual installa-tions and new-media masterpieces.

❻ Pace Cathedral Street

Cathedral Street, the heart of Woolloomooloo, glows purple with jacarandas in November. Walk along the street to get a feel for the suburb and how it is chang-ing, with spiffy renovated terraces alongside social housing buildings.

❼ Settle in at the Old Fitzroy

Islington meets Melbourne in the back streets of Woolloomooloo: this totally unpretentious theatre pub (p139) is also a decent old-fashioned boozer in its own right.

For reviews see

⊙ Sights	p135
✗ Eating	p136
🖻 Drinking	p139
★ Entertainment	p141

Sights

Elizabeth Bay House

HISTORIC BUILDING

1 ◉ MAP P134, D3

Now dwarfed by 20th-century apartments, Colonial Secretary Alexander Macleay's elegant Greek Revival mansion was one of the finest houses in the colony when it was completed in 1839. The architectural highlight is an exquisite oval saloon with a curved and cantilevered staircase. There are lovely views over the harbour from the upstairs rooms. Drop down to the twin cellars for an introductory audiovisual with a weird beginning.

The grounds – a sort of botanical garden for Macleay, who collected plants from around the world – extended from the harbour all the way up the hill to Kings Cross. Traces remain, including a little **hidden grotto** reached by taking a path between 16 and 18 Onslow Ave. (☏02-9356 3022; www.sydneylivingmuseums.com.au; 7 Onslow Ave, Elizabeth Bay; adult/child $12/8; ⊙11am-4pm Fri-Sun; 🚌311, 🚆Kings Cross)

Woolloomooloo Wharf

HISTORIC BUILDING

2 ◉ MAP P134, A2

A former wool and cargo dock, this beautiful Edwardian wharf faced oblivion for decades before a 2½-year demolition-workers' green ban on the site in the late 1980s saved it. It received a huge sprucing up in the late 1990s and has emerged as one of Sydney's most exclusive eating, sleeping and marina addresses.

It's still a public space, so feel free to explore the innards, past industrial conveyor-belt relics and a **hotel** (☏02-9331 9000; www.ovolohotels.com.au; 6 Cowper Wharf Rdwy; r $400-700; 🅿➡❄@🛜🏊). Along the way the wharf's history is etched into glass walls. You might even squeeze in some star-spotting – everyman-megastar Russell Crowe is one of several personalities to have a plush pad here. (Finger Wharf; Cowper Wharf Roadway, Woolloomooloo; 🚌311, 🚆Kings Cross)

Artspace

GALLERY

3 ◉ MAP P134, A3

Artspace is spacey: its eternal quest is to fill the void with vigorous, engaging Australian and international contemporary art. Things here are decidedly avant-garde – expect lots of conceptual art, audio-visual installations and new-media pieces. It's an admirable attempt to liven things up in Sydney's art scene, experimenting with sometimes disturbing concepts. Disabled access is excellent. (☏02-9356 0555; www.artspace.org.au; 43-51 Cowper Wharf Rd, Woolloomooloo; admission free; ⊙11am-5pm Mon-Fri, to 6pm Sat & Sun; 🚌311, 🚆Kings Cross)

Coca-Cola Sign

LANDMARK

4 ◉ MAP P134, B6

A Sydney landmark, this huge sign marks the entrance to Kings Cross. You're actually looking at the 2016 model: the previous one was replaced, then auctioned off letter by letter for local homeless charity the Wayside Chapel. (Darlinghurst Rd, Kings Cross; Kings Cross)

Eating

Room 10

CAFE $

5 MAP P134, C4

With a real neighbourhood feel, this tiny cafe is the sort of place where staff know all the locals by name. The coffee is delicious and the menu limited to sandwiches, salads and such – tasty and uncomplicated. Watch them make it in front of you as you sit at impossibly tiny tables or do some people-watching on this lovable laneway. (0432 445 342; www.facebook.com/room10espresso; 10 Llankelly Pl, Kings Cross; mains $8-14; 7am-4pm Mon-Fri, 8am-4pm Sat & Sun; ; Kings Cross)

What's in a Name?

Where exactly is Kings Cross? Although technically it's just the intersection of William and Victoria Sts, in reality it's more of a mindset than an exact geographical place. Much of what most people call Kings Cross falls within the suburb of Potts Point; businesses tend to use a Potts Point address if they want to sound classy and Kings Cross if they want to emphasise their party cred. Either way, you'll know Kings Cross when you see it.

Douce France

CAFE $

6 MAP P134, C5

Locals love the croissants at this welcoming cafe on the main strip through the Cross. Other tempting patisserie options and pleasing coffee make this a top stop. Grab an outdoor table to watch the Cross characters parade past. (www.facebook.com/coffeefrench DouceFrance; 7 Darlinghurst Rd, Kings Cross; breakfasts $6-14; 7am-7pm Mon-Fri, 8am-5.30pm Sat & Sun; ; 311, Kings Cross)

Harry's Cafe de Wheels

FAST FOOD $

7 MAP P134, B3

Open since 1938 (except for a few years when founder Harry 'Tiger' Edwards was on active service), Harry's has been serving meat pies to everyone from Pamela Anderson to Frank Sinatra and Colonel Sanders. You can't leave without trying a 'Tiger': a hot meat pie with sloppy peas, mashed potato, gravy and tomato sauce. (02-9357 3074; www.harryscafedewheels.com.au; Cowper Wharf Roadway, Woolloomooloo; pies $5-8; 8.30am-2am Mon & Tue, to 3am Wed & Thu, to 4am Fri, 9am-4am Sat, 9am-1am Sun; 311, Kings Cross)

Piccolo Bar

CAFE $

8 MAP P134, C5

A surviving slice of the old bohemian Cross, this tiny cafe hasn't changed much in over 60 years. The walls are covered in movie-star memorabilia, and its latest owners are faithful to the unique atmosphere created by locally legendary former owner Vittorio, who still drops by for a chat. (☎02-9368 1356; www.facebook.com/piccolobarcafe; 6 Roslyn St, Kings Cross; light meals $5-10; ☻6am-midnight Wed-Fri, 7am-midnight Sat & Sun; ☎; ☒Kings Cross)

Cho Cho San   JAPANESE $$

9 ☒ MAP P134, C3

Glide through the shiny brass sliding door and take a seat at the communal table that runs the length of this stylish Japanese restaurant, all polished concrete and blond wood. The food is just as artful as the surrounds, with tasty izakaya-style bites emanating from both the raw bar and the hibachi grill. There's a good sake selection, too. (☎02-9331 6601; www.chochosan.com.au; 73 Macleay St, Potts Point; mains $22-38; ☻5.30-11pm Mon-Thu, noon-11pm Fri-Sun; ☒311, ☒Kings Cross)

Farmhouse   MODERN AUSTRALIAN $$

10 ☒ MAP P134, C6

Occupying a space between restaurant and supper club, this narrow sliver of a place has a tiny kitchen and a charming host. Diners sit at one long table and eat a set menu that features uncomplicated, delicious dishes from high-quality produce. There are good wines and a buzzy, fun atmosphere. Prebooking is essential. (☎0448 413 791; www.farmhousekingscross.com.au; 4/40 Bayswater Rd, Kings Cross; set menu $60; ☻sittings 6.30pm & 8.30pm Wed-Sat, 2pm & 6.30pm Sun; ☒Kings Cross)

Fratelli Paradiso   ITALIAN $$

11 ☒ MAP P134, C2

This underlit trattoria has them queuing at the door (especially on weekends). The intimate room showcases seasonal Italian dishes cooked with Mediterranean zing. Lots of busy black-clad waiters, lots of Italian chatter, lots of oversized sunglasses. No bookings. (☎02-9357 1744; www.fratelliparadiso.com; 12-16 Challis Ave, Potts Point; breakfast $12-17, mains $25-39; ☻7am-11pm Mon-Sat, to 10pm Sun; ☒311, ☒Kings Cross)

Fish Shop   SEAFOOD $$

12 ☒ MAP P134, C2

Decked out in bright Hamptons style, this brings a coastal breeze to Challis Ave with casual but high-quality fish dishes served all day, and some nice wines to accompany them. It's also great for a quick snack – some oysters or a fish burger – and a glass of something. (☎02-9114 7340; www.merivale.com.au/thefishshop; 22 Challis Ave, Potts Point; mains $28-38; ☻noon-10pm Mon-Fri, to 11pm Sat, to 9pm Sun; ☒311, ☒Kings Cross)

Butler   LATIN AMERICAN $$

13 ☒ MAP P134, B4

There's a real wow factor to the verdant back terrace of this Potts Point bar-restaurant, with its spectacular city skyline views. The breezy vibe and furniture make it a prime spot to get stuck into share plates that take influences from across the Caribbean and Latin America. (📞02-8354 0742; www.butlersydney.com.au; 123 Victoria St, Potts Point; large share plates $30-36; ⏱4-11pm Mon, noon-midnight Tue-Sat, noon-10pm Sun; 🛜; 🚇Kings Cross)

Chester White ITALIAN $$

14 MAP P134, B4

Calling itself a 'cured diner', this diminutive corner eatery, named after a breed of pig, serves nine different kinds of cured meats, a large variety of pickled vegetables and a few simple mains (pasta and the like). Grab a chrome stool by the kitchen/bar, sip on an Italian wine and watch the hipster lads slicing and dicing away. (📞02-9332 3692; www.chesterwhitediner.com.au; 3 Orwell St, Kings Cross; dishes $14-23;

Old Fitzroy Hotel

⏱5-11pm Tue-Thu, noon-11pm Fri & Sat; 🚇Kings Cross)

Apollo GREEK $$

15 MAP P134, C4

An excellent exemplar of modern Greek cooking, this taverna has stylish and fashionable decor, a well-priced menu of share plates and a bustling vibe. Starters are particularly impressive, especially the pitta bread hot from the oven, the fried saganaki cheese with honey and oregano, and the wildweed and cheese pie. (📞02-8354 0888; www.theapollo.com.au; 44 Macleay St, Elizabeth Bay; mains $26-38; ⏱6-11pm Mon-Thu, noon-11pm Fri & Sat, noon-9.30pm Sun; 🚌311, 🚇Kings Cross)

Ms G's ASIAN $$

16 MAP P134, B4

Offering a cheeky, irreverent take on Asian cooking (hence the name – geddit?), Ms G's is nothing if not an experience. It can be loud, frantic and painfully hip, but the adventurous combinations of pan-Asian and European flavours have certainly got some spark. (📞02-9114 7342; www.merivale.com/msgs; 155 Victoria St, Potts Point; mains $22-36; ⏱6-11pm Mon-Thu, noon-3pm & 6-11pm Fri & Sat, 1-9pm Sun; 🛜; 🚇Kings Cross)

Yellow VEGETARIAN $$$

17 MAP P134, C2

This sunflower-yellow former artists' residence is now a top-notch contemporary vegetarian restaurant. Dishes are prepared with real panache, and excellent flavour combinations are present throughout. The tasting menus, which can be vegan, take the Sydney meat-free scene to new levels and the service is not too formal. Weekend brunch is also a highlight, as is the wine list. (📞02-9332 2344; www.yellowsydney. com.au; 57 Macleay St, Potts Point; 5-/7-course degustation menu $75/95; ⏱6-11pm Mon-Fri, 11am-3pm & 6-11pm Sat & Sun; 🗲; 🚌311, 🚊Kings Cross)

China Doll ASIAN $$$

18 MAP P134, A2

Gaze over the Woolloomooloo marina and city skyline as you tuck into deliciously inventive dishes drawing inspiration from all over Asia. The setting on the finger wharf is memorable, but the food keeps up, with delicious textures and flavour combinations. Plates are designed to be shared; there are also a few dim-sum-style options. (📞02-9380 6744; www.chinadoll.com. au; 4/6 Cowper Wharf Roadway, Woolloomooloo; mains $36-46; ⏱noon-3pm & 6-10.30pm; 🚌311, 🚊Kings Cross)

Otto Ristorante ITALIAN $$$

19 MAP P134, A2

Forget the glamorous waterfront location and the A-list crowd – Otto will be remembered for single-handedly dragging Sydney's Italian cooking into the new century with dishes such as artisan *strozzapreti* pasta with fresh Yamba prawns, tomato, chilli and black olives. Its opening hours

mean you can often grab a table here on spec mid-afternoon, but booking at meal times is essential. (📞02-9368 7488; www.ottoristorante. com.au; 8/6 Cowper Wharf Rdwy, Woolloomooloo; mains $43-56; ⏱noon-10pm; 🚌311, 🚊Kings Cross)

Aki's INDIAN $$$

20 MAP P134, A2

The first cab off the rank as you walk onto Woolloomooloo's wharf is Aki's. This is beautifully presented, intuitively constructed high-Indian cuisine, supplemented by a six-page wine list showcasing local and international drops. And the setting, of course, is just marvellous. (📞02-9332 4600; www.akisindian. com.au; 1/6 Cowper Wharf Roadway, Woolloomooloo; mains $32-34; ⏱noon-3pm & 6-10.30pm Sun-Fri, 6-10.30pm Sat; 🗲; 🚌311, 🚊Kings Cross)

Drinking

Old Fitzroy Hotel PUB

21 MAP P134, A5

A gem hidden in the backstreets of Woolloomooloo, this totally unpretentious theatre (p141) is also a decent old-fashioned boozer in its own right, with a great variety of beers on tap and a convivial welcome. Prop up the bar, grab a seat at a streetside table or head upstairs to the bistro, pool table and couches. (📞02-9356 3848; www.oldfitzroy.com.au; 129 Dowling St, Woolloomooloo; ⏱11am-midnight Mon-Fri, noon-midnight Sat, 3-10pm Sun; 🛜; 🚊Kings Cross)

Monopole WINE BAR

22 MAP P134, C3

Dark and sexy, Monopole seduces with its stylish interior, complete with hanging strips of black sound-absorption material and discreet front screen. A fabulous wine list of Australian and international producers offers over 20 vintages by the glass or carafe, so an impromptu tasting session is easy. The food is great too, with house-cured charcuterie and intriguing cheeses a highlight. (☑02-9360 4410; www.monopolesydney.com.au; 71a Macleay St, Potts Point; ☺5pm-midnight Mon-Fri, noon-midnight Sat, noon-10pm Sun; ☜; ☐311, ☒Kings Cross)

Roosevelt COCKTAIL BAR

23 MAP P134, C4

The low-lit seductive glamour of this sleek and stylish cocktail bar takes you right back to the '20s, though it's named for a local postwar gangster's haunt. They take their cocktails seriously here,

Party's Over

Formerly Sydney's premier party precinct, this neighbourhood has had much of the life sucked out of it by the central Sydney licensing laws introduced in 2014. Most of the late-night clubs have closed, though a couple are still going. On the upside, the streets look less like a war zone in the wee hours.

making them in front of you with great panache – and they are seriously good. (☑0423 203 119; www.theroosevelt.com.au; 32 Orwell St, Kings Cross; ☺5pm-midnight Mon-Fri, noon-midnight Sat, 3-10pm Sun; ☜; ☐311, ☒Kings Cross)

Kings Cross Hotel PUB

24 MAP P134, B6

This grand old brick building guards the entrance to the Cross and is one of the area's best pubs, with several levels of boozy entertainment. The balcony bar is a very pleasant spot for lunch, while the rooftop that opens weekend evenings has the drawcard vistas. Saturdays are good, with DJs on all levels. (☑02-9331 9900; www.kingscrosshotel.com.au; 244-248 William St, Kings Cross; ☺10am-1am Mon-Thu, to 3.30am Fri & Sat, to midnight Sun; ☜; ☒Kings Cross)

Tilbury PUB

25 MAP P134, A3

Once the dank domain of burly sailors and salty ne'er-do-wells, the Tilbury now sparkles. An upmarket crowd of Potts Pointers and yachties populate the light, bright interiors, sipping G&Ts and glasses of imported wine. The restaurant does top-notch contemporary fare; the seats out the front, in the upstairs bar and in the gin garden are particularly popular on lazy Sunday afternoons. (☑02-9368 1955; www.tilburyhotel.com.au; 12-18 Nicholson St, Woolloomooloo; ☺11am-10pm Mon-Wed, 11am-midnight Thu & Fri,

10am-midnight Sat, 10am-10pm Sun; 🛜; 🚌 311, 🚇 Kings Cross)

Candy's Apartment CLUB

26 🚇 MAP P134, C6

It's dark and very sweaty in this subterranean venue with two bars, a dance floor with DJs spinning house and other electronica, and a space for bands to play. They pack 'em in and you'll find plenty of guys and gals scanning the crowd hoping they won't go home alone. (📞 02-9380 5600; www.candys.com.au; 22 Bayswater Rd, Kings Cross; ⏲8pm-4am Fri & Sat; 🚇 Kings Cross)

East Sydney Hotel PUB

27 🚇 MAP P134, A5

Not a poker machine is in sight at this beautiful traditional corner boozer in a quiet area of Woolloomooloo. Open since 1856, it's a place of great character, perfect for sipping a quiet schooner of beer while reading the paper. Uncomplicated pub grub is also available. (📞02-9358 1975; www.eastsydneyhotel.com; cnr Crown & Cathedral Sts, Woolloomooloo; ⏲11.30am-midnight Sun-Tue, to 1am Wed & Thu, to 3am Fri & Sat; 🛜; 🚌 311, 🚇 St James)

Entertainment

Old Fitz Theatre THEATRE

Is it a pub? A theatre? A bistro? Actually, it's all three. Grassroots company Red Line Productions stages loads of new Australian plays at this likeable venue (see 21 🚇 Map

Coca-Cola Sign (p135)

ALIZADA STUDIOS/SHUTTERSTOCK ©

p134, A5) in a quiet Woolloomooloo street. (📞0416 044 413; www.redline-productions.com.au; 129 Dowling St, Woolloomooloo; $25-48; 🚇 Kings Cross)

Happy Endings Comedy Club COMEDY

28 ⭐ MAP P134, B6

Between 1955 and 1969 this was the city's premier finger-snappin', beret-wearing boho cellar bar, hosting performances by Frank Sinatra and Sarah Vaughan. Those heady days are long gone but good-quality stand-up comedy keeps this intimate venue buzzing. Book ahead for discounted admission. (El Rocco Room; 📞02-9130 5150; www.happyendingscomedyclub.com.au; 154 Brougham St, Potts Point; $27.50; ⏲shows 8.30pm Fri & Sat; 🚇 Kings Cross)

Explore ⊗

Bondi to Coogee

Sydney sheds its suit and tie, ditches the strappy heels and chills out in the eastern suburbs. Beach after golden-sand beach, alternating with sheer sandstone cliffs, are the classic vistas of this beautiful, laid-back and egalitarian stretch of the city.

Improbably good-looking arcs of sand framed by jagged cliffs, the eastern beaches are a big part of the Sydney experience. Most famous of all is the broad sweep of Bondi Beach, where Sydney comes to see and be seen. South of Bondi, Bronte is a steep-sided beach 'burb, its bowl-shaped park strewn with picnic tables and barbecues. Further south is the concrete-fringed, safe-swimming inlet of Clovelly: a great place to dust off your snorkel. Next stop, heading south, is Coogee, with a wide, handsome beach and lively backpacker and local scene in the pubs and shops.

Getting There & Away

🚆 The Eastern Suburbs train line heads to Bondi Junction, which is 2.5km from Bondi Beach, 3km from Bronte Beach and 4km from Coogee Beach.

🚌 For Bondi, take bus 333 (express) or 380 from Circular Quay via Oxford St. For Coogee, take bus M50, 373 or 372 among others. It's quicker to get a bus from Bondi Junction station.

Bondi to Coogee Map on p148

Top Experience 📷
Ride the Waves at Bondi Beach

Definitively Sydney, Bondi is one of the world's great beaches: ocean and land collide, the Pacific arrives in great foaming swells and all people are equal, as democratic as sand. It's the closest ocean beach to the city centre (8km away), has consistently good (though crowded) waves, and is great for a rough-and-tumble swim.

◉ MAP P148, E2

Campbell Pde, Bondi

🚌 333, 380-2

Surf's Up

Two surf clubs patrol the beach between sets of red-and-yellow flags, positioned to avoid the worst rips and holes. Thousands of unfortunates have to be rescued from the surf each year, so don't become a statistic – swim between the flags. Surfers carve up sandbar breaks at either end of the beach; it's a good place for learners too.

Icebergs Pool

This famous saltwater **pool** (☏02-9130 4804; www.icebergs.com.au; 1 Notts Ave; adult/child $7/5; ◷6am-6.30pm Mon-Wed & Fri, from 6.30am Sat & Sun), regularly doused by the breakers, commands the best view in Bondi and has a cute cafe (p153). There's a more sheltered pool for kids. It closes on Thursdays so they can clean the seaweed out.

The Pavilion

Built in a blended Mediterranean/Georgian Revival style in 1929, 'The Pav' is more a cultural centre than a changing shed, although it does have changing rooms, showers and lockers (small/large $4/6). There's a free art gallery upstairs, a theatre out the back, and various cafes and a bar lining the ocean frontage, including the extremely popular Bucket List (p156). Redevelopment plans had been put on hold at time of research.

Other Features

In summer there's an outdoor cinema (p157) behind the beach while at the southern end is a skate park. There's an outdoor workout area at the northern end, plus a park with barbecues. Alcohol is banned throughout.

★ Top Tips

o Swim between the red-and-yellow flags, which indicate areas patrolled by lifeguards.

o If the sea's angry or you have small children in tow, try the saltwater sea baths at either end of the beach.

o Surfers carve up sandbar breaks at either end of the beach; there's a **skate ramp** (Queen Elizabeth Dr; 🚌333, 380-2) at the beach's southern tip.

o At the beach's northern end there's a grassy spot with coin-operated barbecues. Note that booze is banned on the beach.

✕ Take a Break

Once you've had your fill of the surf, head to the North Bondi RSL (p156) at the northern end of the beach.

Or at the trendier southern end, hit the Crabbe Hole cafe (p153) by the Icebergs pool.

Walking Tour 🥾

Bondi to Coogee

Arguably Sydney's most famous, most popular and best walk, this coastal path shouldn't be missed. Both ends are well connected to bus routes, as are most points in between should you feel too hot and bothered to continue – although a cooling dip at any of the beaches en route should cure that (pack your swimmers). There's little shade on this track, so make sure you dive into a tub of sunscreen before setting out.

Walk Facts

Start Bondi Beach
End Coogee Beach
Length 6km; three hours

❶ Bondi Beach

Starting at iconic Bondi Beach (p144), take the stairs up the south end to Notts Ave, passing above the glistening Icebergs pool complex. Step onto the clifftop trail at the end of Notts Ave. Walking south, the windswept sandstone cliffs and boisterous Pacific Ocean couldn't be more spectacular (watch for dolphins, whales and surfers).

❷ Tamarama Beach

Small but perfectly formed Tamarama (p150) has a deep reach of sand that is totally disproportionate to its width.

❸ Bronte Beach

Descend from the cliff tops onto Bronte Beach (p150). Take a dip, lay out a picnic under the Norfolk Island pines or head to a cafe for a caffeine hit. After your break, pick up the path on the southern side of the beach.

❹ Waverley Cemetery

Some famous Australians are among the subterranean denizens of the amazing cliff-edge Waverley Cemetery (p150). On a clear winter's day this is a prime vantage point for whale-watchers.

❺ Clovelly Beach

Pass the locals enjoying a beer or a game of lawn bowls at the Clovelly Bowling Club, then breeze past the cockatoos and canoodling lovers in Burrows Park to sheltered Clovelly Beach (p150).

❻ Gordons Bay

Follow the footpath up through the car park, along Cliffbrook Pde, then down the steps to the upturned dinghies lining Gordons Bay, one of Sydney's best shore-dive spots.

❼ Dolphin Point

The trail continues past **Dolphin Point** (Baden St, Coogee; 🚌 313-14, 353, 370•4), which offers great ocean views and the Giles Baths ocean pool (p151). A sobering shrine commemorates the 2002 Bali bombings that killed many locals. The park's name was changed to honour the six members of the Coogee Dolphins rugby league team who died in the blast.

❽ Coogee Beach

The trail then lands you smack-bang on glorious Coogee Beach (p150). Swagger into the Coogee Bay Hotel (p156) and toast your efforts with a cold beverage.

Bondi to Coogee

Cooper Park

Bellevue Rd

Bellevue Park

Birriga Rd

Edgecliff Rd

Syd Einfeld Dr

Old South Head Rd

BONDI JUNCTION

Paul St

Council St

Bronte Rd

Birrell St

Carrington Rd

Queens Park

Darley Rd

Gipps St

Gardyne St

Brae St

Bronte Rd

BRONTE

Bronte Rd

Bronte Park

Palmerston Ave

Hewlett St

Murray St

WAVERLEY

Henrietta St

Wiley St

Waverley Park

Park Pde

King St

Stephen St

Ewell St

Birrell St

Watson St

Avoca St

Belgrave St

Read St

Alfred St

Bronte St

Bayview St

Hewlett St

Tamarama Beach

Tamarama Bay

Bronte Beach

Marks Park

Mackenzies Bay

Gerroch Ave

TAMARAMA

Tamarama Park

Glen St

Dudley St

Wilga St

Hunter Park

BONDI

Bondi Rd

Wellington St N

Ocean St N

Penkivil St

Martins Ave

Anglesea St

Bondi Rd

Francis St

Edward St

Lamrock Ave

Curlewis St

Hall St

O'Brien St

Roscoe St

Wellington St

Hall St

Glenayr Ave

Beach Rd

Gould St

Warners Ave

Blair St

Wairoa Ave

Wallis Pde

Hastings Pde

Brighton Blvd

Ramsgate Ave

Military Rd

Bondi Golf Club

Bay St

Ben Buckler Point

Bondi Bay

Bondi Beach

Campbell Pde

BONDI BEACH

12
22
18
25
26
29
9
7
8
15
21
30
28
27
11
16
20
17
1
2

Bondi to Coogee

SOUTH PACIFIC OCEAN

500 m
0.25 miles

Macpherson St
Trafalgar St
St Thomas St
St Thomas St
Keith St
Waverley Cemetery
Clga R=serve
Boundary St
Ocean St
Barrows Park
Shark Point

Winchester Rd
Clifton Rd
Burnie St
Eastbourne Ave
Melrose Pde
Clovelly Beach
Gordons Bay

CLOVELLY
Kent St
Varna St
Varna Park
Greville St
Clovelly Rd
Battery St
Bundock Park
Arcadia St
Dunningham Reserve
Dolphin Point

Fern St
Douglas Rd
Carrington Rd
Hooper St
Marcel Ave
Division St
Brook St
COOGEE
Arden St
Baden St
Coogee Bay
Coogee Beach

Alison Rd
Coogee Bay Rd
Bream St
Dolphin St
Coogee Oval
Arden St
Mount St
Melody St
Byron St
Mount St
Carr St
Brook St

Sights

Tamarama Beach

BEACH

1 MAP P148, D4

Surrounded by high cliffs, Tamarama has a deep tongue of sand with just 80m of shoreline. Diminutive, yes, but ever-present rips make Tamarama the most dangerous patrolled beach in New South Wales; it's often closed to swimmers. Make sure you pay attention to the lifesavers. It's hard to picture now, but between 1887 and 1911 a rollercoaster looped out over the water as part of an amusement park. (Pacific Ave, Tamarama; 361)

Bronte Beach

BEACH

2 MAP P148, C4

A winning family-oriented beach hemmed in by sandstone cliffs and a grassy park, Bronte lays claims to the title of the oldest surf lifesaving club in the world (1903). Contrary to popular belief, the beach is named after Lord Nelson, who doubled as the Duke of Bronte (a place in Sicily), and not the famous literary sorority. There's a kiosk and a changing room attached to the surf club, and covered picnic tables near the public barbecues. (Bronte Rd, Bronte; 379)

Waverley Cemetery

CEMETERY

3 MAP P148, C5

Many Sydneysiders would die for these views...and that's the only way they're going to get them. Blanketing the clifftops between Bronte and Clovelly beaches, the white marble gravestones here are dazzling in the sunlight. Eighty thousand people have been interred here since 1877, including writers Henry Lawson and Dorothea Mackellar, and cricketer Victor Trumper. It's an engrossing (and surprisingly uncreepy) place to explore, and maybe to spot a whale offshore during winter. The Bondi to Coogee coastal walk (p146) heads past it. (02-9083 8899; www.waverleycemetery.com; St Thomas St, Bronte; 7am-5pm May-Sep, to 7pm Oct-Apr; 360, 379)

Clovelly Beach

BEACH

4 MAP P148, C6

It might seem odd, but this concrete-edged ocean channel is a great place to swim, sunbathe and snorkel. It's safe for the kids, and despite the swell surging into the inlet, underwater visibility is great. Bring your goggles, but don't go killing anything...a beloved friendly grouper fish lived here for many years until he was speared by a tourist. (Clovelly Rd, Clovelly; 338-9)

Coogee Beach

BEACH

5 MAP P148, B8

Bondi without the glitz and the posers, Coogee (locals pronounce the 'oo' as in the word 'took') has a deep sweep of sand, historic ocean baths and plenty of green space for barbecues and Frisbee hurling. There are lockers and showers here. Between the world wars, Coogee had an English-style pier, with a 1400-seat theatre and a 600-seat ballroom...until the surf took it.

At Coogee Beach's northern end, below Dolphin Point, **Giles Baths** is what's known as a 'bogey hole' – a semiformal rock pool open to the surging surf. At the beach's southern end, **Ross Jones Memorial Pool** has sandcastle-like concrete turrets. Both have free admission.

A short walk beyond the beach are the sea pools known as **McIver's** (Beach St; $2; ☼sunrise-sunset; 🚌352, 372-7) and **Wylie's** (📞02-9665 2838; www.wylies.com.au; 4b Neptune St; adult/child $5/2.50;

☼7am-7pm Oct-Mar, to 5pm Apr-Sep; 🚌353, 376-7).

Offshore, compromising the surf here a little, is craggy Wedding Cake Island, immortalised in a surf-guitar instrumental by Midnight Oil. (Arden St, Coogee; www.randwick.nsw.gov.au; 🚌313-14, 353, 370-4)

Mahon Pool
SWIMMING

6 👁 MAP P148, B8

Hidden within the cliffs, 500m north of Maroubra Beach, Mahon Pool is an idyllic rock pool where the surf crashes over the edges at high tide. It's quite possibly Sydney's most beautiful bogey hole (sea bath). (www.randwick.nsw.gov.au; Marine Pde, Maroubra; admission free; 🚌353, 376-77)

Beach Culture

In the mid-1990s an enthusiastic businesswoman obtained a concession to rent loungers on Tamarama Beach and offer waiter service. Needless to say, it didn't last long. Even at what was considered at the time to be Sydney's most glamorous beach, nobody was interested in that kind of malarkey.

For Australians, going to the beach is all about rolling out a towel on the sand with a minimum of fuss. And they're certainly not prepared to pay for the privilege. Sandy-toed ice-cream vendors are acceptable; martini luggers are not. In summer one of the more unusual sights is the little coffee and ice-cream boat pulling up to Lady Bay (and other harbour beaches) and a polite queue of nude gentlemen forming to purchase their icy poles.

Surf lifesavers have a hallowed place in the culture and you'd do well to heed their instructions, not least of all because they're likely to be in your best interest. They're an Australian institution.

Waverley Cemetery (p150)

RUBEN MARTINEZ BARRICARTE/SHUTTERSTOCK ©

Eating

Lox Stock & Barrel

JEWISH, CAFE $$

7 MAP P148, D1

Stare down the barrel of a smoking hot bagel and ask yourself one question: Wagyu corned-beef Reuben, or homemade pastrami and Russian coleslaw?

In the evening the menu sets its sights on steak, lamb shoulder and slow-roasted eggplant. It's always busy, even on a wet Monday. (☑02-9300 0368; www.loxstockandbarrel.com.au; 140 Glenayr Ave, Bondi Beach; breakfast & lunch dishes $10-22, dinner $18-29; ☺7am-3.30pm daily plus 6-10pm Wed & Thu, to 11pm Fri & Sat; 🛜🖉🚻; 🚍379)

Funky Pies

VEGAN, BAKERY $

8 MAP P148, D1

Taking the meat out of a meat pie would be considered un-Australian in some quarters but this tiny place does a great job of it. Really tasty vegan combinations can be accompanied by huge smoothies; grab one of the two outdoor tables or take away to the beach. The place has a social conscience too, supporting several charities. (☑0451 944 404; www.funkypies.com.au; 144 Glenayr Ave, Bondi Beach; pies $6.50; ☺8.30am-8.30pm Mon-Fri, from 10am Sat & Sun; 🖉; 🚍379)

Bonditony's Burger Joint

BURGERS $

The squelch comes oozing out as you bite down on one of these sinfully tasty burgers from a rock 'n' roll–themed spot (see 9 Map p148, D1) a couple of blocks back from the beach. Prepare to wait a long time at weekends, as it's so popular. It's got a drinks licence though, so you can kick back with a beer while you do. (☑0410 893 003; www.bonditonysburgerjoint.com; 144 Glenayr Ave, Bondi Beach; burgers $15-17; ☺noon-10pm Mon-Fri, 11am-10pm Sat, 11am-9pm Sun; 🚻; 🚍379)

La Piadina

ITALIAN $

9 MAP P148, D1

A piadina is a filled flat bread common in northern Italy, and the Zizioli brothers are the only ones serving them in Sydney. Fillings include prosciutto, rocket, mozzarella and *nduja*, a spicy, spreadable Italian sausage. Have them for breakfast, lunch or dinner, but whatever you do, have them – they're delicious! (📞 02-9300 0160; www.lapiadina.com.au; 106 Glenayr Ave, Bondi Beach; mains $13-18; ⏰ 8am-5pm Mon, to 10pm Tue-Sun; 🚌 379)

Crabbe Hole
CAFE $

Tucked within the Icebergs pool complex (there's no need to pay admission if you're only eating), this crab-sized nook (see 18 🗺 Map p148, D3) is the kind of place locals would prefer we didn't let you know about. Toasted sandwiches, muesli, and banana bread star on the small but perfectly formed menu, coffees are automatic double shots unless you specify otherwise. The views are blissful. (📞 0450 272 223; www.facebook.com/thecrabbehole; Lower Level, 1 Notts Ave, Bondi Beach; breakfasts $8-15; ⏰ 7am-3pm Mon-Fri, to 5pm Sat & Sun; 🚌 333, 380-2)

Three Blue Ducks
CAFE $$

10 🗺 MAP P148, C5

These ducks are a fair waddle from the water at Bronte Beach, but that doesn't stop queues forming outside the graffiti-covered walls for weekend breakfasts across two seating areas. The adventurous chefs have a strong commitment to using local, organic and fair trade food whenever possible. It's part of a nice little eating strip. (📞 02-9389 0010; www.threeblueducks.com; 141-143 Macpherson St, Bronte; breakfasts $14-22, lunches $20-32, dinners $28-38; ⏰ 6.30am-2.30pm daily plus 6-11pm Wed-Sat; 🚌 379)

Trio
CAFE $$

11 🗺 MAP P148, D2

Brunch in Bondi has become de rigueur in Sydney in recent years, and this friendly, unpretentious cafe is one of the top spots to do it. The menu covers several global influences, from Mexican chilaquiles to Middle Eastern shakshouka via some Italian bruschetta. It's a great way to start a day by the sea. (📞 02-9365 6044; www.triocafe.com.au; 56 Campbell Pde, Bondi Beach; dishes $18-27; ⏰ 7am-3pm Mon-Fri, 7.30am-3.30pm Sat & Sun; 🚌 333, 380-2)

Bondi's Best
SEAFOOD $$

12 🗺 MAP P148, F1

In an appealing block of cafes close to the beach action but more peaceful, this little square place has more kitchen than customer space, but it's worth finding a spot for all-day fish 'n' chips as well as more elaborate fish and seafood, plus mealtime sushi and sashimi choices. It's all casual and tasty; there's a more restaurant-y outlet on Hall St in Bondi too. (📞 02-9300 9886; www.bondisbest.com.au; 39-53 Campbell Pde, North Bondi; meals $15-30; ⏰ noon-9pm; 🚻 🚌 333, 379, 380-2)

Cafe de France
FRENCH, CAFE $$

13 🗺 MAP P148, A8

An art nouveau building, posters of Paris, crêpes, croissants and croques monsieur...this friendly cafe is as French as South Coogee can get. There are breakfasts all day, as well as salads and classics such as steak frites for lunch. Dinners are memorable, with blackboard bistro specials like coq au vin. (📞02-9664 4005; www.cafedefrancecoogee.com.au; 19 Havelock Ave, Coogee; breakfast $11-17, dinner mains $29-36; ⏰7am-3.30pm Mon-Wed, 7am-3.30pm & 6-10pm Thu & Fri, 7.30am-10pm Sat, 7.30am-5pm Sun; 🚌353, 376-7)

Little Kitchen
CAFE $$

14 MAP P148, B8

Confident modern Australian fare, strong on presentation, vibrant flavours and quality ingredients, is on offer in this tiny spot. A cheerful, family-run business with an open kitchen and some outdoor seating, it fits well with Coogee's likeably casual beach vibe. Pre-beach breakfasts are a great option here too. (📞02-8021 3424; www.thelittlekitchen.com.au; 275

Arden St, Coogee; lunch mains $19-26, dinner mains $25-31; ⏰7am-3pm daily plus 6-9pm Thu, 6-10pm Fri & Sat; 🚌353, 376-7)

A Tavola
ITALIAN $$

15 MAP P148, D1

Carrying on the tradition of its Darlinghurst **sister** (📞02-9331 7871; 348 Victoria St, Darlinghurst; mains $22-35; ⏰noon-3pm & 6-11pm Mon-Sat; 🚉Kings Cross), Bondi's A Tavola gathers around a big communal marble table where, before the doors open, the pasta-making action happens. Expect robust flavours, impeccably groomed waiters and delicious homemade pasta. There's some pleasant outdoor seating on this interesting street. (📞02-9130 1246; www.atavola.com.au; 75 Hall St, Bondi Beach; mains $25-37; ⏰5.30-11pm Mon & Tue, noon-3pm & 5.30-11pm Wed-Sun; 📱; 🚌379)

Bondi Trattoria
ITALIAN $$

16 MAP P148, D2

For an all-day Bondi option with vistas, you can't go past the trusty 'Trat', as it's known in these parts. Tables spill out onto Campbell Pde for those hungry for beach views. There are quality antipasto options and excellent salads as well as pizzas, pasta and daily fish specials. (📞02-9365 4303; www.bonditrattoria.com.au; 34 Campbell Pde, Bondi Beach; breakfast $11-20, lunch & dinner $28-37; ⏰8am-10pm; 🅿; 🚌333, 380-2)

Beach Eats
🍽️

There are plentiful eating options in the beach suburbs, though heading away from the beachfront strip is often a good idea. Bondi has the biggest range of options, from brunchy cafes to upmarket restaurants. Coogee is another likely spot, while Bronte has a decent eating strip on Macpherson St, west of St Thomas St, which is a 10-minute walk back from the sand.

Icebergs Dining Room ITALIAN $$$

 17 MAP P148, D3

Poised above the famous Icebergs swimming pool (p145), Icebergs' views sweep across the Bondi Beach arc to the sea. Inside, bow-tied waiters deliver fresh, sustainably sourced seafood and steaks cooked with elan. There's also an elegant cocktail bar. In the same building, the Icebergs club has a bistro and bar with simpler, cheaper fare. (02-9365 9000; www.idrb.com; 1 Notts Ave, Bondi Beach; mains $46-52; noon-3pm & 6.30-11pm, from 10am Sun, 333, 380-2)

Sean's Panaroma MODERN AUSTRALIAN $$$

18 MAP P148, E1

Sean Moran's ever-changing menu is chalked on a blackboard in this modest little dining room that packs out with happy diners. Ocean views, hearty seasonal dishes and friendly service make it a deservedly popular, buzzy spot. (02-9365 4924; www.seanspanaroma.co; 270 Campbell Pde, Bondi Beach; mains $39-45; 6-10pm Wed-Sat, noon-4pm Sat & Sun; 333, 380-2)

Drinking

Coogee Pavilion BAR

19 MAP P148, B7

With numerous indoor and outdoor bars, a kids' play area and a glorious adults-only rooftop, this vast complex has brought a touch of inner-city glam to Coogee. Built in 1887, the building originally housed an aquarium and swimming pools. Now, space, light and white wood give a breezy feel. Great eating options run from Mediterranean-inspired bar food to fish 'n' chips and sashimi.

It gets totally packed at weekends. (02-9114 7321; www.merivale.com.au/coogeepavilion; 169 Dolphin St, Coogee; 7.30am-midnight; 313-14, 353, 370-4)

Anchor BAR

 20 MAP P148, D2

Surfers, backpackers and the local cool kids slurp down icy margaritas at this bustling bar at the south end of the Bondi strip. It sports a dark-wood nautical piratey feel and is also a great spot for a late snack. The two-hour happy hour from 5pm weekdays is a good way to start the post-surf debrief. (02-8084 3145; www.facebook.com/anchorbarbondi; 8 Campbell Pde, Bondi Beach; 5pm-midnight Mon-Fri, from noon Sat & Sun; 333, 380-382)

Neighbourhood BAR

21 MAP P148, D1

This smart food and wine bar has a brick interior giving way to a wood-lined courtyard. Bondi Radio broadcasts live from a booth near the kitchen, which specialises in burgers. It's a cool place with a great weekend vibe. (02-9365 2872; www.neighbourhoodbondi.com.au; 143 Curlewis St, Bondi Beach; 5-11pm Mon-Thu, from 4pm Fri, from noon Sat, 10am-10pm Sun; 333, 380-382)

Icebergs Bar
BAR

The neighbouring eatery is more famous, but the casual-chic Icebergs Bar (see 18 ⊗ Map p148, D3) is a brilliant place for a drink. Colourful sofas and ritzy cocktails do little to distract from the killer views from floor-to-ceiling windows looking north across Bondi Beach. A small astroturf terrace adds an outdoor vibe. (☑02-9365 9000; www. idrb.com; 1 Notts Ave, Bondi Beach; ⊙noon-midnight Mon-Sat, 10am-10pm Sun; 🚌333, 380-382)

North Bondi RSL
BAR

22 🚇 MAP P148, F2

This Returned & Services League bar ain't fancy, but with views no one can afford and drinks that everyone can, who cares? The kitchen serves good cheap nosh, including a dedicated kids' menu. Bring ID, as nonmembers theoretically need to prove that they live at least 5km away. Grab a balcony seat for the perfect beach vistas. (☑02-9130 3152; www.northbondirsl. com.au; 120 Ramsgate Ave, North Bondi; ⊙noon-10pm Mon-Thu, noon-11pm Fri, 10am-11pm Sat, 10am-10pm Sun; 👫; 🚌380-382, 379)

Clovelly Hotel
PUB

23 🚇 MAP P148, C6

A renovated megalith on the hill above Clovelly Beach, this pub has a shady terrace and water views – perfect for post-beach Sunday-afternoon bevvies (drinks). If you fancy being in-

doors, the cosy front bar or ultra-spacious lounge will do the trick. Food, now that it's under the Matt Moran empire, is on the up. (☑02-9665 1214; www.clovellyhotel. com.au; 381 Clovelly Rd, Clovelly; ⊙10am-midnight Mon-Sat, to 10pm Sun; 🗻; 🚌338-9)

Coogee Bay Hotel
PUB

24 🚇 MAP P148, B8

This enormous, rambling, rowdy complex packs in the backpackers for live music, open-mic nights, comedy and big-screen sports in the beaut beer garden, sports bar and Selina's nightclub. Sit on a stool at the window overlooking the beach and sip on a cold one. (☑02-9665 0000; www.coogeebay hotel.com.au; 253 Coogee Bay Rd, Coogee; ⊙8am-4am Mon-Thu, to 6am Fri & Sat, to 10pm Sun; 🗻; 🚌313-14, 353, 372-4)

Bucket List
BAR

25 🚇 MAP P148, E2

By no means subtle, Bucket List blares out beachy pop over its excellent in-demand terrace and promotes a hedonistic good-times atmosphere. Sip on an ice-cold beverage while watching the passing parade or gazing aimlessly out to sea. The interior doesn't lack for views either, with a big wraparound window giving it a conservatory feel. (☑02-9365 4122; www.thebucket listbondi.com; Bondi Pavilion, Bondi Beach; ⊙11am-midnight; 🗻; 🚌333, 380-2)

Entertainment

Bondi Openair Cinema
CINEMA

26 ⭐ MAP P148, E2

Enjoy open-air screenings by the sea, with live bands providing prescreening entertainment. Online bookings are cheaper and recommended anyway. (www.openaircinemas.com.au; Dolphin Lawn, next to Bondi Pavilion, Bondi Beach; adult/concession $25/17; ⊙mid-Jan–Feb; 🚌333, 380-2)

Shopping

Surfection
FASHION & ACCESSORIES

27 🔒 MAP P148, D2

Selling boardies, bikinis, sunnies, shoes, watches, tees…even luggage – Bondi's coolest surf shop has just about everything the stylish surfer's heart might desire. Old boards hang from the ceiling, while new boards fill the racks. (✆02-9300 6619; 31 Hall St, Bondi Beach; ⊙9.30am-6pm Mon-Wed & Sat, to 9pm Thu, to 7pm Fri, 10am-6pm Sun; 🚌333, 380-382)

Gertrude & Alice
BOOKS

28 🔒 MAP P148, D2

This second-hand bookshop and cafe sees locals, students and academics hang out reading and drinking excellent coffee. Join them for comfort food and discourse around communal tables. (✆02-9130 5155; www.gertrudeandalice.com.au; 46 Hall St, Bondi Beach; ⊙6.45am-9pm; 🛜; 🚌379)

Bondi Markets
MARKET

29 🔒 MAP P148, E1

On Sundays, when the kids are at the beach, their school fills up with characters rummaging through tie-dyed secondhand clothes, original fashion, books, beads, earrings, aromatherapy oils, candles, old records and more. There's a farmers market here on Saturdays (9am to 1pm). (www.bondimarkets.com.au; Bondi Beach Public School, Campbell Pde, Bondi Beach; ⊙10am-4pm Sun, to 5pm Dec & Jan; 🚌380-382)

Aquabumps
ART

30 🔒 MAP P148, D1

Photographer/surfer Eugene Tan has been snapping photos of Sydney's sunrises, surf and sand for 20 years. His colourful prints hang in this cool space, just a splash from Bondi Beach. (✆02-9130 7788; www.aquabumps.com; 151 Curlewis St, Bondi Beach; ⊙10am-6pm; 🚌333, 380-2)

Walking Tour 🥾

A Day in Watsons Bay

The narrow peninsula ending in South Head is one of Sydney's most sublime spots. The view of the harbour from the Bondi approach, as Old South Head Rd leaves the sheer ocean cliffs to descend to Watsons Bay, is breathtaking. Watsons Bay was once a small fishing village, as evidenced by the tiny heritage cottages that pepper the narrow streets.

Getting There

⚓ Regular ferries run between Circular Quay and Watsons Bay.

🚌 Routes to Watsons Bay include the 325 via Vaucluse and the 380 via Bondi.

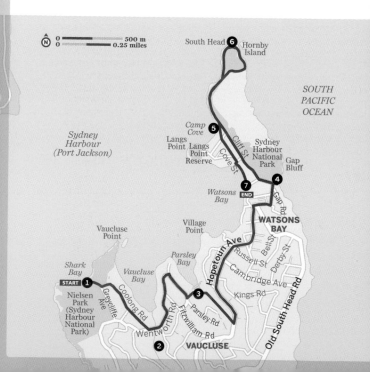

❶ Nielsen Park

Something of a hidden gem, this leafy harbourside **park** (Vaucluse Rd, Vaucluse; ⊙national park area 5am-10pm; 🚌325) with a sandy beach was once part of the 206-hectare Vaucluse House estate. Visit on a weekday when it's not too busy. The park encloses **Shark Beach** – a great spot for a swim, despite the ominous name – and **Greycliffe House**, an 1851 Gothic sandstone pile (not open to visitors).

❷ Vaucluse House

Vaucluse House (📞02-9388 7922; www.sydneylivingmuseums.com.au; Wentworth Rd, Vaucluse; adult/child $12/8; ⊙10am-4pm Wed-Sun; 🚌325) is an imposing specimen of Gothic Australiana set among 10 hectares of lush gardens. Building commenced in 1805 but the house was tinkered with into the 1860s. Decorated with European period pieces, it offers visitors a rare glimpse into early (albeit privileged) colonial life.

❸ Parsley Bay

A hidden gem, this little **bay** (Vaucluse; 🚌325) has a calm swimming beach, a lawn dotted with sculptures for picnics and play, and a cute suspension bridge. Keep an eye out for water dragons as you walk down through the bush.

❹ The Gap

On the ocean side of Watsons Bay, the Gap is a dramatic cliff-top lookout. See if you can spot one of the frequent proposals taking place.

❺ Camp Cove

Immediately north of Watsons Bay, this **swimming beach** (Cliff St, Watsons Bay; 🚌324, 325, 380, ⛴Watsons Bay) is popular with both families and topless sunbathers. When Governor Phillip realised Botany Bay didn't cut it as a site for a settlement, he sailed north into Sydney Harbour, dropped anchor and stepped onto Camp Cove's golden sand on 21 January 1788.

❻ South Head

The **South Head Heritage Trail** passes old battlements and a path heading down to **Lady Bay**, a diminutive gay nudist beach, before continuing on to the candy-striped Hornby Lighthouse and the sandstone Lightkeepers' Cottages (1858) on South Head itself. The harbour views, whale-watching opportunities and crashing surf on the ocean side make this a very dramatic and beautiful spot indeed.

❼ Watsons Bay Beach Club

One of the great pleasures in Sydney life is languishing in the beer garden of the **Watsons Bay Hotel** (📞02-9337 5444; www.watsonsbayhotel.com.au; 1 Military Rd; ⊙10am-midnight Mon-Sat, to 10pm Sun; 🚌324, 325, 380, ⛴Watsons Bay) after a day at the beach. Stay to watch the sun go down over the city. Adjacent **Doyles** (📞02-9337 2007; www.doyles.com.au; 11 Marine Pde, Watsons Bay; mains $41-49; ⊙noon-3pm & 5.30-9pm Mon-Fri, noon-4pm & 5.30-9pm Sat & Sun) is a famous fish restaurant with a takeaway outlet.

Explore ✦
Manly

With both a harbour side and a glorious ocean beach, Manly is Sydney's only ferry destination with surf. Capping off the harbour with scrappy charm, it's a place worth visiting for the ferry ride alone. The surf's good, there are appealing contemporary bars and eateries and, as the gateway to the Northern Beaches, it makes a popular base for the board-riding brigade. There's also some great walking to be done.

The Corso connects Manly's ocean and harbour beaches; here surf shops, burger joints, juice bars and pubs are plentiful. The refurbished Manly Wharf has classier pubs and restaurants, and there are some good cafes and small bars scattered around the back streets.

The great walks on North Head (p162) and the Manly Scenic Walkway (p164) to the Spit Bridge are very worthwhile at any time.

Getting There & Around

🚢 Frequent direct ferries head from Circular Quay to Manly, making this the best (and most scenic) way to go. Regular Sydney ferries take 30 minutes for the journey, while fast ferries take just 18 minutes.

🚌 Express bus E70 takes 35 to 40 minutes to get to Manly Wharf from near Wynyard Station, while its weekend equivalent, the 170, takes longer.

Manly Map on p166

The Corso, connecting Manly's two beaches
ALEKSANDAR TODOROVIC/SHUTTERSTOCK ©

Top Experience 📷
Bike Around North Head

About 3km south of Manly, spectacular North Head offers dramatic cliffs, lookouts, pretty paths through the native scrub and sweeping views of the ocean, the harbour and the city. It's great to explore by bike or on foot. Grab a map and plot your own path through the headland, taking in former military barracks, WWII gun emplacements, a quarantine cemetery and a military memorial walk. At the tip, Fairfax Lookouts offer dramatic clifftop views.

◎ MAP P166, D5

📞 1300 072 757

www.nationalparks.nsw.gov.au

North Head Scenic Dr

admission free

🕐 sunrise-sunset

🚌 135

Viewpoints

Just before the roundabout by the Q Station (p167), take the metal walkway leading off to the left. Follow it up through attractive native scrub, then take a right at the T-junction near the Barracks complex to reach a couple of spectacular viewpoints, one along the Northern Beaches, one across the harbour. The path then arrives at the evocative Third Quarantine Cemetery, with more marvellous harbour vistas.

A Military History

North Head was long a major army base and a key part of Sydney Harbour's defensive system; there are numerous gun emplacements and fortifications. The North Fort complex has a network of tunnels that can be visited by tour as well as an information centre and cafe (open until 4pm). From here begins **Australia's Memorial Walk**, a commemorative brick footpath honouring the armed forces. It passes a series of WWII gun emplacements and links up with a scenic, partly cobbled road that was designed in the 1920s as a WWI memorial.

Fairfax Lookouts

At the end of the headland, a circular track with more defensive fortifications plus information on flora and fauna runs out to the very mouth of Sydney Harbour, where, atop impressive sandstone cliffs, you can gaze your heart out at sea, harbour, city skyline and the parallel bulk of South Head, opposite. Watching one of the big cruise ships sail in or out is quite a sight.

Bluefish Track

The best way to leave is via this spectacular short path that winds across sandstone outcrops, offering magnificent sea views. Squeeze through a low door in a sturdy wall and you'll emerge in the carpark just above Shelly Beach (p167).

★ **Top Tips**

○ At Manly ferry wharf, pick up a map from the Hello Manly information centre as you pass.

○ You can walk here easily enough from Manly Wharf, but the 135 bus will also bring you here.

✖ **Take a Break**

There's a cafe at the North Fort complex in the heart of the headland and eating options at the Q Station (p167).

Finish your exploration by descending the Bluefish Track down to Shelly Beach and tasty seafood at the Boathouse (p169).

Walking Tour 🥾

Manly Scenic Walkway

This epic walk traces the coast west from Manly past million-dollar harbour-view properties and then through a rugged 2.5km section of Sydney Harbour National Park that remains much as it was when the First Fleet sailed in. Make sure you carry plenty of water, slop on some sunscreen, slap on a hat and wear sturdy shoes.

Walk Facts
Start Manly Cove
End Spit Bridge
Length 9km; four hours

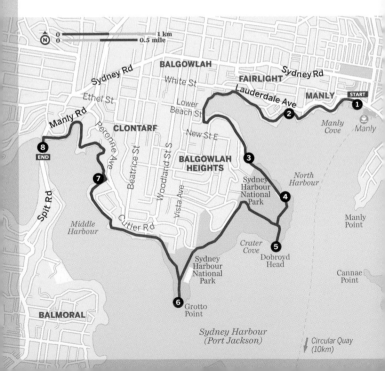

❶ Manly Cove

Pick up a walk brochure (which includes a detailed map) from the visitor information centre by Manly Wharf. Walk along Manly Cove (p168) and find the path at the end of the beach.

❷ Fairlight Beach

After 700m you'll reach Fairlight Beach, where you can scan the view through the heads. Yachts tug at their moorings as you trace the North Harbour inlet for the next 2km.

❸ Forty Baskets Beach

Forty Baskets Beach sits at the point where the well-heeled streets of Balgowlah Heights end and bushclad Sydney Harbour National Park commences. The picnic area is cut off at high tide.

❹ Reef Beach

Kookaburras cackle as you enter the national park and approach Reef Beach, a beautiful cove with turquoise water and great views back to Manly.

❺ Dobroyd Head

The track becomes steep, sandy and rocky further into the park –

keep an eye out for wildflowers, spiders in bottlebrush trees and fat goannas sunning themselves. The views from Dobroyd Head are unforgettable. Check out the deserted 1930s sea shacks at the base of Crater Cove cliff.

❻ Grotto Point

Look for Aboriginal rock carvings on a ledge left of the track before the turn-off to Grotto Point Lighthouse. Rugged and beautiful, Washaway Beach is a secluded little spot on the point's eastern edge.

❼ Clontarf Beach

Booalmed Castle Rock Beach is at the western end of the national park. From here the path winds around the rear of houses to Clontarf Beach, where there's a wide stretch of sand and the walk's only real eating stop.

❽ Spit Bridge

Sandy Bay follows and then Fisher Bay before you reach Spit Bridge, a bascule bridge that connects Manly to Mosman and opens periodically to let boats through to Middle Harbour. From here you can bus back to Manly or into the city.

Manly

A

Pittwater Rd 🔒20
Raglan St
Ivanhoe Park
Sydney Rd
Manly
**Art Gallery
& Museum**
7
Manly
Bike
Tours
11
8
14 16
15 9
17
Manly
Cove 12 🍴
13
18
5

B

North Steyne
1 Manly
Beach
The Corso
Wentworth
St
Victoria
Pde
19 🔒
Manly
Kayak
Centre
East Esp
Ashburner St
South
Steyne
Reddall St
Cliff St
Addison
Rd
MANLY
Darley Rd
High St
Osborne Rd
Woods St
Marshall St
Stuart St
Cove Ave
Addison Rd
North Head Scenic Dr
6 St Patrick's
College

C

Manly Surf School
(350m)

Cabbage Tree
Bay
Shelly
Beach
Bower St

D

SOUTH
PACIFIC
OCEAN

Shelly
Beach 4
Park
10

Sydney
Harbour
National
Park

Manly
Cove

Manly

Circular Quay
(10km)

Smedleys
Point

Manly
Point

North
Harbour

Little
Manly
Point

Cannae
Point

Collins
Flat
Beach

Collins Beach Rd

Store
Beach
2 ◎

North Head Scenic Dr

3 ◎
Q Station

Sydney
Harbour
National
Park

**North
Head**
◎

For reviews see	
◉ Top Experiences	p162
◎ Sights	p167
🍴 Eating	p168
🍺 Drinking	p170
🔒 Shopping	p171

N
0 ——————— 500 m
0 ——————— 0.25 miles

A   **B**   **C**   **D**

Sights

Manly Beach   BEACH

1 🔘 MAP P166, B1

Sydney's second most famous
beach is a magnificent strand that
stretches for nearly two golden
kilometres, lined by Norfolk Island
pines and midrise apartment
blocks. The southern end of the
beach, nearest the Corso, is known
as South Steyne, with North Steyne
in the centre and Queenscliff at the
northern end; each has its own surf
lifesaving club. (🏊Manly)

Store Beach   BEACH

2 🔘 MAP P166, B4

A hidden jewel on North Head,
magical Store Beach can only be
reached by kayak (you can hire
them from Manly Kayak Centre;
p170) or boat. It's a breeding
ground for **fairy penguins**, so access is prohibited from dusk, when
the birds waddle in to settle down
for the night. (🕐dawn-dusk; 🏊Manly)

Q Station   HISTORIC BUILDING

3 🔘 MAP P166, C5

From 1837 to 1984 this sprawling
historic complex in beautiful North
Head bushland was used to isolate
new arrivals suspected of carrying
disease. These days it has been
reborn as a tourist destination,
offering appealing **accommodation** (📞02-9466 1500; r $259-399;
🅿️🚐❄️📶; 🚌135, 🏊Manly) and
tours. Shuttle buses whisk you
from reception down to the wharf,

where there's a lovely beach, a
museum in the old luggage store
telling the site's story, an information desk and a cafe. Nearby is a
bar and restaurant.

The quarantine station was
an attempt to limit the spread of
cholera, smallpox, influenza and
bubonic plague. Passengers were
accommodated according to the
class of their ticket. Sandstone
inscriptions record the names of
ships laid up here; gravestones
the names of those who never
left.Tours run to a daily or weekly
schedule and must be prebooked;
contact the office. The 2½-hour
Ghostly Encounters tour ($40 to
$55) runs nightly and rattles some
skeletons; three-hour Extreme
Ghost Tours ($75) take it a step fur-
ther and try to summon the spirits.
The two-hour daytime Quarantine
Station Story tour ($35) highlights
the personal stories of those who
worked and waited here, while the
45-minute Wharf Wander ($18) is
a truncated version for those short
on time. (Quarantine Station; 📞02-
9466 1551; www.qstation.com.au; 1
North Head Scenic Dr, Manly; admission
free; 🕐museum 10am-4pm; 🚌135)

Shelly Beach   BEACH

4 🔘 MAP P166, D2

This pretty, sheltered, north-facing
ocean cove is an appealing 1km
walk from the busy Manly beach
strip. The tranquil waters are a
protected haven for marine life, so it
offers wonderful **snorkelling**. It's a
popular place for picnickers. (Bower
St, Manly; 🏊Manly)

Manly Cove

BEACH

5 MAP P166, A2

Split in two by Manly Wharf, this sheltered enclave has shark nets and calm water, making it a popular choice for families with toddlers. Despite the busy location, the clear waters have plenty of appeal. (Manly)

St Patrick's College

HISTORIC BUILDING

6 MAP P166, C3

Southeast of Manly's centre, this enormous Gothic Revival college (1889) lords over the rooftops from its hillside position. It used to be a seminary but is now a management college; it doubled as Jay Gatsby's house for Baz Luhrmann's 2013 film version of *The Great Gatsby*. You can roam the grounds and admire the building from outside.

Australian PM Tony Abbott (in office 2013–15) was a student here in the 1980s, which gave rise to his nickname, the Mad Monk. (www.stpatricksestate.org.au; 151 Darley Rd, Manly; grounds sunrise-sunset; 135, Manly)

Manly Art Gallery & Museum

MUSEUM

7 MAP P166, A2

A short stroll from Manly Wharf, this passionately managed community gallery maintains a local focus, with changing, locally relevant exhibitions and a small permanent collection that includes an excellent ceramics gallery. There are lots of old Manly photos to peer at too. (02-9976 1421; www.northern beaches.nsw.gov.au; West Esplanade, Manly; admission free; 10am-5pm Tue-Sun; Manly)

Eating

Chica Bonita

MEXICAN $

8 MAP P166, B1

This upbeat place rises above its unprepossessing location: straddling the end of a dingy shopping arcade, with carpark views. It offers zingy, inventive Mexican fare from lunchtime burritos to evening tacos, with good margaritas and other cocktails on hand to wash them down. It's easiest to enter from the corner of Whistler St and Market Pl. (02-9976 5255; www.chicabonita.com.au; Shop 9, 9 The Corso, Manly; tacos $6, other dishes $10-16; 11.30am-3.30pm & 6-10.30pm Tue-Fri, 11am-3.30pm & 5.30-10.30pm Sat & Sun; Manly)

Barefoot Coffee Traders

CAFE $

9 MAP P166, B1

Run by surfer lads serving fair-trade organic coffee from a closet-sized open-to-the-breeze shop, Barefoot epitomises Manly cool. Food is limited but the Belgian chocolate waffles go magically well with a macchiato. The coffee is deliciously smooth. There's a larger cafe (p169) on Wentworth St. (0415 816 061; www.barefootcoffee.com.au; 18 Whistler St, Manly; snacks $3-7; 6.30am-5pm Mon-Fri, 7am-5pm Sat & Sun; ; Manly)

Boathouse Shelly Beach

CAFE $$

10 ✕ MAP P166, D2

This sweet little spot on picturesque Shelly Beach makes a top venue for breakfast juices, brunches, fish 'n' chips, oysters or daily fish specials, served either in the restaurant section or from the kiosk. There's pleasantly shady outdoor seating. No bookings taken. (☑02-9974 5440; www.theboathousesb.com.au; 1 Marine Pde, Manly; kiosk mains $12-19, restaurant mains $18-29; ☺7am-4pm; 🛜📶)

Belgrave Cartel

CAFE $$

11 ✕ MAP P166, B1

This established cafe does perhaps Manly's best espresso in a soothing vintage atmosphere with laneway-style outdoor tables. Breakfasts and Sunday brunches are guaranteed to please, as is the selection of Italian share plates. By night, there's an appealing small-bar scene with cocktails and wine. (☑02-9976 6548; www.belgravecartel.com.au; 6 Belgrave St, Manly; small plates $6-18, mains $16-26; ☺6am-2pm Mon & Tue, 6am-midnight Wed-Fri, 7am-midnight Sat, 7am-10pm Sun; 🛜; 🚢Manly)

Hugos

MODERN AUSTRALIAN $$$

12 ✕ MAP P166, A2

Occupying Manly's primo wharf location, Hugos has super views from its open windows and sought-after outdoor deck. Relax on the banquette seating and sip a cocktail, then tuck in to delicious pizzas or an Italian-inflected menu of sea-

St Patrick's College

food and yummy desserts. It serves pizza all day; it's also a decent place to just slide in for a beer. (☑02-8116 8555; www.hugos.com.au; Manly Wharf, Manly; pizzas $25-29, mains $34-39; ⊙noon-midnight Mon-Fri, 11.30am-midnight Sat & Sun; 🛜; 🛳Manly)

Drinking

Manly Wharf Hotel PUB

13 ⓦ MAP P166, B2

Just along the wharf from the ferry, this remodelled pub is all glass and water vistas, with loads of seating so you've a good chance of grabbing a share of the view. It's a perfect spot for sunny afternoon beers. There's good pub food, too (mains $22 to $30), with pizzas, fried fish and succulent rotisserie chicken all worthwhile. (☑02-9977 1266; www.manlywharfhotel.com.au; East Esplanade, Manly;

⊙11.30am-midnight Mon-Fri, 11am-1am Sat, 11am-midnight Sun; 🛜🚻; 🛳Manly)

Donny's COCKTAIL BAR

14 ⓦ MAP P166, B1

This two-level bar-restaurant is an atmospheric spot for a great night-time cocktail if you can read the menu in the low-lit ambience. Sweet-toothers will love the sugar-and-coffee hit that is the Sticky Date Espresso, while the ginned-up 'detox' option is served to look like you're having a pot of tea in case your personal trainer drops by.

It does some smart fusion food, too, and has regular live bands. (☑02-9977 1887; www.donnys.com.au; 7 Market Lane, Manly; ⊙6-11pm Mon, 4pm-midnight Tue-Fri, noon-midnight Sat, noon-10pm Sun; 🛳Manly)

Out & Active

Manly is a great place to get out on a surfboard and several places near the beach hire out equipment. It's also a popular spot to learn, with **Manly Surf School** (Map p166 ☑02-9932 7000; www.manlysurfschool. com; North Steyne Surf Club; 🚌136, 139, 🛳Manly) a reliable operator. Other watery activities are also available, including from **Manly Kayak Centre** (Map p166, B2; ☑02-9976 5057; www.manlykayakcentre.com.au; Manly Wharf; hire per 1/2/4/8hr from $25/45/55/75; ⊙9am-5pm; 🛳Manly), **Manly Ocean Adventures** (☑1300 062 659; www.manlyoceanadventures.com.au) and **Dive Centre Manly** (Map p166, see 11 ◎; ☑02-9977 4355; www.divesydney. com.au; 10 Belgrave St; ⊙8.30am-6pm Mon-Fri, 8am-6pm Sat & Sun; 🛳Manly).

On land, there are excellent walks available, while **Manly Bike Tours** (Map p166, A2; ☑02-8005 7368; www.manlybiketours.com.au; Belgrave St, Manly; hire per hr/day from $16/33; ⊙9am-6pm Oct-Mar, to 5pm Apr-Sep; 🛳Manly) hires out bikes and provides maps for self-guided tours.

4 Pines

MICROBREWERY

15 MAP P166, B2

Local brewing concern 4 Pines has set up this handsome two-storey venue opposite the ferry wharf. Some of the beer is brewed here, and you can sip it on the balcony while munching on a pulled-pork burger or a range of other pricey but tasty bar fare. Evening-only downstairs has the same menu, but with table service and no outlook. (☑02-9976 2300; www.4pinesbeer. com.au; 29/43-45 East Esplanade, Manly; ☺11am-midnight; 🛜; 🛳Manly)

Hotel Steyne

PUB

16 🚇 MAP P166, B1

With something for everyone, the Steyne is a Manly classic that's big enough to get lost in: it's like a village of its own with various bars and eating areas around the sociable central courtyard, which goes loud and late most nights. The rum-focused Moonshine bar has a balcony with beach views. (☑02-9977 4977; www.hotelsteyne.com.au; 75 The Corso, Manly; ☺9am-2am Mon-Sat, to 3am Thu, to midnight Sun; 🛜; 🛳Manly)

Bavarian

BEER HALL

17 🚇 MAP P166, A2

At the ferry wharf, this open-sided bar offers numerous local and imported brews. The pork knuckles and pretzels are delicious; sausages are the best option. (☑02-9977 8088; www.thebavarian.com.au; Manly Wharf, Manly; ☺11am-midnight Mon-Fri, 9am-midnight Sat & Sun; 🛜; 🛳Manly)

Shopping

Budgy Smugglers

SPORTS & OUTDOORS

18 🔒 MAP P166, B2

This cheeky Northern Beaches swimwear brand appropriates a well-known Australian slang term for Speedos (think it through) and runs with it. Colourful men's and women's swimmers come in national colours, thematic designs or create-your-own. (☑0404 026 836; www.budgysmuggler.com.au; 22 Darley Rd, Manly; ☺9am-5pm; 🛳Manly)

Manly Life Saving Club

SPORTS & OUTDOORS

19 🔒 MAP P166, C2

Support this local institution by nipping upstairs to check out its worthwhile surf shop. (☑02-9977 2742; www.manlylsc.com; South Steyne, Manly; ☺shop 10am-4pm Mon & Fri, 10.30am-4.30pm Tue-Thu, 9.30am-2.30pm Sat, 8am-3.30pm Sun; 🛳Manly)

Aloha Surf

SPORTS & OUTDOORS

20 🔒 MAP P166, B1

This quality surf shop offers longboards, shortboards, bodyboards, skateboards and surfing fashion. The owner is a proper surfer and can give local advice. (☑02-9977 3777; www.alohasurfmanly.com; 42 Pittwater Rd, Manly; ☺9am-6pm Fri-Wed, to 7pm Thu; 🛳Manly)

Walking Tour 🥾

Northern Beaches

Wilder and more distant than Sydney's eastern strands, the Northern Beaches are a must-see, especially for surfers. Although you'll most likely approach them as a day trip, they're very much a part of the city, with the suburbs pushing right up to the water's edge. Some neighbourhoods are ritzier than others, but what they all have in common is a devotion to the beach.

Trip Details

The quickest route to the Northern Beaches is to get the B-Line bus from Wynyard station. Once there, use the 199 bus, which hops along the beach suburbs.

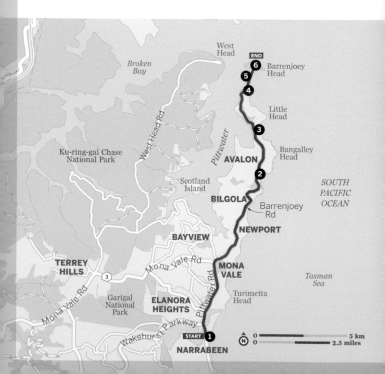

❶ Narrabeen

Immortalised by the Beach Boys in 'Surfin' USA', long, spectacular **Narrabeen** is hard-core surf turf – get some experience before hitting the breaks. At the far northern end of the beach, there's good paddling for young children on the lagoon side of the strand. Back from the centre of the beach, the lagoon has an 8.4km trail and kayaks for hire.

❷ Avalon

Caught in a sandy '70s time warp, **Avalon** is the mythical Australian beach you always dreamed of but could never find. Challenging surf and sloping, tangerine-gold sand have a jutting headland for a backdrop. There's a sea pool at the southern end. Good, cheap eating options abound in the streets behind.

❸ Whale Beach

Walk or bus from Avalon to sleepy **Whale Beach** (Whale Beach Rd, Whale Beach; 🚌 199, L90), off the beaten track and well worth seeking out. A paradisiacal slice of deep, orange-tinted sand backed by pines and flanked by steep cliffs, it's a good beach for surfers and families. There's a sea pool at its southern end. High above, **Jonah's** (📞02-9974 5599; www.jonahs.com.au; 69 Bynya Rd, Whale Beach; 2/3/4 courses $88/115/130; ⊗7.30-9am, noon-2.30pm & 6.30-11pm; 🛜; 🚌199, L90) is a noted destination restaurant.

❹ Palm Beach

Long, lovely Palm Beach is a crescent of bliss, famous as the setting for cheesy TV soap *Home & Away*. The suburb has two sides: the magnificent ocean beach, and a pleasant strip on Pittwater, where the calmer strands are good for young kids. From here you can get ferries to other picturesque Pittwater destinations, including glorious **Ku-ring-gai Chase National Park**.

❺ Lunch at the Boathouse

Sit on the large timber deck right by the sand at Pittwater or grab a table on the lawn at Palm Beach's most popular **cafe** (📞02-9974 5440; www.theboathousepb.com.au; Governor Phillip Park; mains $18-29; ⊗7am-4pm, 🛜 🥬; 🚌199, L90). The food (try the legendary fish and chips) is nearly as impressive as the views – and that's really saying something. No bookings are taken.

❻ Barrenjoey Lighthouse

This historic sandstone lighthouse (1881; 📞02-9451 3479; www.nationalparks.nsw.gov.au; Palm Beach; admission free; 🚌L90, 199) sits at the northern tip of the peninsula in an annexe of Ku-ring-gai Chase National Park. For the steep hike to the top, take either the shorter stairs or a winding track: majestic views across Pittwater and down the peninsula are worth the effort.

The route starts from the reserve car park at the northern end of Palm Beach. There are no toilets at the top.

Survival Guide

Ferry approaching Circular Quay (p31)
POMINOZ/SHUTTERSTOCK ©

Before You Go

Book Your Stay

○ Sydney offers a vast quantity and variety of accommodation, especially concentrated in the downtown, Rocks and Darling Harbour areas.

○ Even so, the supply shrivels up under the summer sun, particularly around weekends and big events, so be sure to book ahead.

○ Prices, even in the budget class, are high; city-centre hotels charge stratospheric rates.

Useful Websites

Destination NSW (www.sydney.com) Official visitors guide.

TripView The handiest app for planning public transport journeys.

Time Out (www.timeout.com/sydney) 'What's on' information and reviews.

Not Quite Nigella (www.notquitenigella.com) Entertaining food blog.

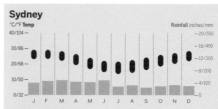

Sydney
°C/°F Temp
Rainfall inches/mm

When to Go

○ **Summer** (Dec–Feb) The peak season is from Christmas until the end of January, which coincides with school holidays and the hot weather.

○ **Spring** (Sep–Nov) Usually dry and warm.

○ **Autumn** (Mar–May) Sydney's wettest months, but not cold until May. Mardi Gras fills hotels in early March.

○ **Winter** (Jun–Aug) Cold, short days. Film festivals, arts festivals and footy.

FBI Radio (https://fbiradio.com) Underground music and arts scene coverage.

Lonely Planet (www.lonelyplanet.com/sydney) Destination information, hotel bookings, traveller forum and more.

Best Budget

○ **Blue Parrot Backpackers** (☏02-9356 4888; www.blueparrot.com.au; 87 Macleay St, Potts Point; dm $35-46; 🚌@🛜; ⓇKings Cross) As homelike as a hostel can get.

○ **Sydney Harbour YHA** (☏02-8272 0900; www.yha.com.au; 110 Cumberland St; dm $41-69, d $165-250; 🚌❄@🛜; ⓇWynyard) Upmarket hostelling with super views of the city's harbour.

○ **Cockatoo Island** (☏02-8969 2111; www.cockatooisland.gov.au; Cockatoo Island; campsites $45-50, simple tents $89-99, 2-bed tents $130-175, apt/house from $265/625; 🛜; ⛴Cockatoo Island) Glamping in the middle of the harbour.

Best Midrange

○ Tara Guest House
(www.taraguesthouse.com.
au) Strikingly good Inner
West B&B.

○ Dive Hotel (☑02-9665
5538; www.divehotel.com.
au; 234 Arden St, Coogee;
standard r from $230,
ocean-view r from $355;
🅿️ 🚌 ❄️ @ 🛜; 🚍313, 314,
353, 372, 373) Right across
from Coogee Beach.

**○ Watsons Bay Bou-
tique Hotel** (☑02-9337
5444; www.watsonsbay-
hotel.com.au; 1 Military
Rd, Watsons Bay; d from
$299, with harbour view
from $329, ste from $489;
🅿️ 🚌 ❄️ 🛜; 🚍324, 325,
L90, 🚢Watsons Bay) Spa-
cious, light rooms in a
marvellous location.

Best Top End

○ QT Sydney (☑02-8262
0000; www.qthotelsan-
dresorts.com/sydney-cbd;
49 Market St; r $360-540;
🅿️ 🚌 ❄️ @ 🛜; 🚍Queen
Victoria Building, 🚆Town
Hall) Stylish, glamorous,
fun and central.

**○ ADGE Boutique
Apartment Hotel**
(☑02-8093 9888; www.
adgehotel.com.au; 222 Riley
St, Surry Hills; apt $350-700;
🅿️ 🚌 ❄️ 🛜; 🚍301, 302,
352, 🚆Central) Check out
that fabulous carpet!

○ Ovolo 1888 (☑02-
8586 1888; www.ovoloho-
tels.com.au; 139 Murray
St, Pyrmont; r $239-539;
🚌 ❄️ @ 🛜 🐾; 🚍Conven-
tion) Brilliant industrial
conversion near Darling
Harbour.

Arriving in Sydney

Sydney Airport

Also known as King-
sford Smith Airport,
Sydney Airport
(Kingsford Smith Airport,
Mascot Airport; ☑02-9667
9111; www.sydneyairport.
com.au; Airport Dr, Mascot;
🚆Domestic Airport,
🚆International Airport),
just 10km south of the
centre, has separate
international (T1) and
domestic (T2 and T3)
sections, 4km apart
on either side of the
runways. A free shuttle
bus runs between
the two terminals,
taking around 10
minutes. They are also
connected by train
($6.70). Each has
left-luggage services
(☑02-9667 0926; www.
baggagestorage.com.
au; Sydney Airport; 24hr
suitcase/carry-on $17/14;

⏱6am-9.30pm), ATMs,
currency-exchange
bureaux and rental-car
counters; trains, buses
and shuttles depart
from both.

Central Station

Intercity trains pull
into the old (Country
Trains) section of Syd-
ney's historic **Central
Station** (☑02-9379 1777;
Eddy Ave; 🚆Central), in
the Haymarket area
of the southern inner
city. From here you can
connect to the sub-
urban train network,
catch the light rail, or
follow the signs to Rail-
way Sq or Eddy Ave for
suburban buses.

Sydney Coach Terminal

Long-distance coaches
arrive outside Central
Station. From here you
can access the sub-
urban train network,
buses and light rail.

Overseas Passenger Terminal

Many cruise ships
dock at the **Overseas
Passenger Terminal**
(☑02-9296 4999; www.
portauthoritynsw.com.au;
Circular Quay West;

The Opal Card

Sydney's public transport network runs on a ticketing system called Opal (www.opal.com.au).

The easiest way to use the system is to tap on and off with a contactless credit or debit card (Visa, MasterCard or Amex), or linked device; you'll be charged an adult fare. Most contactless cards issued overseas can be used, though you may be charged an overseas transaction fee by your card issuer.

You tap on when you start your trip at an electronic reader, and then tap off when you complete your trip, and the system calculates and deducts the correct fare. Readers are located at train and metro station gates, inside the doors of buses, on light-rail platforms and at ferry wharves.

You can also obtain dedicated Opal cards (for free) online or at numerous newsagencies and convenience stores across Sydney. They must be loaded with credit (minimum $10/5 for adult/child; $35 at airport stations). Child/youth Opal cards offer discounted travel for kids aged four to 15 years; kids three and under travel free. For student and pensioner discount Opal cards (available only to Australians or those studying in Australia), you have to apply online. You can still buy single adult or child tickets (Opal single-trip tickets) from machines at many train stations, ferry wharves and light-rail stops, or from bus drivers. These are more expensive than using a card or device.

You get a discount when transferring between services, and after a certain number of journeys in the week, and daily charges are capped at $16.10 ($2.80 on Sundays). Weekly charges are capped at $50. You can use the Opal system at the airport train stations, but none of these bonuses apply.

Circular Quay) at Circular Quay, in the heart of town, between the Harbour Bridge and the Opera House and near Circular Quay station. Others pull in at **White Bay Cruise Terminal**, in Balmain, from where ferries and taxis can run you into the centre.

Getting Around

Train

o **Sydney Trains** (✆13 15 00; www.transportnsw. info) has a large suburban railway web with relatively frequent services, although there are no lines to the northern or eastern beaches.

o Trains run from around 5am to midnight – check timetables for your line. They run till a little later at weekends. Trains are replaced by NightRide buses in the small hours. These mostly leave from around Town Hall Station and pass through Railway Sq at Central Station.

o Trains are significantly more expensive at peak hours, which are from 7am to 9am and 4pm to 6.30pm, Monday to Friday.

o Trains use the Opal ticketing system; a short one-way trip costs $3.61, or $2.52 off-peak.

Bus

o **Transport NSW** (☑13 15 00; www.transportnsw. info) has an extensive bus network, operating from around 4.30am to midnight, when less frequent NightRide services commence.

o Bus routes starting with an M or E indicate express routes; those with an L have similarly limited stops; all are somewhat quicker than the regular bus lines.

o There are several bus hubs in the city centre: Wynyard Park by Wynyard train station; Railway Sq by Central Station; the QVB close to Town Hall Station; and Circular Quay by the ferry, train and light-rail

stops of the same name.

o Use your contactless credit card, linked device or Opal card to ride buses (adult fares start at $2.24); tap on when you board, and remember to tap off when you alight, or you'll be charged the maximum fare.

Ferry

o Most **Transport NSW ferries** (☑13 15 00; www. transportnsw.info) operate between 6am and midnight. The standard adult one-way fare for most harbour destinations is $6.12; ferries to Manly, Sydney Olympic Park and Parramatta cost $7.65. Ferries use the Opal ticketing system.

o Private company **Manly Fast Ferry** (☑02-9583 1199; www.manlyfastferry. com.au; Wharf 2, Circular Quay; adult one way $9.90) offers boats that blast from Circular Quay to Manly in 18 minutes. Other routes link Manly with Darling Harbour, Barangaroo and Watsons Bay.

o **Captain Cook Cruises** (☑02-9206 1111; www.captaincook.com. au; Wharf 6, Circular Quay; from $35; ℞Circular Quay)

offers services with several stops around the harbour and all the way to Lane Cove.

Light Rail (Tram)

o Trams run on two connecting routes. One runs between Central Station and Dulwich Hill, stopping at Chinatown, Darling Harbour, the Star casino, Sydney Fish Market, Glebe and Leichhardt en route. The second runs from Circular Quay through the city centre to Central Station, then shoots east through Surry Hills heads past the Sydney Cricket Ground and on to Kingsford, with a branch veering to Randwick.

o Tickets use the Opal system and cost $2.24 to $4.80.

Bicycle

o Sydney traffic can be intimidating, but there is an increasing number of separated bike lanes; see www.cityofsydney. nsw.gov.au. Helmets are compulsory.

o Bicycles can travel on suburban trains for free. Bikes also ride for free on Sydney's ferries but are banned from buses.

o Many cycle-hire shops require a hefty credit-card deposit. For hire, see the following; there are many more operators around town:

Bike Buffs (☑ 0414 960 332; www.bikebuffs.com.au; adult/child $95/70; ☒ Circular Quay)

Bonza Bike Tours (☑ 02-9247 8800; www.bonzabiketours.com; 30 Harrington St; tours from $99; ☺ office 9am-5pm; ☒ Circular Quay)

Manly Bike Tours (☑ 02-8005 7368; www.manlybiketours.com.au; Belgrave St, Manly; hire per hour/day from $18/35, extra days from $15; ☺ 9am-6pm Oct-Mar, to 5pm Apr-Sep; ☒ Manly)

Skater HQ (☑ 02-8667 7892; www.skaterhq.com.au; Bent St, Entertainment Quarter, Centennial Park; hire with safety gear per hour/day $20/30; ☺ 9am-6pm Mon-Wed, Fri & Sat, to 7pm Thu, to 5pm Sun; ☒ 355, ☒ Moore Park)

o Dockless bike-share schemes have come, failed, then come again. You may or may not find them around; if you do, download the app and ride away.

Car & Motorcycle

Avoid driving in central Sydney if you can: there's a confusing one-way-street system, parking's elusive and expensive, and parking inspectors, tolls and tow-away zones proliferate. Conversely, a car is handy for accessing Sydney's outer reaches (particularly the beaches) and for day trips.

Taxi

Metered taxis are easy to flag down in the central city and inner suburbs, except at changeover times (3pm and 3am). Fares are regulated, so all companies charge the same. Flagfall is $3.60, with a $2.50 'night owl surcharge' after 10pm on a Friday and Saturday until 6am the following morning. After that the fare is $2.19 per kilometre, with an additional surcharge of $2.63 per kilometre between 10pm and 6am.

Ride-sharing apps like Uber (www.uber.com) and Ola (https://ola.com.au) operate in Sydney and are very popular. Shebah (www.shebah.com.au) is an all-women (and children) ride-share service. Other apps such as GoCatch and Rydo offer taxi bookings, which can be very handy on busy evenings.

Zero200 (☑ 02-8332 0200; www.zero200.com.au) is a wheelchair-accessible taxi service.

Major taxi companies:

13CABS (☑ 13 22 27; www.13cabs.com.au)

Premier Cabs (☑ 13 10 17; www.premiercabs.com.au)

RSL Cabs (☑ 02-9581 1111; www.rslcabs.com.au)

Silver Service (☑ 13 31 00; www.silverservice.com.au)

Water Taxi

Water taxis are a fast way to shunt around the harbour (Circular Quay to Watsons Bay in as little as 15 minutes, for example). Companies will quote on any pick-up point within the harbour and the river, including private jetties, islands and other boats. All have a quote genera-lor on their websites; you can add in extra cruise time for a bit of sightseeing. It's much better value for groups than singles or couples.

The following is a list of water-taxi companies:

Fantasea Yellow Water Taxis (☎1800 326 822; www.yellowwatertaxis.com.au; ⏰8am-9pm, prebooking required for services outside these hours)

H2O Maxi Taxis (☎1300 420 829; www.h2owatertaxis.com.au)

Water Taxis Combined (☎02-9555 8888; www.watertaxis.com.au)

Metro

Sydney Metro (www.sydneymetro.info) is a massive new infrastructure project. The first phase, running from Chatswood to Sydney's northwest, should be operational in mid- to late 2019. The second phase, linking Chatswood to three new central underground stations via a new harbour tunnel and on out to the west, will take longer. Opal cards will be used on the service.

Essential Information

Business Hours

Opening hours vary very widely. The following opening times are approximations:

Restaurants noon to 2.30pm and 6pm to 10pm, sometimes shut Sunday or Monday

Cafes 7am to 4pm

Pubs 11am to midnight Monday to Saturday, noon to 10pm Sunday

Shops 9.30am to 6pm Monday to Wednesday, Friday and Saturday; 9.30am to 8pm Thursday; 11am to 5pm Sunday

Banks 9.30am to 4pm Monday to Thursday, 9.30am to 5pm Friday

Offices 9am to 5.30pm Monday to Friday

Discount Cards

Sydney Museums Pass (www.sydneylivingmuseums.com.au; adult/child $35/28) Allows a single visit to each of 12 museums in and around Sydney, including the Museum of Sydney, Hyde Park Barracks, Justice & Police Museum and Susannah Place. It's valid for a month and available at each of the participating museums. It's a good deal.

Four Attraction Pass (adult/child $75/53) Provides access to the high-profile, costly attractions operated by British-based Merlin Entertainment: Sydney Tower Eye, Sydney Sea Life Aquarium, Wild Life Sydney Zoo and Madame Tussauds. It's available from each of the venues, but is often considerably cheaper online through the venue websites. If you plan on visiting only some of these attractions, discounted Sydney Attractions Passes are available in any combination you desire.

Electricity

Standard voltage throughout Australia is 220 to 240 volts AC (50Hz). Plugs are flat three-pin types. You can buy converters for US, European and Asian configurations in airports, outdoors stores, hardware stores, luggage shops and some pharmacies.

Type I
230V/50Hz

Money

There are ATMs everywhere and major credit cards are widely accepted, though there's often a surcharge. Cryptocurrency (particularly Bitcoin) is accepted at some major tourist destinations.

ATMs

Central Sydney is chock-full of banks with 24-hour ATMs that will accept debit and credit cards linked to international networks. Most banks place a A$1000 limit on the amount you can withdraw daily. You'll also find ATMs in pubs and clubs, although these usually charge slightly higher fees. Shops and retail outlets usually have EFTPOS facilities, which allow you to pay for purchases with your debit or credit card; contactless is usually available. Some places like supermarkets offer 'cash out', which means they charge your card more and hand over the difference in cash.

Changing Money

o Exchange bureaux are dotted around the city centre, Kings Cross and Bondi.

o Shop around, as rates vary and most charge some sort of commission. The best rates are usually found online.

o The counters at the airport are open until the last flight comes in; rates here are significantly poorer than they are in the city.

Credit & Debit Cards

Sydneysiders rarely seem to use cash these days, with locals going for contactless 'tap' payments. Visa and MasterCard are widely accepted at shops, restaurants, pubs and hotels. Diners Club and American Express are less widely accepted. A credit card surcharge or minimum transaction amount is common.

Currency

o The unit of currency is the Australian dollar, divided into 100 cents.

o Notes are colourful, plastic and washing-machine-proof, in denominations of $100, $50, $20, $10 and $5.

o Coins come in $2, $1, 50c, 20c, 10c and 5c. The old 2c and 1c coins have been out of circulation for years, so shops round prices up (or down) to the nearest 5c.

o Travellers cheques won't be accepted everywhere. It's easier not to bother with them.

Money-saving Tips

o For views, zip up to **Blu Bar** (☑02-9250 6000; www.shangri-la.com; Level 36, 176 Cumberland St; ☺5pm-midnight Mon-Thu, 4pm-1am Fri, from 2.30pm Sat, 3-11pm Sun; ☎; ☒Circular Quay), on the 36th floor of the Shangri-La hotel, or the rotating **O Bar** (☑02-9247 9777; www.obardining.com.au; Level 47, Australia Square, 264 George St; ☺5pm-midnight Sat-Thu, noon-midnight Fri; ☎; ☒Wynyard) on the 47th floor of the Australia Square tower. They're not cheap but a cocktail will cost less than the price of visiting Sydney Tower.

o Rather than booking an expensive cruise, explore the harbour on a **Manly ferry** (☑02-9583 1199; www.manlyfastferry.com.au; Wharf 2, Circular Quay; adult one way $9.90) or take the **Parramatta River service** upstream.

o Instead of the pricey **BridgeClimb** (☑02-8274 7777; www.bridgeclimb.com; 3 Cumberland St; adult $268-388, child $188-278; ☒Circular Quay), head up the **Pylon Lookout** (☑02-9240 1100; www.pylonlookout.com.au; Sydney Harbour Bridge; adult/teen/child $19/12.50/9.50; ☺10am-5pm; ☒Circular Quay) instead.

o Save your expensive public transport for Sundays, when all-day Opal card travel costs just $2.60.

Taxes & Refunds

There's a 10% goods and services tax (GST) automatically added to almost everything you buy, Australia-wide. If you purchase goods with a total minimum value of $300 from any one shop within 60 days of departure from Australia, the Tourist Refund Scheme entitles you to a refund of any GST paid (see www.abf.gov.au/entering-and-leaving-australia/tourist-refund-scheme for more information).

Tipping

In Sydney most service providers don't expect a tip, so you shouldn't feel pressured into giving one.

o **Restaurants** The exception is restaurants, where a tip of 10% or so is standard.

o **Taxis** People tend to round up to the nearest dollar or more.

o **Bars** Tipping in bars is uncommon but on the increase, especially for cocktails..

Public Holidays

On public holidays, government departments, banks, offices and post offices shut up shop. On Good Friday, Easter Sunday, Anzac Day and Christmas Day, most shops are closed.

New Year's Day 1 January

Australia Day 26 January

Easter (Good Friday, Easter Saturday, Easter Monday) March/April

Anzac Day 25 April

Queen's Birthday Second Monday in June

Labour Day First Monday in October

Christmas Day 25 December

Dos & Don'ts

o **Greetings** In non-COVID times, greet both men and women by shaking hands or a kiss/air kiss for friends (it's not custom for straight Aussie blokes to kiss each other though).

o **Dinner** Bring wine, flowers or chocolates if you are invited to someone's house for a meal.

o **Restaurants** Splitting restaurant bills is standard practice.

o **Parties** If you're asked to 'bring a plate' to a party, it means bring food.

o **Public Transport** Offer seats on crowded buses, trains and ferries to older people or parents with kids.

o **Bargaining** Not usual in shops but sometimes OK at some markets.

o **Escalators** Stand on the left, walk on the right.

Boxing Day
26 December

o Many public holidays cleverly morph into long weekends (three days), and if a major holiday such as New Year's Day falls on a weekend, the following Monday is a holiday.

o Something else to consider when planning a Sydney visit is school holidays, when accommodation rates soar and everything gets hectic. Sydney students' holidays include a long summer break that includes Christmas and most of January.

Responsible Travel

Every step you take in Sydney, as in the rest of Australia, is on Indigenous land. Different parts of the city have different Traditional Owner peoples. Showing respect for them includes:
o Learning about Indigenous history and culture and the impact of colonisation - several of the city's museums have good information.

o Getting up-to-date on the important Uluru Statement from the Heart (www.uluru

statement.org) and showing your support for its three key pillars.

o Supporting Aboriginal-owned businesses. A good way to do this and get fascinating insights is by taking a tour with an agency like **Dreamtime Southern X** (✆02-9517 4390; www.dreamtimesouthernx.com.au; adult/child $44/33), **Tribal Warrior** (✆02-9699 3491; www.tribalwarrior.org; adult/child $60/40; ♋ Circular Quay) or Guringai Aboriginal Tours.

Safe Travel

o Sydney's wonderful beaches must be treated with healthy respect. People drown every year from rips and currents. Swim between the flags.

o Police in Sydney have little tolerance for minor transgressions or drug use. Random searches are common in clubs. .

o Sydney's sun is fierce in summer – don a hat and plenty of sunscreen.

Tourist Information

Sydney Visitor Centre – The Rocks (✆ 02-8273 0000; www.sydney.com; cnr Argyle &

Playfair Sts; ⏱9.30am-5.30pm; 🚊Circular Quay) Sydney's principal tourist office is in the heart of the historic Rocks district

○ **City of Sydney Information** The council operates a good tourist information desk in the **Customs House** (www.cityofsydney.nsw.gov.au; Alfred St, Circular Quay; ⏱9am-8pm Mon-Sat, to 5pm Sun; 🚊Circular Quay) as well as kiosks in Martin Place, **Chinatown** (www.cityofsydney.nsw.gov.au; Dixon St; ⏱11am-7pm, 🚊Town Hall) and **Kings Cross** (📞0477 344 125; www.cityofsydney.nsw.gov.au; cnr Darlinghurst Rd & Springfield Ave, Kings Cross; ⏱9am-5pm; 🚊Kings Cross).

○ **Hello Manly** (📞02-9976 1430; www.hellomanly.com.au; East Esplanade, Manly; ⏱9am-5pm Mon-Fri, 10am-4pm Sat & Sun; 🚢Manly) This helpful visitor centre, just outside the ferry wharf and alongside the bus interchange, has free pamphlets covering the **Manly Scenic Walkway** (www.manly.nsw.gov.au; 🚢Manly) and other Manly attractions, plus loads of local bus information.

○ **Parramatta Heritage & Visitor Information Centre** (📞02-8839 3311; www.discoverparramatta.com; 346a Church St, Parramatta; ⏱9am-5pm; 🚊Parramatta) Knowledgeable staff will point you in the right direction with loads of brochures and leaflets, info on access for visitors with impaired mobility, and details on local Aboriginal cultural sites.

Travellers with Disabilities

Compared with many other major cities, Sydney has great access for citizens and visitors with disabilities. Central districts and suburban centres are well endowed with kerb cuts and tactile pavement indicators.

Download Lonely Planet's free Accessible Travel guide from http://lptravel.to/AccessibleTravel.

Hearing-impaired travellers Most of Sydney's major attractions offer hearing loops and some can arrange sign-language interpreters. To make sure your needs can be met, contact venue staff in advance.

Vision-impaired travellers Many new buildings incorporate helpful architectural features, such as tactile floor indicators at the top and bottom of stairs. Sydney's pedestrian crossings feature beep-and-buzz sound cues.

Wheelchair access Most of Sydney's main attractions are accessible by wheelchair, and all new or renovated buildings must, by law, include wheelchair access. Older buildings can pose some problems, however, and some restaurants and entertainment venues aren't quite up to scratch. Most of the National Trust's historic houses are at least partially accessible.

Parking permits Contact **Roads & Maritime Services** (📞13 22 13; www.rms.nsw.gov.au), who can supply temporary parking permits for international drivers with disabilities.

Visas

All visitors to Australia need a visa – only New Zealand nationals are exempt, and even they receive a 'special category' visa on arrival.

Index

See also separate subindexes for:

⊗ **Eating p188**

⊙ **Drinking p189**

✪ **Entertainment p190**

🔒 **Shopping p190**

Index

Behind the Scenes

Send Us Your Feedback

We love to hear from travellers – your comments help make our books better. We read every word, and we guarantee that your feedback goes straight to the authors. Visit **lonelyplanet.com/contact** to submit your updates and suggestions.

Note: We may edit, reproduce and incorporate your comments in Lonely Planet products such as guidebooks, websites and digital products, so let us know if you don't want your comments reproduced or your name acknowledged. For a copy of our privacy policy visit lonelyplanet.com/privacy.

Andy's Thanks

It's always a great pleasure roaming around Sydney; thanks to many extremely helpful people along the way. I am particularly grateful to Corinna Mazurek for excellent cafe investigations, to Toni Sheridan, Daniel Beech, Portia Tshegofatso Loeto, Matt Beech and Peter Smith for sterling research company, to Raquel Bloom and colleagues for so much information, to my family for their support.

Acknowledgements

Cover photograph: Harbour Bridge, sharonxie/Shutterstock ©;
Back cover photograph: Swimming Pool, Bondi Beach, Barnaby Chambers/Shutterstock ©;
Photographs pp26–7 (from left): Nenad Basic/Shutterstock, M. Letscher/Shutterstock, Kompasskind.de/Shutterstock ©

This Book

This 6th edition of Lonely Planet's *Pocket Sydney* guidebook was researched and written by Andy Symington. This guidebook was produced by the following:

Destination Editors Niamh O'Brien, Tasmin Waby

Series Designer Campbell McKenzie

Cartographic Series Designer Wayne Murphy

Senior Product Editor Amy Lynch

Product Editors Clare Healy, Alison Killilea, Alex Conroy

Cartographers Valentina Kremenchutskaya, Julie Sheridan

Book Designer Gwen Cotter

Assisting Editors Melanie Dankel, Rebecca Dyer, Trent Holden, Ali Lemer, Lorna Parkes, Monique Perrin

Cover Researcher Gwen Cotter

Thanks to Ronan Abayawickrema, Imogen Bannister, Laura Crawford, Grace Dobell, Blaze Hadzik, James Hardy, Liz Heynes, Simon Hoskins, Sandie Kestell, Chris Lee Ack, Harsha Maheshwari, Jean-Pierre Masclef, Liam McGrellis, Dan Moore, Virginia Moreno, Darren O'Connell, Martine Power, Kirsten Rawlings, Wibowo Rusli, Dianne Schallmeiner, Ellie Simpson, Victoria Smith, John Taufa, Angela Tinson, Juan Winata

Our Writer

Andy Symington

Andy has written or worked on more than a hundred books and other updates for Lonely Planet (especially in Europe and Latin America) and other publishing companies, and has published articles on numerous subjects for a variety of newspapers, magazines and websites. He part-owns and operates a rock bar, has written a novel and is currently working on several fiction and nonfiction writing projects. Andy first became involved in writing when someone cannily contracted him to contribute to a pub guide: his formidable research on that title broke a man but launched a career.

Originally from Australia, Andy moved to northern Spain many years ago. When he's not off with a backpack in some far-flung corner of the world, he can probably be found watching the tragically poor local football side or tasting local wines after a long walk in the nearby mountains.

Published by Lonely Planet Global Limited
CRN 554153
6th edition – March 2022
ISBN 9781787017566
© Lonely Planet 2022 Photographs © as indicated 2022
10 9 8 7 6 5 4 3 2 1
Printed in Malaysia